Complete Guide
to Professional Woodworking:
Including Projects and Schematics

Ken Calhoun

*Professor of Technology
and Industrial Education
Central Washington University*

PRENTICE HALL, Englewood Cliffs, New Jersey 07632

Library of Congress Cataloging-in-Publication Data

CALHOUN, KEN
  Complete guide to professional woodworking : including projects
    and schematics / Ken Calhoun.
    p. cm.
  Includes index.
  ISBN 0-13-160193-8
    1. Woodwork. I. Title.
TT180.C35 1989
684′ .08--dc19   88-11121
                                                   CIP

Editorial/production supervision and
  interior design: Tom Aloisi
Cover design: 20/20 Services, Inc.
Manufacturing buyer: Bob Anderson

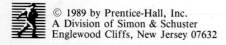 © 1989 by Prentice-Hall, Inc.
A Division of Simon & Schuster
Englewood Cliffs, New Jersey 07632

Printed in the United States of America

10 9 8 7 6 5 4 3 2 1

ISBN: 0-13-160193-8

PRENTICE-HALL International (UK) Limited, *London*
PRENTICE-HALL of Australia Pty. Limited, *Sydney*
PRENTICE-HALL   Canada Inc., *Toronto*
PRENTICE-HALL Hispanoamericana, S.A., *Mexico*
PRENTICE-HALLof India Private Limited, *New Delhi*
PRENTICE-HALL of Japan, Inc., *Tokyo*
SIMON & SCHUSTER Asia Pte. Ltd., *Singapore*
EDITORA PRENTICE-HALL do Brasil, Ltda., *Rio de Janeiro*

Contents

3 WOODWORKING MACHINES   75

4 ADHESIVES, ABRASIVES, AND HARDWARE 215

5 WOOD FINISHING 240

6 EQUIPPING THE HOME SHOP 257

7 EQUIPMENT ADJUSTMENT AND MAINTENANCE 289

8 PROJECTS 315

Preface

This book is for people of all ability levels who enjoy woodworking. It is designed to help you increase your woodworking skills and your enjoyment of woodworking. Certain basic fundamentals that are necessary for successful woodworking are reviewed, and then many advanced operations are presented. Many professional woodworking techniques can benefit hobby woodworkers, and these are presented and illustrated.

We examine the many available supplies, such as abrasives, adhesives, and hardware, and learn how to select those that are best for each situation.

Wood finishing is probably one of the least understood aspects of woodworking. The available options are discussed and criteria for making the best choice are presented.

We devote a great deal of attention to the exciting task of starting and equipping your own home workshop. Recommendations are made on equipment selection based on your woodworking objectives. Once the equipment has been acquired, the all-important subject of maintenance and adjustment must be addressed.

Finally, a selection of interesting projects is presented that will challenge woodworkers of all ability levels.

Most of the photography was done by Debbie Storlie, and I would like to thank her for her work.

Ken Calhoun

1 Introduction

Woodworking can be one of the most fascinating and rewarding of hobbies. It is a hobby that can be enjoyed by people of all ages and skill levels. Many woodworkers have built all the furniture and cabinets for their own homes. However, woodworking is not necessarily all furniture making. There are many other useful items that woodworkers can make and enjoy. Children's toys, work benches, tool boxes or cabinets, planter boxes, and storage sheds are just a few of the many things that woodworkers can make.

The satisfaction comes from many sources. There is the satisfaction that results from starting with rough lumber and transforming it into an attractive piece of furniture or other items. Not to mention the compliments of friends! There is also the satisfaction provided by using the completed project.

Like many other worthwhile pursuits, it takes time to become proficient at woodworking. So there is a certain satisfaction in seeing your skill level develop with each project.

Many people also enjoy using high-quality, functional tools and machines. There has probably never been a better selection of high-quality woodworking tools available to the woodworking enthusiast than at the present time. There is a certain enjoyment in owning and using these tools that perform their intended function well and are well constructed.

Many woodworkers have been able to sell some of their work to buy other needed tools and equipment. The savings realized by making your own furniture, cabinets, and other items rather than buying them may also help pay for your equipment.

It is not always necessary to have a fully equipped shop to enjoy woodworking. Many communities offer evening woodworking classes in local high school or community college shops. Taking such a class will give you access to machines that you may not have at home. If you plan your work, you can use your time to get work done that requires special machines and then do the rest of it at home. Some people do all their woodworking in these classes, rather than invest in their own equipment.

One of the most important qualities that a person can develop to enhance woodworking skills is the patience to do each step right. Take the time to measure accurately, cut accurately (make test cuts on scrap lumber if necessary), check for squareness, and sand all machine marks from the wood. Maintaining sharp cutting tools and having properly adjusted machines are also very important. If these requirements are met, there is no reason that amateur woodworkers cannot produce results comparable to those of professional woodworkers. The main difference is that the professional will be faster. It is much easier to start working slowly, but accurately, and then develop speed with practice, than it is to do fast, sloppy work and try to develop accuracy.

It is, of course, best to start with projects that are within your skill level and then advance to more complex projects. Many people have lost their enthusiasm for woodworking by starting a very complex project before they were ready for it. Study project plans carefully before starting. If you can go through the steps of making each part of the project mentally, you will probably be successful. "Building the project in your mind" is a good practice before starting actual construction in any case. It usually makes the construction process much smoother.

Chapter 8 has a selection of project plans ranging from fairly easy to quite challenging.

Most of the photography was done by Debbie Storlie and I would like to thank her for her work.

2 Construction Techniques

Before beginning our discussion of construction techniques, a brief review of wood properties will help in our selection of appropriate construction methods for various projects.

WOOD PROPERTIES

Cell Structure

Wood cells are long, tubular elements running vertically in the tree. They are bound together with a natural adhesivelike substance know as lignin. Their length, thickness, and physical makeup vary considerably between hardwoods and softwoods and even between species of wood. This, in part, accounts for the great differences in hardness, strength, and shock resistance among different species of wood. Interestingly enough, the chemical makeup of the cell wall material is quite similar for all woods. This cell structure is shown in Fig. 2–1.

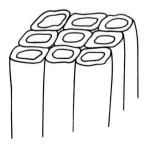

Figure 2–1 Wood cell structure.

The following characteristics of wood are due, at least in part, to this unique cell construction.

- Wood is much stronger in the direction of the wood grain than across the grain.
- Wood expands and contracts greatly with changes in moisture content.
- Wood cells shrink or expand very little in length, but a great deal in diameter.
- Wood pieces may be bonded together with adhesives and the resultant glue joint will be stronger than the wood. To achieve this strength, the wood cells of the two adjoining surfaces must be parallel (Fig. 2–2).
- Wood is a fair insulator against the passage of heat and sound.
- Wood is very strong in relation to its weight.
- Wood is very resistant to fatigue failure.

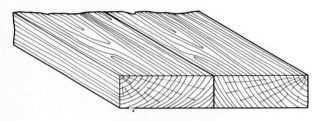

Edge-to-edge gluing results
in strong glue joint

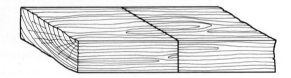

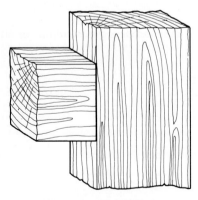

End-to-end and end-to-edge
gluing produces weak joints

Figure 2–2 Edge joints versus end joints.

Moisture, Shrinkage, and Expansion

One of the biggest problems in woodworking is controlling the shrinkage and expansion of wood. Wood is a hygroscopic material, meaning that it readily takes on and gives off moisture in both liquid and vapor forms. Wet wood shrinks when placed in a dry environment, and dry wood expands or swells when placed in a humid environment. If precautions are not taken, moisture content changes can cause the following changes to the wood:

- Warping, including cup, twist, and bow.
- Splits and checks in the wood.
- Joint failure due to swelling of wood parts.
- Raised grain, causing a rough surface.
- Premature finish failure.
- A high level of frustration on the part of the woodworker!

It is important that the woodworker understand how this shrinkage occurs and how to minimize its effects. The long, tubular cells shown in Fig. 2–1 tend to shrink in diameter (but not length) as the wood dries. No shrinkage occurs on the initial drying of very wet (green) lumber until the wood is dried to approximately 30% moisture content (moisture content is expressed as the percentage of water weight to dry wood weight). From this point on, the shrinkage becomes substantial. The objective is to dry the wood to a point that is in equilibrium with its environment. At this point, it will no longer give off or take on moisture. For outdoor furniture or a deck on a house, this might be anywhere between 12% and 20% moisture content, depending on the climate in various parts of the country. Wood for interior furniture should be between $6\frac{1}{2}\%$ and 8% moisture content.

The way in which a board is cut from a log will also determine its shrinkage characteristics. For example, a board that is plain sawn (cut tangent to the growth rings) shrinks approximately twice as much in width as a board that is quarter sawn (cut radially, as in Fig. 2–3). Boards that are plain sawn (Fig. 2–3) will also tend to cup away from the center of the tree.

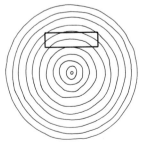

Board cut tangent
to growth rings
(plain sawn)

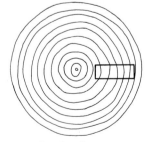

Board cut in
radial direction
(quarter-sawn)

Figure 2–3 Tangent versus radial cut.

You should know the moisture content of the wood that you are working with. Your lumber yard should be able to tell you. However, if the lumber has been stored in an unheated shed in a rainy climate, for example, the moisture content may have increased since it was kiln dried. You can do your own moisture content check if you have a way of weighing a small sample accurately. Use the following procedure:

Cut a sample from a board that you wish to check. This sample should not be near the end of the board since the ends dry faster and will not be representative of the actual moisture content of the board. Weigh the sample and record its weight. Then place the sample in an oven at about 200°F. Weight the sample periodically. When it stops losing weight, you know it is completely dry. To determine the original moisture content of the sample, apply the following formula:

$$\text{moisture content (\%)} = \frac{\text{wet weight} - \text{oven dry weight}}{\text{oven dry weight}} \times 100$$

For example, if we have a sample that weighs 0.5 pound wet and 0.46 pound dry, the calculation would be done as follows:

$$\text{moisture content} = \frac{0.5 \text{ lb} - 0.46 \text{ lb}}{0.46} \times 100$$

$$= \frac{0.04}{0.46} = 0.087 \times 100 = 8.7\%$$

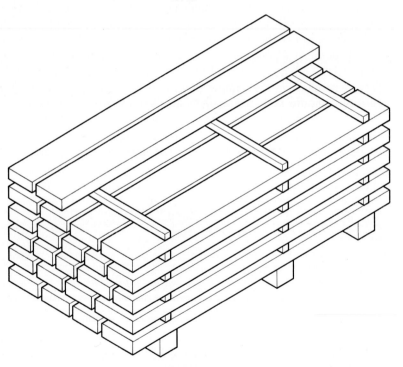

Figure 2-4 Lumber stacked with stickers for air circulation.

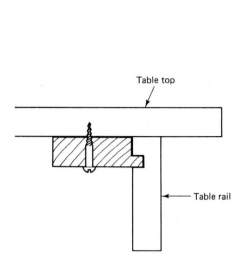

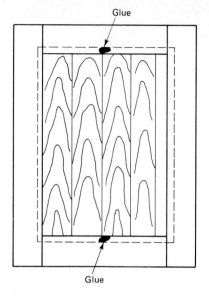

Figure 2-5 Method of attaching a table top that allows it to expand and contract.

Figure 2-6 Glue applied to the center of a door panel to allow it to expand and contract.

This sample at 8.7% moisture content is still slightly too wet for best results for furniture.

There are also moisture meters available for quickly checking moisture content and, although they are quite expensive, some serious woodworkers use them.

Once you have determined that your wood is at the proper moisture content, there are other precautions that can be taken to prevent warpage. Lumber should be stored carefully while awaiting construction and while in construction. Obviously, boards should not be stored so that they can sag or twist, but they should also be stacked so that air can circulate between boards (Fig. 2-4). Avoid laying boards flat on the floor where they can draw moisture. Also avoid leaning them against exterior walls in the winter.

There are also precautions that can be taken during construction to minimize the effects of shrinkage or expansion. These generally consist of techniques designed to allow the wood to shrink or expand, rather than trying to prevent it. These include such techniques as attaching a table top to a table so that the top can expand or contract as in Fig. 2-5, mounting panels in doors so that they can expand (Fig. 2-6) or contract, allowing drawer bottoms to "float" in a groove, and cutting wide boards into relatively narrow boards, alternating growth rings and regluing (Fig. 2-7).

Figure 2-7 Growth rings should be alternated when edge gluing.

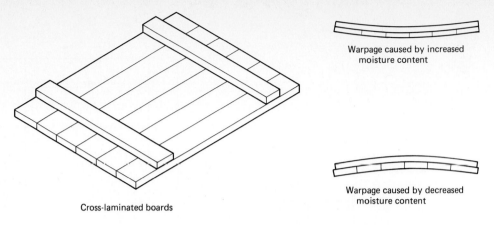

Warpage caused by increased
moisture content

Warpage caused by decreased
moisture content

Cross-laminated boards

Figure 2–8 Cross-laminating boards increases chance of warpage.

In light of this, you can see that some of the commonly tried remedies for warping actually promote warping. For example, gluing "stabilizing" boards (Fig. 2–8) perpendicular to the grain direction on a laminated table top actually increases the likelihood of warpage. Since boards shrink and expand much more in width than in length, the top shown will cup away from the cross boards if it shrinks or will cup toward them if it expands.

The familiar "bread board" ends (Fig. 2–9) when used on wide laminated boards also cause problems. If the wide laminated surface expands, the bread board joint will crack and the edge will extend beyond the bread board ends, and if the board shrinks, it will crack or split.

When the time comes for finishing a project, you can take another step to prevent moisture-related problems by finishing both the front and back surfaces of all parts of the project. Even though finishes do not completely seal the wood against moisture changes, they slow down the rate of moisture change. Leaving the underside of a table top, for example, unfinished will allow it to expand or contract faster than the top side, resulting in warpage.

In summary, you can avoid many moisture-related problems by making sure that the wood is at the proper moisture content when you start working it, taking care in its storage, building so that wide surfaces are allowed to expand and contract, and, finally, finishing all sides of wood surfaces.

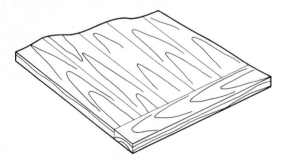

Figure 2–9 "Bread board" end.

Construction Techniques   Chap. 2

OPTIONS FOR MAKING UP LARGE SURFACES

One of the first decisions that you must make when starting a larger project is how to make up the large surfaces. These large surfaces could include table, desk, or cabinet tops, sides and backs of cabinets or furniture pieces, and cabinet or furniture doors. There are three basic methods of making up these surfaces. They are edge gluing solid lumber, frame and panel, and using standard manufactured sheet materials. Each system has advantages and disadvantages, and no one system is best for all applications. You will need to consider such factors as strength, stability, and durability requirements for your finished project, as well as cost, time, appearance, and availability of materials. The type of equipment that you have may also determine which system is best for a particular project. In fact, many projects combine systems. We will briefly discuss the advantages and disadvantages of each system and then look at the actual construction method used with each.

Edge-glued Solid Lumber

Edge-glued solid boards offer some significant advantages to the woodworker. They do not require the special care in cutting and sanding that hardwood plywoods do, with their very thin face veneers. They also do not require that edge plys be covered as plywood does. They allow cutting molded edges directly on the edge of the board. There is also the connotation of quality associated with furniture made of solid lumber.

There are, of course, disadvantages associated with wide surfaces made up of solid lumber. Because of the tendency for boards to shrink and expand in width, this is the least stable method of the three. Care must be taken to allow the finished parts to expand or contract after they are part of the finished project. Glued solid boards are also the most likely to cup, warp, twist, and develop splits in the ends.

It is also somewhat more time consuming to build using this method, compared with using sheet materials. If you are using rough lumber, the boards must be face jointed, planed, edge jointed, ripped, glued, and then planed to finish thickness. Alternatively, using lumber already planed to finish thickness requires carefully selecting straight, flat boards and using great care in gluing to keep the glue joints flush.

If you do not have a planer, you are limited to using planed lumber unless you can take your glued panels to a local cabinet shop for planing.

Frame and Panel Construction

Frame and panel construction is very popular for cabinet and furniture doors, but it can also be used for cabinet and furniture sides and is often used for dust panels between drawers in furniture. Frame and panel construction consists of a wood frame and a panel, which may be edge-glued solid lumber, plywood, or even plastic or glass. This system is much more stable than using solid lumber only. If the panel is solid lumber, it is set in a groove in such a way that it is free to expand and contract. Frame and panel construction offers many options to enhance the appearance of what otherwise might be a flat, uninteresting surface. Figure 2–10 shows some options for chang-

(a)

(b)

(c)

(d)

Figure 2-10 Examples of frame and panel construction.

Construction Techniques   Chap. 2

ing the appearance of surfaces using frame and panel construction. Frame and panel construction may also be lighter in weight, especially if thin plywood panels are used.

Some disadvantages of frame and panel include the fact that it can also be time consuming to construct, usually even more so than the previously mentioned glued lumber system, since each frame and panel unit is made up of a minimum of five parts (two stiles, two rails, and a panel). There are also construction problems in machining and joining the stiles and rails. These will be discussed in more detail in the section on frame and panel construction.

Sheet Material

In light of the just mentioned problems associated with glued lumber and frame and panel construction, the use of sheet material, especially plywood, would seem to be very appealing. It comes in large sheets (usually 4 ft × 8 ft) and is usually sanded so that all we need to do is cut parts to size, machine any needed joints, and assemble the project. Plywood also offers some other advantages because of its cross-banded construction. It is more stable than solid lumber, and its strength across the grain is more nearly equal to its strength in the face grain direction. It has no tendency to split near the ends, even when nails are driven near the edge of the sheet.

People often think of solid wood as providing a more attractive appearance than plywood, but some of the better grades of hardwood plywoods, especially plane sliced or quarter sliced, are truly beautiful. The veneers used on the faces of these sheets are cut in sequence and book matched to provide an appearance that would be impossible to achieve by edge gluing solid boards. Figure 2-11 shows such a sheet. See the section on veneers for more examples of veneer cuts and veneer matches.

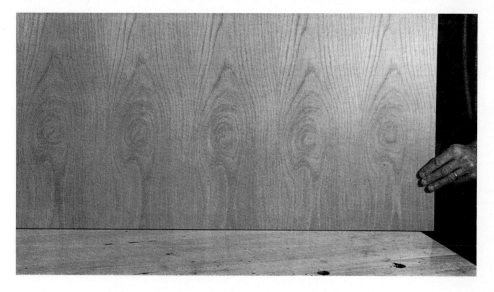

Figure 2-11 Example of book-matched veneer on plywood.

Other sheet materials are often used on certain projects. Particle board, hardboard, medium-density fiberboard, and cabinet liner boards are some of the more popular ones. Some of these are covered with wood veneers and are used much like plywood. Others have vinyl or polyester films or other wood-grain prints and are used in furniture and cabinets. Some have no coverings and are used for interior or hidden parts of cabinets and other applications where appearance is not a prime concern.

Plywoods and other sheet materials have their limitations and disadvantages also. Plywood has to have its edges covered when used for furniture or cabinets. This involves applying wood tape or making wood strips or moldings to cover the edge plys. Most hardwood plywoods have very thin face veneers, which tend to make them more prone to chipping than solid lumber. The thin face veneer chips easily, especially when cutting across the face grain, if the proper saw blade is not used. Even then, chipping sometimes occurs unless special precautions are observed. (See following section on working with sheet material.) When plywood parts are joined, they must be accurately fitted since the veneer is so thin that they cannot be "sanded to fit" later (Fig. 2-12). Another disadvantage is that the surface of plywood cannot be carved nor can the edges be molded, as is possible on solid wood.

So there we have the three major systems for making large surfaces with no clear-cut winner. Sheet material is almost always used in cabinetmaking because it is so fast and relatively inexpensive. However, in furniture making, any of the three systems may be used, often in combinations. For example, a hutch may have solid lumber or plywood sides and frame and panel doors.

You need to weigh the advantages and disadvantages of each system and select the best one (or ones) for your situation. Your own shop facilities may dictate your decision. For example, if you do not have a way of planing large glued up surfaces flat, you may want to consider plywood (or frame and plywood panel). On the other hand, if you do not have the room to handle large plywood sheets or have a saw suitable for cutting them, you may want to glue up solid lumber and take it to a cabinet shop for planing.

We will next examine the procedures for using each of the three systems.

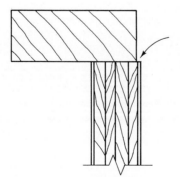

Figure 2-12 Improperly fitted plywood joint cannot be "sanded to fit."

Making Large Panels by Gluing Solid Stock

Since solid lumber is more likely to warp than other material, we must take certain precautions when using this type of construction. Boards should ideally be cut into relatively narrow widths and then glued to make up the wide surface. Widths of $2\frac{1}{2}$ in. or less are ideal, but widths up to 4 in. are usually satisfactory. The growth rings on the end of the boards should be alternated as shown in Fig. 2-13. The color and grain pattern of the boards should be matched as closely as possible. If it is necessary to use boards with sapwood on the edges, for instance, try to put two boards with sapwood on the edges together to avoid having a sharp line transition between the lighter sapwood and the darker heartwood (Fig. 2-14).

If you have a jointer and a surface planer and are working with rough lumber, the procedure for getting the wood ready for gluing is as follows: The lumber is first cut to rough lengths, usually $\frac{1}{2}$ in. to 1 in. longer than the finished panel length.

Figure 2-13 Alternating growth ring direction when edge gluing boards.

Figure 2-14 Avoid putting dark wood next to light wood when gluing boards.

Figure 2–15 Using the jointer to establish a flat surface on a rough board.

The boards are then face jointed on the jointer to establish a flat surface (Fig. 2–15). If the boards are too wide for the jointer or if they are badly cupped or twisted, they will need to be ripped to narrower widths first. After all the pieces have been face jointed, they are planed to a uniform thickness, but should be left thicker than the eventual finished thickness of the panel (Fig. 2–16). For example, if the finished

Figure 2–16 Planing rough board to thickness after first face has been jointed flat on jointer.

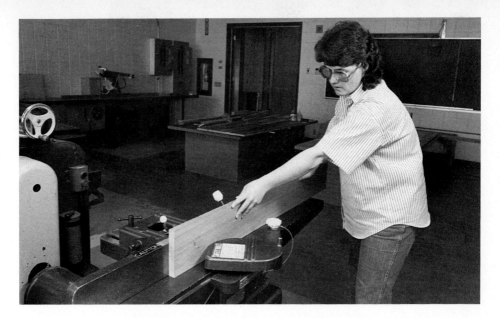

Figure 2-17 Jointing one edge of board on jointer.

thickness of a panel is to be ¾ in. and you are working with 1-in. rough lumber, the lumber would be planed to ¹³⁄₁₆ in. or ⅞ in. before gluing. The next step is to joint one edge straight on each board on the jointer (Fig. 2-17). Great care must be taken at this point to make sure that the jointer fence is exactly perpendicular to the table (Fig. 2-18) and that each board is held flat against the fence while it

Figure 2-18 Checking to see that the jointer fence is perpendicular to the table.

is run through the machine. Otherwise, the edge of the board will not be square, and the resulting glued panel will be cupped.

The next step is to rip the boards to the desired widths. This is usually done with the table saw (Fig. 2–19). The individual boards should be cut wide enough so that the total panel will be somewhat wider than its eventual finished width. The final machining process before gluing is to run the sawn edges across the jointer to remove the saw marks and provide a flat surface. (*Note:* Some of the smoother-cutting circular saw blades will leave a surface suitable for gluing, provided that the wood is pushed smoothly through the saw with no sideways movement.)

Once the boards are all cut to size, we are ready to lay the panel up for gluing. Bar clamps or pipe clamps may be used to clamp the panel. Clamps are set on a table in a row, as shown in Fig. 2–20. If the boards to be glued are 3 in. wide, the clamps should be placed about 12 in. apart. (After the boards are set in the clamps, we will put clamps on top of the boards between each of the bottom clamps. This will give us a spacing of 6 in. between clamps. The final spacing between clamps should be about two times the width of the boards being glued.)

The boards can now be set in the clamps and matched for color and grain pattern. You should try to alternate growth ring direction as shown in Fig. 2–13. However, sometimes it may be necessary to turn one of the boards the "wrong" way to get the desired color match.

Figure 2-19 Ripping board to width.

Figure 2-20 Clamps set up for edge gluing boards.

There is normally no need to put dowels or other reinforcements in joints to be edge glued. Most modern adhesives create a glue joint that is stronger than the wood, so the only reason for using dowels would be to hold the boards in place while tightening the clamps. For instance, if you are working with planed lumber that is ¾ in. thick and you want the finished panel to be ¾ in. thick, you may want to put dowels in the edges to keep the surfaces from slipping when the clamps are tightened.

When the pieces are all matched, they are turned up on edge and given a coat of glue (Fig. 2-21). Aliphatic resin wood glue works very well for this purpose if the joint does not have to be waterproof. The boards are then laid back down and pushed together to spread the glue on both surfaces. The remaining clamps are then placed on top of the boards, and they are all tightened uniformly to keep the panel from cupping (Fig. 2-22).

Any excess glue that is squeezed from the joint should be left to dry. Do *not* wipe it up. Wiping the glue forces it into the pores of the wood and affects the way the wood accepts a finish in that area. The glue beads can be scraped off later with a scraper. The boards are left in the clamps for 30 minutes to 1 hour using the aliphatic resin glue at normal room temperature. Most other wood glues take longer.

The procedure is similar when working with planed lumber, except the first steps of face jointing and surface planing are eliminated. Since planed lumber is already at its finished thickness and no "straightening" can be done, you should try to select

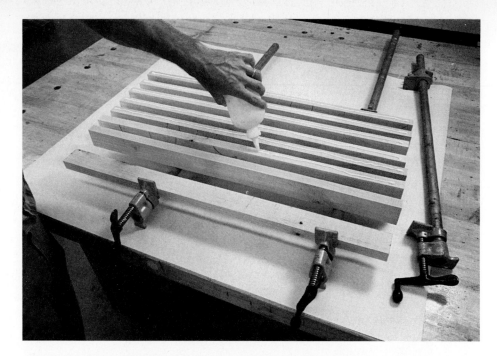

Figure 2–21 Glue is applied to the edges of boards.

Figure 2–22 Alternately tightening the clamps to prevent cupping the board.

straight boards for gluing. The edges should be jointed to get a smooth, flat gluing surface, and great care must be taken to keep the boards flat and flush when gluing.

After the glue has cured and the panels have been removed from the clamps, the glue can be scraped from the surface. If you have a planer, the glued-up boards are then planed (Fig. 2–23). If you do not have a planer, you can take them to a cabinet shop for planing and even sanding if they have a wide belt sander. (*Note:* If the finished panel is wider than the available planer, it is easier to glue up two panels that will fit through the planer, plane them to final thickness, and then glue them together. This way you have only one glue joint to keep flush and to scrape by hand.)

If planed lumber was used to make up the panel, then no further planing can be done. In this case, the panel must be scraped with a hand scraper. This little understood tool takes a little practice to master, but it is one of the most useful hand tools in woodworking. The hand scraper can be used to smooth slightly uneven glue joints and to remove planer mill marks (Fig. 2–24). It will also smooth the surface to the point where only the finer grits of abrasive paper are needed before finishing. Chapter 7 tells how to sharpen and use the hand scraper.

Once the panel is planed and scraped or rough sanded, it is cut to finished size. It should be cut to width first using the table saw and then cut to final length. Chapter 3 shows several techniques for trimming the uneven ends on glued panels. The panels are now ready for machining any necessary joints.

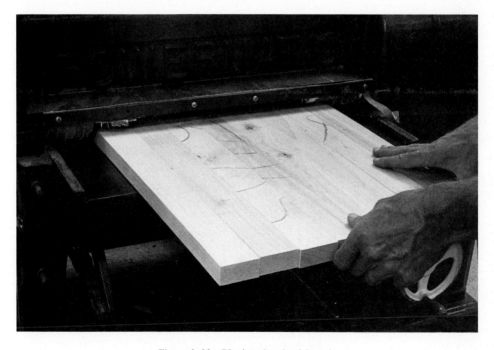

Figure 2–23   Planing the glued boards.

Figure 2-24 Using a hand scraper to smooth a surface.

Constructing a Frame and Panel Unit

Frame and panel construction offers the woodworker many options, in fact so many that it is sometimes bewildering. For instance, the frame members can be assembled with mortise and tenon joints, butt joints with dowels, miter joints, or cope cut joints. The panels may be raised on one side or both sides or may even be flat, or the panel may be another material such as glass or caning.

The basic frame and panel unit is made of two stiles (vertical frame members), two rails (horizontal frame members), and a panel as shown in Fig. 2–25. The stiles

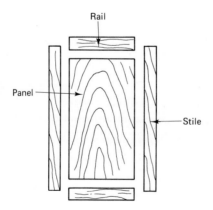

Figure 2-25 Frame and panel components.

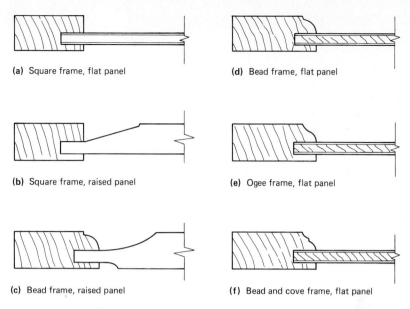

(a) Square frame, flat panel

(d) Bead frame, flat panel

(b) Square frame, raised panel

(e) Ogee frame, flat panel

(c) Bead frame, raised panel

(f) Bead and cove frame, flat panel

Figure 2-26 Typical frame and panel details.

and rails often have a molding on the inside edge. This molding is called sticking. Figure 2–26 shows some of the common sticking shapes, along with some common panel designs. The sticking can enhance the appearance of the frame and panel unit, but it also causes one of the major problems associated with frame and panel construction, that of joining the stiles and rails.

If the stiles and rails have square edges (no sticking), a simple butt joint with dowels or a mortise and tenon joint may be used. However, when the stiles and rails have sticking, the options for joining them become somewhat more difficult. If you have a shaper available, you can get matched stile and rail cutter sets. One cutter makes the sticking cut on the inside edge of the stiles and rails and the other cutter makes the cope cut on the end of the rails (Fig. 2–27). These cutters (Fig. 2–28) are

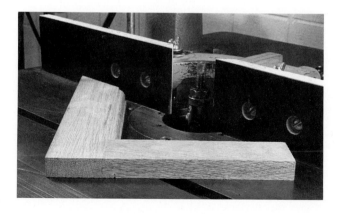

Figure 2-27 Stile and rail fitted with a cope cut.

Options for Making Up Large Surfaces

Figure 2-28 Stile and rail cutter set.

quite expensive, but if you anticipate doing a lot of frame and panel work, they offer the best solution. With just two different cuts, the frame is ready to assemble, complete with a groove for the panel.

There are several other options for joining stiles and rails. One option is to cut away the stile sticking in the area where the rail joins the stile, as shown in Fig. 2-29. Dowels may be used to reinforce the joint.

Another option is to miter the stiles and rails together, as shown in Fig. 2-30. The joint is usually reinforced with dowels and must be assembled with miter clamps or must be clamped in both directions with bar or pipe clamps.

Another option is to leave the edges of the stiles and rails square until after assembly. This allows the corners to be assembled with the normal dowel or mortise and tenon joint. The inside edge of the assembled frame is then molded with a router. The back of the frame may be rabbeted for the panel. This method has the disadvantage of leaving a rounded corner detail on the sticking, as shown in Fig. 2-31.

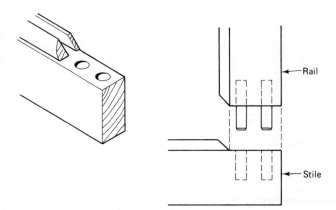

Figure 2-29 Sticking cut away from the stile and mitered to fit the rail sticking.

Figure 2–30 Stile and rail assembled with a miter joint.

Figure 2–31 Sticking machined with a router after frame has been assembled.

Another method is to again assemble the frame and panel without any sticking on the stiles and rails. A quarter-round molding, as shown in Fig. 2–32, is glued to the inside of the stiles and rails.

The panel for a frame and panel unit may be thin plywood (usually ¼ in.) or it may be made of edge-glued lumber, as described in the previous section. Panels made of solid stock are usually raised (actually tapered around the edges), as shown in Fig. 2–26.

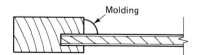

Molding

Figure 2–32 Molding applied after assembly of frame and panel.

Raised panels may be made on the table saw, as shown in Chapter 3, or they may be made on a heavy-duty shaper using a suitable panel raising cutter (Fig. 2–33). There are also router cutters for making small pattern raised panels. The panel and its cove or tapered edge should be sanded before assembly.

Once the parts are all cut and machined, we are ready to assemble them. (It is best to cut the stiles and rails so that the assembled frame and panel unit will be approximately ⅛ in. oversize in width and height. This will allow it to be accurately trimmed to finish size.) Two bar clamps or pipe clamps are used unless the frame corners are mitered.

The clamps are set on a bench, and the frame and panel unit is placed in the clamps so that the clamping is done across the rails. After a trial fitting to make sure everything fits properly, glue is applied to the frame joints, and a spot of glue is applied to the center of the panel at the top and bottom. This will hold the panel securely in place, but will allow it to expand or contract with moisture changes. As soon as the frame is clamped, it should be checked for squareness. This is best done by measuring the frame diagonals as shown in Fig. 2–34. If the frame is not square, it can be pulled square by angling the clamps slightly in the direction of the long diagonal, as shown in Fig. 2–35.

Figure 2-33 Raised panel shaper cutter.

Figure 2–34 Measuring the diagonals to make sure the frame and panel assembly is square.

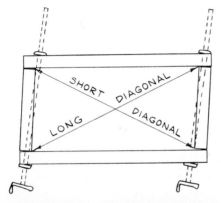

Figure 2–35 Clamps angled to pull frame and panel assembly square.

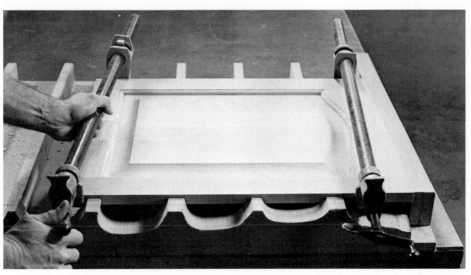

Figure 2–36 Sanding frame and panel rails with belt sander.

Figure 2–37 Sanding stiles with belt sander.

Figure 2-38 Final sanding with finish sander.

When the frame and panel units are dry and removed from the clamps, they are ready for sanding. If you have a number of frame and panel units to be sanded, you may want to have them sanded by a cabinet shop with a wide belt sander. This machine will sand any uneven joints flat, and you will only need to remove the final cross-sanding scratches from the rails.

If you sand them yourself, you will need a belt sander if the joints are not perfectly even. The rails are sanded first, sanding across the joint as shown in Fig. 2-36. The stiles are then sanded. You must sand right to the edge of the rail, as shown in Fig. 2-37, to remove cross-grain scratches. The stiles and rails are then sanded with a finish sander (Fig. 2-38).

If the joints were flush, the belt sanding step could be omitted and all the sanding could be done with the finish sander. A final hand sanding with the grain is always recommended to remove any swirl marks left by the finish sander.

If the panels were made slightly oversize, they can now be trimmed to exact size.

Frame and panel units used for glass or plastic should have a rabbet for the glass rather than a groove so that the glass can be installed after the finish is applied, and so that the glass can be replaced in the event it is broken.

Construction with Sheet Material

Construction with sheet material such as plywood is generally somewhat simpler than the other two methods just described. It basically consists of cutting parts to size, machining any needed joints, and then assembling the project. However, some important precautions must be observed to obtain satisfactory results when working with plywood:

1. All cutting and machining must be very accurate since the thin face veneers do not allow sanding to make things fit.
2. Care must be taken to keep these thin veneers from chipping when cutting.
3. Exposed plywood edges should be covered with wood tape, wood strips, or moldings or otherwise hidden.
4. Cutting must be carefully planned to get best utilization of the sheet and to make sure that the grain is running in the desired direction on each part.

Some techniques for achieving these requirements are discussed next.

Accurate cutting.   A good table saw, along with a table behind the saw and a support rail to the left of the saw, is best for cutting plywood sheets. Figure 2–39 shows such a setup. The saw should also be capable of cutting at least 48 in. to the right of the blade to allow cutting to the center of a 96-in. sheet. The rip fence must

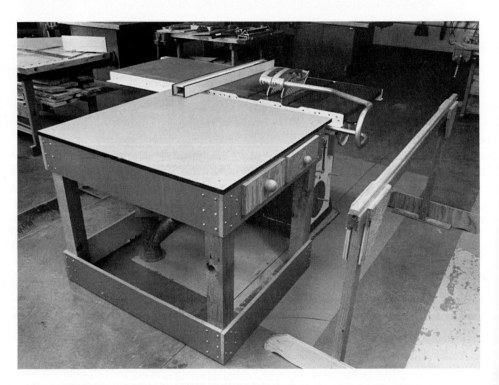

Figure 2–39   Table saw with off-bearing table and rail for cutting large plywood sheets.

lock in place so that it is exactly parallel with the blade. If it does not automatically line up with the blade, it must be checked on each cut. You can check this by measuring from the fence to one of the miter gage slots. Measurements must be taken at both the front and rear of the table.

With such a setup, one person can make cuts across the sheet or in the long direction. If there are to be cuts across the sheet, it is often best to make these first so that you do not have to try to cross cut 8-ft long pieces with a miter gage.

To make a cut across a 4 ft by 8 ft sheet of plywood, the end of the sheet is placed against the saw fence, and you stand slightly to the left of the center of the sheet, as shown in Fig. 2–40. As the sheet is pushed through the saw, the edge sliding along the fence must be watched to be sure it stays in contact with the fence. Standing near the center of the sheet, you can push harder with either your left or right hand as necessary to bring the plywood back against the fence if it pulls away. As you near the end of the cut, you should move to your right enough so that you can use your right hand to push the piece between the blade and fence past the rear of the blade (Fig. 2–41). The pressure being applied with your left hand should be gradually released as the cut is completed to avoid pinching the plywood on the saw blade.

Figure 2–40 The operator should stand near the center of the sheet when crosscutting plywood sheets on the table saw. (The saw guard has been removed for clarity in showing this operation.)

Options for Making Up Large Surfaces

Figure 2-41   Completing the plywood crosscut.

If the rip fence will not move far enough from the blade for the cut you want to make or if you want to make a taper cut on sheet material, the following technique may be used. Check to see if the left edge of the saw table is smooth, straight, and parallel with the blade. If it is, you can clamp a board with a straight edge on the underside of the sheet and use it as a guide on the edge of the saw table (Fig. 2-42).

Lacking a large enough table saw, you can also cut plywood sheets to a more manageable size with a portable circular saw with a plywood cutting blade and a straight-edge guide clamped to the sheet (Fig. 2-43). The results are usually not as accurate or straight as when done on a table saw, so parts are often cut oversize and trimmed to final size on the table saw. A sliding crosscut jig, such as the one shown in Fig. 2-44, can be used to cut long, narrow plywood parts to length.

One final note on cutting plywood parts: the factory edge often shows the effects of wear and tear from shipping and handling. If you were to try, for instance, to apply edge banding to this edge, you would probably not get a good, tight joint. Therefore, the factory edge is usually trimmed off by making the first cut $\frac{1}{8}$ to $\frac{1}{4}$ in. oversize and then turning the piece around and cutting to final size, removing the factory edge. All other parts are cut right to final size.

Figure 2-42 Using a board clamped to plywood sheet as a cutting guide. (The guide board runs against the edge of the saw table.)

Figure 2-43 Using a portable circular saw to cut plywood parts to smaller sizes.

Figure 2-44 Using a sliding crosscut jig to cut long plywood parts.

Avoid chipping. The thin face veneers found on most hardwood plywood are very prone to chipping when being cut across the grain on the sheet (Fig. 2-45). A major factor affecting chipping is the shape of the saw blade teeth. Special blades are made for cutting plywood and they should always be used whenever possible. Figure 2-46 shows two plywood cutting blades.

The plywood sheet should be cut with the good face up on a table saw (so that the cutting teeth are coming down on the face veneer). The good face is placed down when cutting with a portable circular saw for the same reason.

Figure 2-45 Chipping that often occurs when cutting across the grain on plywood.

Figure 2–46 Plywood cutting blades.

Many of the large industrial saws designed for cutting plywood have a small scoring blade just ahead of the main blade. This small blade cuts through the first veneer on the bottom of the sheet and keeps it from chipping when the main sawteeth break through the veneer. You can do essentially the same thing on your own table saw. When you are ready to make a cross-grain cut on plywood, first raise the blade just slightly higher than the thickness of the first veneer layer. Set the fence for the desired width and slowly run the plywood over the blade. The blade teeth are just scoring the surface and are much less likely to chip than if they are breaking through the veneer from behind. Now raise the blade a little higher than the thickness of the plywood sheet and, without moving the fence, complete the cut by running the sheet through the saw again. This is one of the best techniques to get clean, chip-free cuts in hardwood plywoods.

Another technique that will help reduce chipping on the underside of the cut is to use a wood throat plate that fits tightly around the saw blade, as shown in Fig. 2–47. This throat plate supports the wood fibers of the plywood at the cutting point

Figure 2–47 A wood throat plate that fits tightly around the blade will minimize chipping on plywood.

and helps prevent chipping. The throat plate is made by using the standard saw throat plate as a pattern and tracing its outline on a piece of wood or plywood of suitable thickness. The new throat plate is cut out and mounted in the opening with the blade down (plywood blade). The rip fence is then locked over the throat plate but to the side of the blade. The saw is then started and the blade is raised through the throat plate to cutting height. The rip fence holds the throat plate in place during this operation. This wood throat plate should only be used when necessary to prevent splitting. If you leave it on the saw and then try to tilt the blade for a bevel cut, you will bend the blade!

Another method sometimes used to prevent chipping is to place masking tape on the plywood along the path of the cut. This seems to help in some situations, but does not always guarantee chip-free cuts.

Covering Exposed Plywood Edges

Any exposed plywood edges on furniture or cabinets should be covered. There are several ways to do this. One of the most popular is to use one of the commercially available wood tape edge bandings. Some of these have a heat-activated adhesive and can be applied with an ordinary clothes iron (Fig. 2–48). Others are applied with contact cement or an ordinary wood glue, in which case they must be clamped while the glue dries.

Figure 2–48 Applying edge banding to plywood edge. The wood banding has a heat-sensitive adhesive.

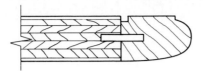

Figure 2-49 Wood molding on edge of plywood.

Another option is to cut thin strips of edging material from a solid wood that matches the plywood face veneer. These strips are usually ¼ or ⅜ in. thick. They are applied with contact cement or glued and clamped or, in some cases, they may be glued and nailed with small brads.

In situations requiring a molded edge, a solid wood molding may be glued to the edge of the plywood sheet to cover the edge plys, as shown in Fig. 2-49. In this case, a spline (often ⅛-in. plywood) is usually used to reinforce the joint. Also notice the "shadow line" (the groove where the molding joins the plywood). This is often done so that, in case the plywood and molding surfaces are not exactly flush, it will not show. It also makes it easier to do final sanding on the molding without cross-sanding on the plywood surface. Such moldings are often used on table tops or desk tops. Plywood edges are also, often covered by face frames on cabinets and some furniture items.

After any edge banding has been applied, the surface should be cleaned of any excess glue and then scraped or sanded. A hand scraper may be used, as described in Chapter 7, or a portable belt sander with a fine belt may be used to sand the edge banding flush with the face of the plywood. Great care must be taken not to sand through the plywood face veneer. A finish sander may be used for a final sanding.

WOODWORKING JOINTS

A brief review of the common woodworking joints may be helpful before going on to construction techniques. As was mentioned in the section on edge gluing boards, it is true that two pieces of wood, if properly edge glued, will produce a glue joint stronger than the wood itself. However, if it is necessary to join wood parts using end grain surfaces, this no longer holds true. In fact, the resulting glue joint will be very weak. Because of this, it is necessary to cut joints in the wood so that parts can be joined in such a manner that they are not totally dependent on the glue for strength.

Some of these joints are shown in Fig. 2-50. Techniques for machining many of these joints are shown in Chapter 3. Many of these joints require additional reinforcement. This reinforcement may be wood dowels, wood splines, wood keys, or any of a number of metal fasteners.

Another interesting joint-reinforcing system uses wood wafers, as shown in Fig. 2-51. This system was developed in Europe, but has become very popular in the United States. It requires a special machine (Fig. 2-52) that cuts matching elliptical slots in the part to be joined. A special wafer made of compressed wood is used along with a water-base glue. When the compressed wafer is inserted in the slot along with the

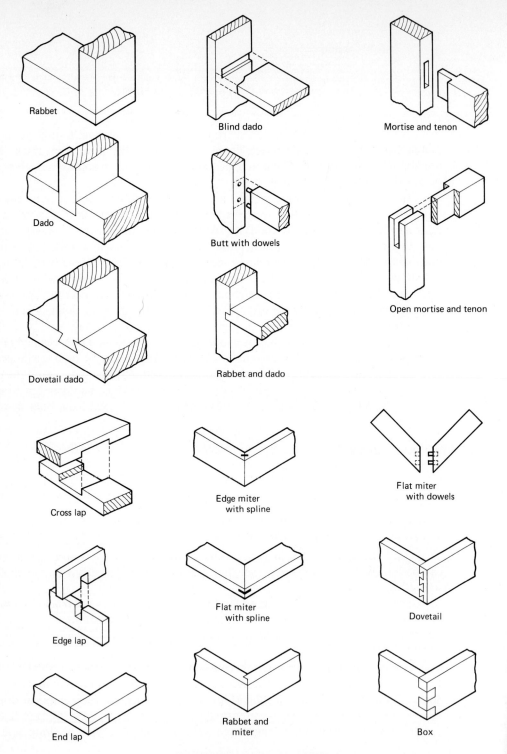

Rabbet

Blind dado

Mortise and tenon

Dado

Butt with dowels

Open mortise and tenon

Dovetail dado

Rabbet and dado

Cross lap

Edge miter
with spline

Flat miter
with dowels

Edge lap

Flat miter
with spline

Dovetail

End lap

Rabbet and
miter

Box

Figure 2–50 Common wood joints.

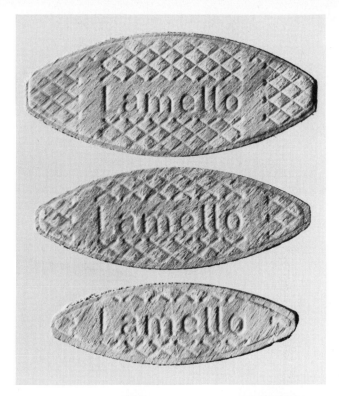

Figure 2-51 Compressed wood wafers for glue joints (Lamello).

Figure 2-52 Machine for cutting wafer joints (Lamello).

water-base glue, it expands, making a very tight fitting joint. This system can often eliminate the need for dado joints, rabbet joints, and many joints that would require dowel reinforcement.

Metal fasteners are also used for joint reinforcement. Nails, wood screws, and bolts may be used in some types of construction. Several other special wood joint fasteners are very useful. These are shown in Figs. 2-53, 2-54, and 2-55.

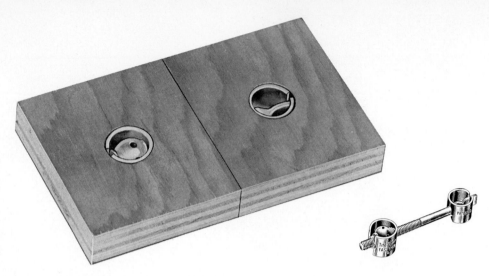

Figure 2-53 Tite-joint fastener (Knape & Vogt).

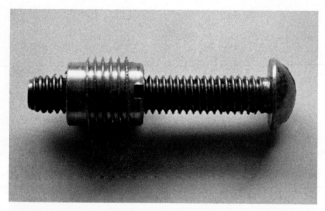

Figure 2-54 Threaded insert.

Figure 2-55 T-nut.

38   Construction Techniques   Chap. 2

BASIC CONSTRUCTION METHODS

Most furniture or cabinet projects are constructed using one of the following methods or some variation of one of the methods:

- Leg and rail
- Box
- Case or carcass
- Frame and cover

Leg and rail construction.   Leg and rail construction, in its simplest form, consists of four legs joined by four rails as shown in Fig. 2–56. This construction method is often used for tables, chairs, benches, and beds, although it is sometimes enclosed to form a cabinet. There may also be bottom rails called stretchers (Fig. 2–57).

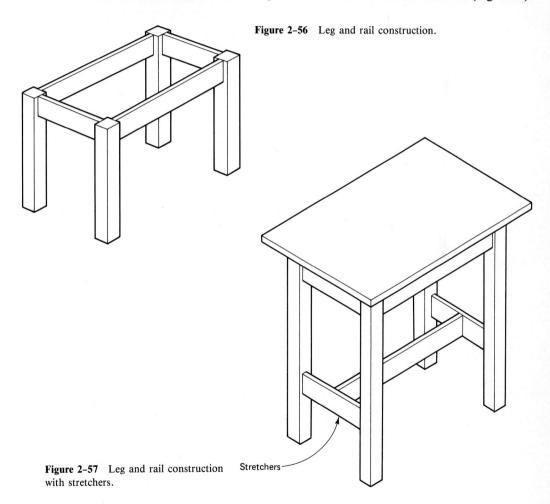

Figure 2-56 Leg and rail construction.

Stretchers

Figure 2-57 Leg and rail construction with stretchers.

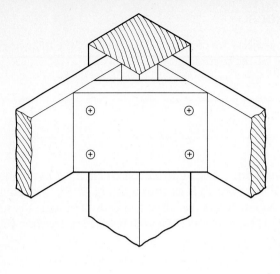

Figure 2-58 Diagonal brace used with leg and rail construction.

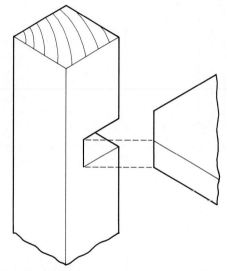

Figure 2-59 Corner dado for installing shelf in leg and rail construction.

The rails and legs may be joined using butt joints with dowels, mortise and tenon joints, or dovetail dado joints. On tables and chairs, the joints are often reinforced with diagonal corner braces, as shown in Fig. 2–58. Shelves may be installed using corner dados, as shown in Fig. 2–59. Drawers are sometimes installed in cutouts in the rails.

Box construction. Box construction is used in the construction of drawers, chests, trunks, jewelry boxes, tool boxes, and other items. In its simplest form, it consists of a bottom, four sides and sometimes a lid. The corners may be joined using rabbet joints, box joints, dovetails, any of several miter joints, or wood corner

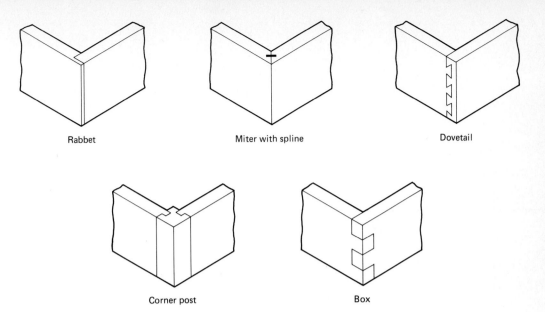

Figure 2-60   Typical joints for assembling corners of a box.

posts. Several of these systems are shown in Fig. 2-60. See Chapter 3 for information on making these joints.

The bottom of the box is usually installed with a rabbet or in a groove in the case of drawers. The box lid may set flat on the top of the box, as in Fig. 2-61, or the box may be assembled with the lid glued in place and the top portion of the box

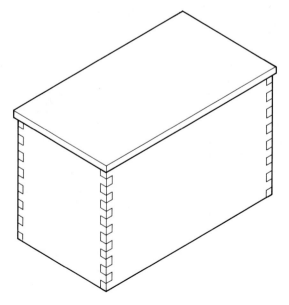

Figure 2-61   Box with separate lid.

Basic Construction Methods

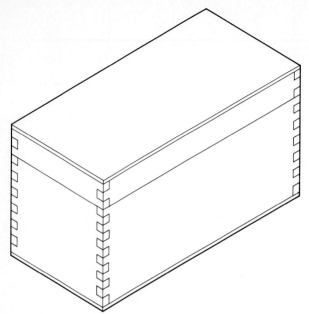

Figure 2–62 Box lid formed by cutting top off box.

cut off later to form a lid (Fig. 2–62). Drawers, shelves, and lift-out trays are often incorporated in box construction.

Case or carcass construction.   These two names are used somewhat interchangeably to designate a large category of furniture and cabinet construction. It includes nearly all cabinet work, chests of drawers units, dressers, china cabinets, linen cabinets, stereo cabinets, gun cabinets, and many others. They can range from a simple box (turned up on edge so that a side is open) to the very finest furniture. Case construction often incorporates drawers, doors, and shelves. The case may be supported by legs, or it may set on a base (sometimes called a plinth).

The sides, tops, and doors on case units may be made using any one of the three construction techniques mentioned earlier. That is, the sides, for example, could be made from plywood, glued solid lumber, or frame and panel construction. The actual joints used to assemble these components into a finished case may vary considerably depending on the final appearance requirement and strength requirement.

The case sides and bottoms are often joined with rabbet joints or dado joints if an integral base is used. The top may be joined to the sides with a rabbet, lock miter, or splined miter if the joint is to be flush. Box joints or dovetail joints are also sometimes used for this purpose. If the top is to overhang the cabinet sides, dowels or one of the special desk top fasteners described in Chapter 4 may be used.

Permanently installed shelves are usually installed with a blind dado, dovetail dado, rabbet and dado, or wafer joints. Adjustable shelf systems are also often used. Figure 2–63 shows some of the common options for joining parts of a case.

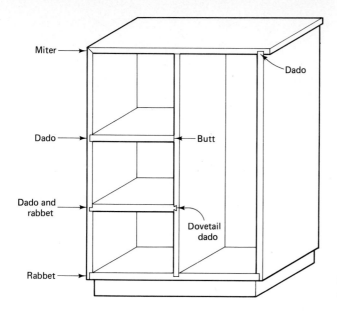

Miter

Dado

Dado

Dado and rabbet

Rabbet

Butt

Dovetail dado

Figure 2-63 Some options for joining case components.

Dust panels are often used between drawers in better furniture construction. These are simply frame and panel units installed much like shelves (Fig. 2-64). Drawer guides are often mounted on these dust panels.

Some larger case goods, such as large hutches, are made in two or more pieces and then attached in final assembly. Some are never permanently attached to allow for easier moving. The top unit just sits on the base unit.

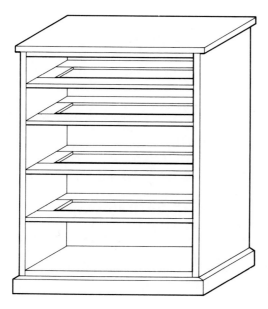

Figure 2-64 Case with dust panels.

Basic Construction Methods

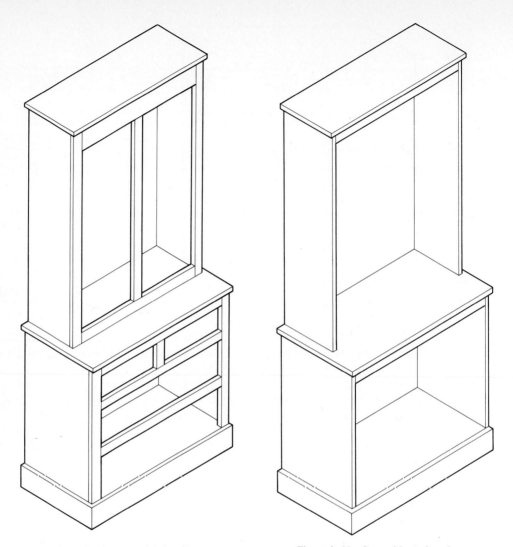

Figure 2-65 Case with face frame.

Figure 2-66 Case without face frame.

Many case units have face frames. The face frame is made up of vertical members (stiles) and horizontal members (rails). The face frame forms the openings for doors and drawers and provides a structure for mounting door hinges and some types of drawer guides.

Figure 2-65 shows a typical case with face frame. When a face frame is used, it is assembled and glued as a unit; then is attached to the cabinet. Some case units do not use a face frame. Figure 2-66 shows a typical case with no face frame.

Frame and cover construction. Cabinets made using frame and cover construction look quite similar to cabinets made using case construction when they are finished. However, there are major structural differences. In the frame and cover method, a skeleton frame is made (usually of 1 in. by 2 in. lumber) such as the one shown in Fig. 2–67. It is then enclosed by being covered with a thin ($\frac{1}{8}$ or $\frac{1}{4}$ in.) plywood. By comparison, the same cabinet using the case or carcass method would be constructed using thicker material ($\frac{3}{4}$ in.), but without a skeleton frame (Fig. 2–68).

The big advantage of frame and cover construction is that the resulting cabinet is much lighter in weight. For this reason this type of construction is popular for cabinets in campers, vacation trailers, and motor homes. It is seldom used where its weight-saving feature is not needed because it takes longer to construct.

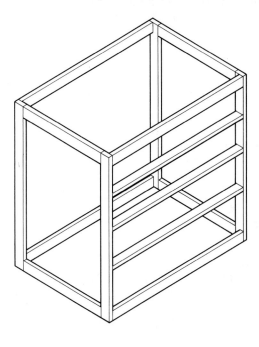

Figure 2–67 Frame for cabinet using frame and cover construction.

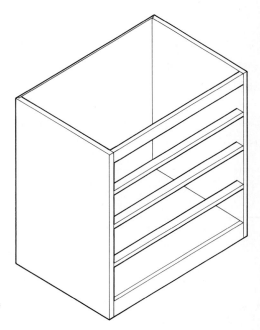

Figure 2–68 Same cabinet using 3/4-in. sheet material.

DOORS

Doors may be used with any of the previously mentioned construction methods. They may be used to enhance the appearance of a cabinet, as well as to hide the contents of the cabinet. They also keep dust out of cabinets. Doors may be hinged, bifold, sliding bypass, or tambour. We will consider hinged doors first.

There are three basic ways of fitting hinged doors to cabinets. These are lip, flush, and overlay (Fig. 2–69). Lip doors (sometimes called inset doors) are made with a rabbet around the edge of the door so that it fits the face frame, as shown in Fig. 2–69. This rabbet is usually ⅜ by ⅜ in. since most hinges for lip doors are made for that size (Fig. 2–70). This system is quite easy to fit, since any slight irregularity in the door opening is covered by the door lip. They are only used on cabinets with face frames.

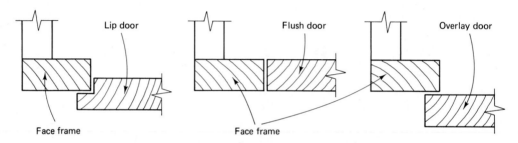

Figure 2–69 Lip, flush, and overlay doors on cabinet with face frame.

Figure 2–70 Hinges for lip doors fit the rabbetted edge.

Flush doors fit inside the door opening so that they are flush with the face of the cabinet. They may be used on cabinets with or without face frames. They are much more difficult to fit accurately since the gap around the door is visible. It is very important that the door opening be perfectly square and that the door be accurately cut to size.

Several types of hinges may be used on flush doors. These range from completely hidden hinges to face-mounted hinges. One of these is shown in Fig. 2–71.

Overlay doors are probably the most popular for furniture and cabinets. They may be used on cabinets with face frames or on cabinets without face frames. For cabinets with face frames, overlay doors are merely cut somewhat larger than the door opening (usually ½ in.) and then mounted on the cabinet face. One of the hinges designed for this purpose is shown in Fig. 2–72.

Figure 2–71 Hidden hinge for flush door (Julius Blum, Inc.).

Figure 2–72 Hinge for mounting overlay door on face frame.

Doors

Figure 2-73 European-style cabinet. Doors and drawer fronts are all that show from the cabinet front.

Overlay doors for cabinets without face frames are designed to completely cover the edges of the cabinet sides, bottom, and partitions. Doors (and drawer fronts) completely cover the cabinet face with this type of construction. This is typical of the popular European-style cabinet shown in Fig. 2-73. The selection of hinges for this style of door is more limited. The semiconcealed pivot hinge shown in Fig. 2-74 may be used, or the European-style concealed hinge (Fig. 2-75) may be used.

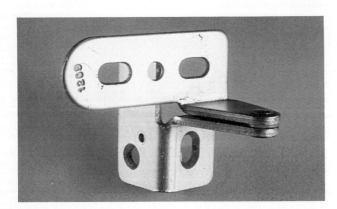

Figure 2-74 Semiconcealed hinge for overlay door.

Figure 2-75 European-style concealed hinges for overlay doors.

Door construction.   Hinged doors may be made from flat sheet material such as plywood, particle board, or medium-density fiberboard. Figure 2-76 shows some doors made from sheet material. These doors are easy to make since no fabrication is required. They are just cut to size and rabbeted in the case of lip doors.

Frame and panel doors are another very popular option for cabinet and furniture construction because of the many appearance options they allow. Figure 2-77 shows an example of a cabinet with frame and panel doors. A detailed discussion of frame and panel construction can be found earlier in this chapter.

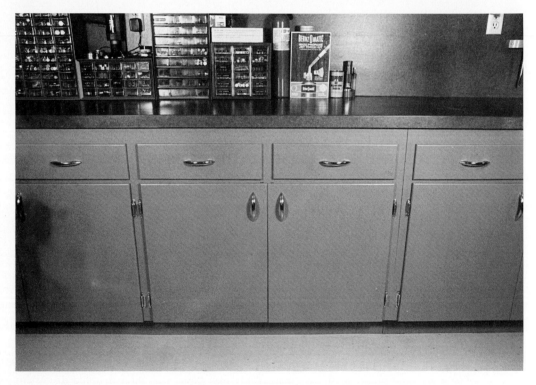

Figure 2-76 Doors made from sheet material.

Figure 2-77 Cabinet with frame and panel doors.

Bifold doors.　Bifold doors may be made of sheet material or of frame and panel construction. They are much like a conventional hinged door except that they have another hinged joint in the middle so that they only require half the room space when open (Fig. 2-78). Special bifold door tracks for larger doors are readily available at lumberyards.

Doors

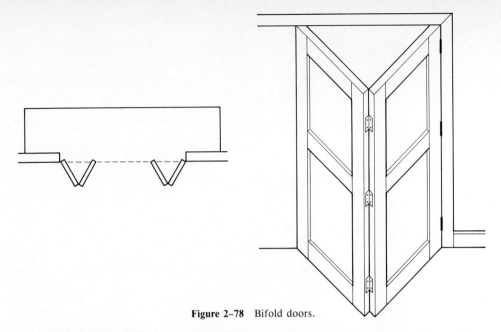

Figure 2-78 Bifold doors.

Sliding bypass doors.   When it is undesirable to have a door swing out into a room or hallway, sliding bypass doors may be used. They are usually made of ¼-in. plywood, glass, or plastic. Figure 2–79 shows a cabinet with sliding bypass doors. They use a track made of wood or plastic or a metal track with rollers. In some cases, the track grooves are cut directly into the cabinet top and bottom.

Figure 2-79   Sliding bypass doors.

When a sliding track is used, the top grooves must be approximately twice as deep as the bottom grooves to allow the door to be installed after the cabinet is assembled. The door is installed by first inserting the top edge of the door into the top track and then pivoting it inward and allowing it to drop into the bottom track.

Tambour doors.   Tambour doors (Fig. 2–80) are flexible doors designed to slide out of sight on a curved track. They are usually made of narrow strips of wood glued to a canvas backing. They may slide horizontally, like the doors shown in Fig. 2–81, or they may slide vertically, as in a roll-top desk. Compared with sliding bypass

Figure 2–80   Tambour doors.

Figure 2–81   Horizontal sliding tambour doors.

doors, tambour doors offer the advantage of being able to open the entire front of a cabinet. With sliding bypass doors, of course, only one side of the cabinet may be open at a time.

INSTALLING DOORS

Lip doors are quite easy to install. The hinges are mounted on the door first, as shown in Fig. 2–82. The spacing of the hinges from the top and bottom of the door will vary somewhat with the size of the door. Hinges are often set about 3 in. from the top or bottom of cabinet doors. To attach the doors to the cabinet, the cabinet is placed on its back on a workbench or on the floor. The doors are then positioned in the opening and the hinges are screwed to the face frame (Fig. 2–83). If self-closing hinges are used, the door will tend to shift away from the hinge side as the hinges are tightened against the cabinet face.

Flush doors are much more difficult to install. The door must be carefully fitted to the opening. A gap about the thickness of a penny all the way around the door should give adequate clearance. The actual installation procedure will vary considerably depending on the type of hinge to be used. The semiconcealed knife hinge shown in Fig. 2–84 requires a recess cut in the top and bottom of the door. Butt hinges (Fig. 2–85) have to be mortised into the edge of the door and the face frame. Invisible hinges require machining on the edge of the door and face frame. Some of the "European" hinges can also be used on flush doors. Face-mounted hinges may also be used. In every case, the manufacturer's directions should be followed.

Figure 2–82   Installing hinge on lip door.

Figure 2-83 Mounting lip door on cabinet.

Figure 2-84 Semiconcealed knife hinge for flush doors.

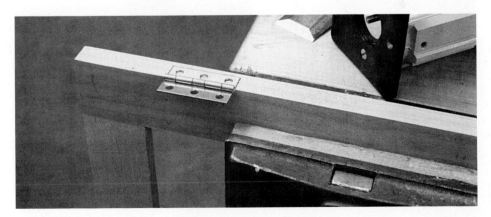

Figure 2-85 Butt hinges are mortised in to the edge of the door.

Overlay doors may be mounted with hinges similar to those used for lip doors. In this case, the door leaf on the hinge will be flat and the mounting procedure will be similar to that for lip doors. Overlay doors on cabinets without face frames may use either the semiconcealed pivot hinge or European-style hinges. The pivot hinge requires a groove cut in the edge of the door, as shown in Fig. 2–86. This may be done on the table saw, as shown in Fig. 2–87.

Figure 2-86 Semiconcealed pivot hinge requires cutting a groove in the door.

Figure 2-87 Cutting the groove for a semiconcealed pivot hinge.

Figure 2–88 Typical European hinge installation.

The pivot hinge is attached to the cabinet first, using the elongated screw hole. The door is then attached, also using the elongated screw hole. The door can then be adjusted up and down or sideways as necessary, and then the remaining screws are installed. If European hinges are used, it is usually necessary to drill a 35-mm hole in the back of the door. A typical European hinge installation is shown in Fig. 2–88.

Installing sliding bypass doors requires either machining grooves in the top and bottom of the cabinet or using one of the commercially available tracks. These tracks may be either nailed with small brads or glued in place. Be sure to put the track with the deeper grooves in the top of the cabinet! Flush finger pulls are available to fit in a ¾-in. hole drilled in each door.

Tambour doors may be installed either by using an extra-deep top groove, allowing them to be inserted in the top groove and then dropped into the bottom groove, or they may be installed from the back of the cabinet if the groove is accessible. (A removable back is sometimes used.) Tambour doors usually require some fine-tuning to make them slide freely around the corners. The ends of the tambour slats may have to be rounded, as shown in Fig. 2–89, if they must take tight-radius turns. After the project is finished, the track should be waxed.

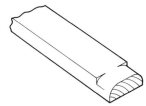

Figure 2–89 Ends of tambour door slots may have to be rounded to allow the door to make tight radius turns.

Hinged glass doors are sometimes used, especially on stereo component cabinets. These glass doors are hung with a special hinge that clamps to the glass.

DRAWERS

Drawers may be fitted to cabinets or furniture using any one of the three basic methods used for doors (lip, flush, or overlay). Drawers present a challenge to woodworkers because they must be quite strong and must slide freely, yet not be "sloppy" in their movement.

Drawer materials. Many materials are used in drawer construction, depending on the application. Hardwoods are often used for drawer sides and backs on fine furniture and better-quality cabinets. Softwoods or plywood may be suitable for other applications. The typical thicknesses listed here are for normal-size cabinets and furniture. Drawers for a small project such as a jewelry box, for example, would be made of thinner material. Typical drawer materials are as follows:

- Fronts: ¾-in. hardwood or hardwood plywood
- Sides: ½-in. hardwood, softwood, plywood, or medium-density fiberboard
- Backs: ½- or ¾-in. hardwood, softwood, plywood, or medium-density fiberboard
- Bottoms: ¼-in. plywood or hardboard

Drawer joints. The joints used to assemble drawers should be selected with the eventual use of the drawer in mind. Drawers that are expected to receive heavy use, such as those for file cabinets or heavy tools, should be assembled with dovetail or dovetail dado joints. Some of the more popular drawer joints are shown in Fig. 2–90. See Chapter 3 for information on machining these joints.

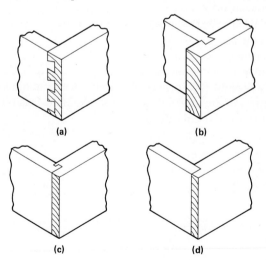

(a)

(b)

(c)

(d)

Figure 2–90 Typical joints for joining drawer fronts to drawer sides.

Drawer assembly.   Drawers may be assembled by gluing and clamping if dovetail or dovetail dado joints are used. For the other joints, nails are often used in addition to gluing. The drawer side is nailed to the drawer front and drawer back. Drawer bottoms are not glued, but are merely trapped in the bottom groove or may be nailed to the underside of the drawer back.

Drawer guides.   Drawer guides must be designed to allow the drawer to slide smoothly without excess sideways motion, yet must allow for some expansion or contraction of the drawer. Shop-built drawer guides are usually either center guides under the drawer or side guides.

Center guides consist of a wood guide rail mounted in the cabinet under the drawer, as shown in Fig. 2–91. A matching grooved hardwood strip may be mounted on the underside of the drawer, as shown in Fig. 2–92. Another very serviceable alternative with the wood center guide is to use a set of commercially available plastic guide tabs (Fig. 2–93). If these plastic guide tabs are to be used, the drawer is made $\frac{1}{4}$ in. smaller than the opening (height and width) to allow space for the plastic tabs.

Drawers made with a bottom guide require a tip rail above the drawer to keep it from tipping forward when it is pulled open. Figure 2–91 shows a typical drawer opening with center guide and tip rail in place.

Figure 2–91   Drawer center guide.

Drawers

Figure 2-92 Grooved hardwood guide on the underside of a drawer to match the center guide rail.

Figure 2-93 Plastic drawer guide tabs.

Installing a drawer with a center guide is quite easy. The center guide is first attached to the front of the cabinet. This may be accomplished by nailing a small $\frac{1}{4}$-in. plywood tab to the front end of the guide rail, inserting it in the cabinet, and then nailing the plywood tab to the back of the face frame (Fig. 2-94).

Figure 2-94 Quarter-inch plywood tab attached to drawer center guide.

Once the drawer guide rail is attached to the front of the cabinet, the drawer is inserted and the back of the guide rail is adjusted until the drawer front closes tightly against the face of the cabinet on all sides. The location of the drawer guide rail is then marked on the cabinet back. The drawer is then removed, and the guide rail is attached as marked, using nails or screws.

The other popular option for shop built drawer guides is the side guide system. This system consists of hardwood rails on both sides of the drawer opening in the cabinet with matching grooves in the drawer sides (Fig. 2-95). This system is somewhat

Figure 2-95 Drawer with hardwood side guides.

Drawers

more difficult to fit, since the guide rails are mounted permanently in the cabinet and the grooves are cut in the drawer sides before the drawer is assembled. It is necessary to be accurate when installing these guides and in cutting grooves in the drawer sides. A coat of hard paste wax on the guides will make them operate smoothly.

In addition to shop-built systems, many commercially made drawer guide systems are available. These, too, are usually either center guides (under the drawer) or side guides.

The center guide system usually consists of a metal channel under the drawer in which a drawer-mounted guide wheel rides (Fig. 2–96). There are also a set of rollers just inside the face frame for the drawer sides to roll on. The directions on the package should be consulted for the required space clearance between the drawer and the drawer opening.

Side roller guides (Fig. 2–97) are usually somewhat more expensive than center guides, but are usually capable of carrying heavier loads and are often smoother in operation. One popular model is rated at 75-pound load capacity, and others are available up to 150-pound capacity. Some side guides are also available in full extension models; that is, the drawer can be opened to its full depth, making it much easier to reach the contents in the rear of the drawer (Fig. 2–98).

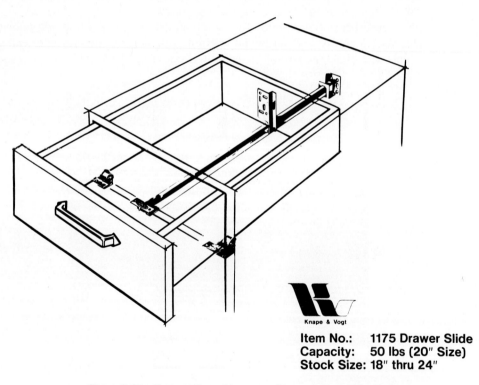

Knape & Vogt

Item No.:   **1175 Drawer Slide**
Capacity: **50 lbs (20″ Size)**
Stock Size: 18″ thru 24″

Figure 2-96   Center-roller guide system (Knape & Vogt Mfg. Co.).

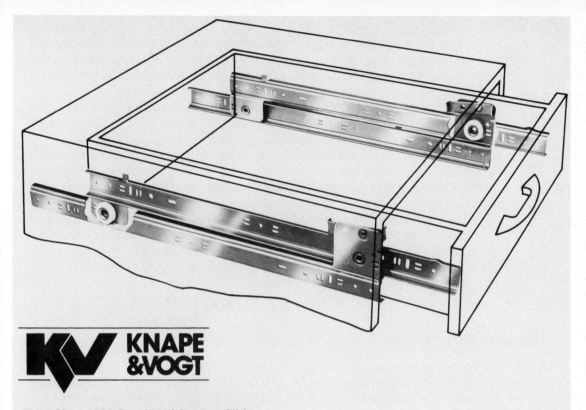

KV KNAPE &VOGT

Item No.: 1300 Pan Head Drawer Slide
Capacity: 75 lbs. (20″ size) (50.8cm)
Sizes: 12″ thru 28″ in two inch increments
Side Clearance: ½″, plus ⅟₃₂″, minus 0 each side   mounts with pan head screws

Figure 2–97 Side-roller guide system (Knape & Vogt Mfg. Co.).

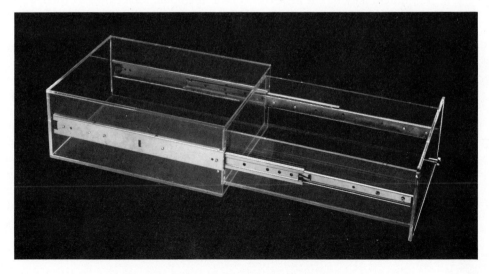

Figure 2–98 Full-extension side guide system (Accuride).

Most side roller guides require ½ in. of space on each side of the drawer, so the drawer must be 1 in. narrower than the drawer opening. Installing drawers with side-mounted guides involves attaching the cabinet rails to each side of the cabinet and the drawer rails to each side of the drawer. The cabinet rails are sometimes installed before the cabinet is assembled. These rails usually come with some of the screw holes elongated vertically and others elongated horizontally to allow for adjustment. If the cabinet rails are installed using the vertically elongated holes and the drawer rails using the horizontally elongated holes, for example, the drawer can be adjusted up or down and in or out before it is permanently locked in place by installing screws in the round holes. If the drawer has too much side play, cardboard shims can be placed behind the guide rails.

There are many side guides on the market offering different features. Some are designed to be nearly silent in operation, some are extra heavy duty for very heavy loads, and some offer full extension convenience. Side roller guides are also used to mount roll-out trays (drawers behind doors) that are often used in cabinets in place of fixed shelves.

VENEERS AND VENEERING

Veneering has been popular for centuries, both with the old master furniture makers and later with furniture manufacturers. It is still a popular art and is not beyond the amateur woodworker who has above-average patience. Veneering involves gluing a very thin piece of wood (veneer) to a thicker piece of a less expensive or less attractive wood, plywood, or particle board. It is done as a method of getting better use of some of the rare or expensive woods or to achieve special effects not available in commercially manufactured plywood. The possibilities are only limited by the imagination of the woodworker. Figure 2–99 shows an example of veneer work.

Veneers are very thin layers of wood, often ½₈ in. thick. The log (referred to as a flitch) may be cut in one of several methods, each designed to give a different appearance. Three methods used for veneer cutting are shown in Fig. 2–100.

The rotary cutting method is by far the most popular and is used almost exclusively in softwood plywood production. It is also used to produce some hardwood veneers and produces the least expensive veneers. Most of the rest of hardwood veneer production is either plain or quarter sliced.

Veneers cut from various parts of a tree can yield some very different and interesting results. Veneer cut from the trunk usually yields a fairly straight uniform grain pattern. Veneer cut at the stump or from a limb crotch yields a very wavy grain pattern. Veneers cut from burls that sometimes occur on trees yield a most interesting pattern of swirls.

In practice, veneers are usually not available in sheets large enough to cover larger surfaces in one continuous piece. Rather, they are cut and edged glued together. The joints are taped to help hold the pieces together until they are glued to the substrate. This joining process allows the woodworker to create some very interesting

Figure 2-99 Example of a veneered bed headboard. (Designed and built by Scott McCulloch)

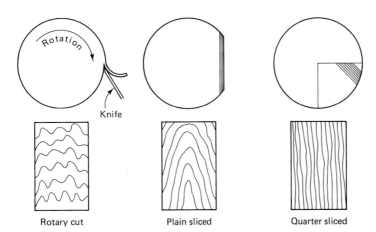

Rotation

Knife

Rotary cut

Plain sliced

Quarter sliced

Figure 2-100 Three common veneer cutting methods and resulting grain patterns.

patterns by selectively matching sections of veneer. Veneers are available in matched sets (successive cuts) to aid in grain matching. Some of the more common veneer matching methods are shown in Fig. 2-101. Some woodworking supply houses sell veneer sheets that have been cut, glued, and taped and are ready to be glued to the substrate.

Veneers and Veneering

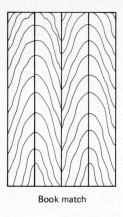
Book match

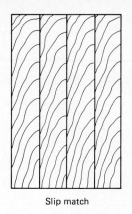
Slip match

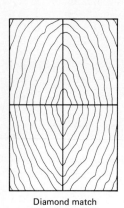
Diamond match

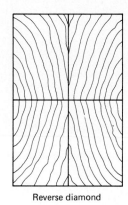
Reverse diamond

Figure 2-101 Four common veneer matching methods.

Working with veneers.   The first problem in working with veneers is cutting them to desired sizes with straight, square edges suitable for gluing. This may be done using a straight edge clamped to the veneer sheet and a veneer saw, dovetail saw, or a very sharp knife. Veneers may also be cut with sheet-metal shears or even paper cutters, but the blades must be *sharp*.

If the edges are not perfectly straight, they can be planed by clamping the veneer between two pieces of scrap lumber and running the edge across the jointer or by using a fixture such as the one shown in Fig. 2-102 and a hand plane.

The veneer pieces are then set in position on the backing (core) material (industrial-grade particle board or medium-density fiberboard make excellent core materials).

If the joints all fit properly, they are taped with masking tape or veneer tape (Fig. 2-103). The veneer sheet is then turned over and the edges are glued using aliphatic resin glue (Fig. 2-104). The back surface is also then taped and the glue allowed to dry. After the glue is dry, the tape is removed from the back surface only. The veneer sheet is then ready to be glued in place.

Figure 2-102 Planing the edge of a piece of veneer.

Figure 2-103 Taping veneer joints.

Figure 2-104 Gluing the veneer edges.

Veneers and Veneering

The best way to glue the veneer down is with a press, using a conventional wood-working glue. Unfortunately, veneer presses are usually only found in large furniture or plywood manufacturing plants; however, small veneer presses are available from some woodworking supply houses.

Lacking a press, the next best method of attaching the veneer to the core stock is to use contact cement. The contact cement is applied to both the back of the veneer and to the core stock. If the core stock is particle board or medium-density fiberboard, a second coat of contact cement should be applied after the first has dried. The contact cement must be allowed to dry before the veneer is installed. The veneer must be positioned and brought into contact with the core very carefully. As soon as the two surfaces touch, they will bond, allowing no further movement. Start at one edge and press the veneer down while holding the rest of the sheet away from the core stock. Gradually press the veneer down working away from the first edge. When the veneer sheet has adhered, the tape may be removed from the face side and the surface rolled with a roller.

Inlaying is sometimes done with veneers. The process involves tracing a pattern on the wood surface and tracing the same pattern on the veneer to be inlaid. The pattern area is then recessed by the thickness of the veneer. A router with a small ($\frac{1}{8}$ in.) bit works well to remove the material from all but the tightest corners, which can be finished with a knife or carving tool. The veneer inlay is then cut to fit with a sharp knife.

Marquetry can be an art form in itself, but is sometimes incorporated into furniture. In marquetry, a picture or pattern is formed by putting pieces of different veneers together to form a picture. Each element of the picture is made from a veneer selected because of its color and grain pattern.

For example, to illustrate a stormy sky, one might use a dark, wavy-grained walnut veneer. Each piece of veneer is cut from a pattern with a sharp knife. They are then taped together and glued to the core stock. Precut marquetry pictures are available from some woodworking supply houses.

CANING

Caning is another process that is often combined with woodworking. Cane is made of thin strips of bamboo bark and is woven into various patterns to form mats or sheets. These are sometimes used for chair seats, chair backs, and cabinet door panels (Fig. 2–105). The cane sheets or mats are available in a number of machine-woven patterns.

Cane is installed in a wood frame with a $\frac{1}{4}$ in. by $\frac{1}{4}$ in. groove cut around the face side. The prewoven cane sheet is cut approximately 2 in. larger than the frame and soaked in warm water until it is pliable (1 to 2 hours). It is then stretched over the frame, and the special caning bead is driven into the groove to hold the caning in place. As the caning dries, it will shrink and become tight.

Figure 2–105 Example of caning.

GLASS

Glass is often used in doors and side panels of woodworking projects. There are several ways of holding the glass in place, but all involve setting the glass in a rabbet in the frame.

The glass may be held in place with a wood molding as shown in Fig. 2–106, or the glass may be glued in place with a clear silicon seal cement. Glass-retaining clips can also be used to mount the glass either flush in a rabbet or on the surface (Fig. 2–107).

Glass doors may be made without a wood frame if special clamp-on hinges and catches are used. These are popular for stereo cabinets.

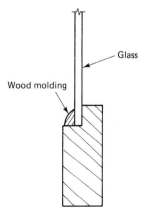

Glass

Wood molding

Figure 2–106 Wood molding used to hold glass in frame.

Glass

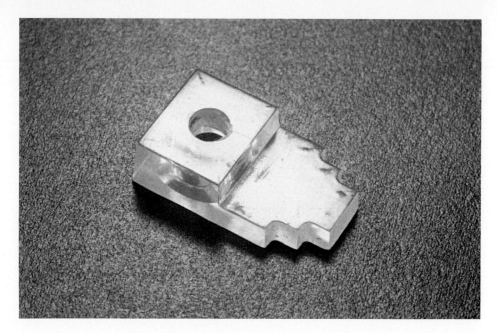

Figure 2–107 Plastic clip for holding glass in frame.

PLASTIC LAMINATES

Plastic laminates, such as Formica and Wilson Art, are often used in furniture and cabinetmaking when a very hard, durable surface is needed. They are especially popular for table, desk, and counter tops. They are sometimes also used as a facing on cabinets.

They are not particularly difficult to install, although a router with laminate trimming bits is very handy. Plastic laminates are usually installed over industrial particle board or plywood using contact cement.

The plastic laminate parts may be cut with a table saw using a carbide plywood or other fine-tooth blade. The parts should be cut somewhat oversize to allow for final trimming after they have been cemented in place. One-quarter-inch oversize is adequate for most smaller parts. If both the edges and the top of a table top, for example, are being covered, the edges are applied first. Contact cement is brushed on the edge of the table top *and* on the back of the plastic laminate. If particle board is used, it should get two coats of contact cement. After the contact cement is dry, the edge strip is applied (Fig. 2–108), and pressure is applied with a roller or by tapping it with a mallet. The excess plastic laminate is then trimmed flush. This is where the router and laminate trimmer bit come in handy (Fig. 2–109). Lacking a router, this can be done with a very sharp block plane or even with a portable belt sander.

Figure 2-108 Applying a plastic laminate edge banding.

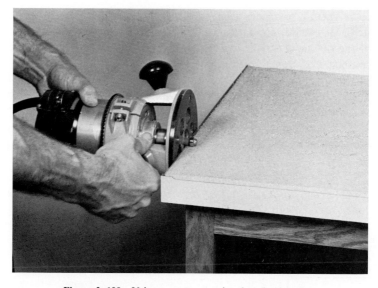

Figure 2-109 Using a router to trim the edge banding.

Plastic Laminates

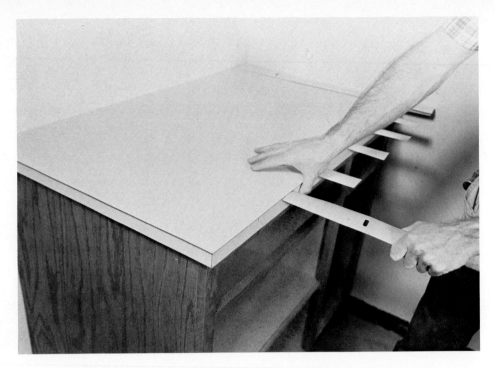

Figure 2-110 Old Venetian blind slats have been used as spacers while the plastic laminate top was positioned. They are then removed, starting at one end of the top.

The top surface is applied last. If the top is very large, it is helpful to have some strips of plastic laminate or wood to lay on the top to allow accurate positioning of the plastic laminate top before the cemented surfaces are allowed to come into contact. Old Venetian blind slats work well for this purpose (Fig. 2-110).

When the top is in position, the first slat is removed and the laminate is pressed down; then the next slat is removed, and so on, until all the slats have been removed and the top is cemented down. A roller is again used to apply pressure.

The excess laminate is trimmed with a beveled laminate trimmer (Fig. 2-111). Finally, the exposed edge should be filed smooth with a fine, single-cut file.

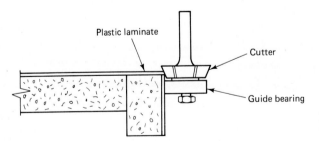

Plastic laminate

Cutter

Guide bearing

Figure 2-111 Router bit for trimming the edge of the laminate sheet.

CUTTING AND DRYING YOUR OWN LUMBER

Many woodworkers cut all or some of the lumber for their own projects. It is often possible to obtain logs from trees that have been blown down or from trees that property owners want removed. These logs can be purchased or sometimes obtained at no charge just for removing the tree.

Several manufacturers make attachments for chainsaws that can be used for cutting these logs into boards. An alternative is to have a local sawmill cut the log into boards to your specifications.

After the boards are cut, they will have to be properly dried before they can be used. The Forest Service, U.S. Department of Agriculture, recommends the following procedure for drying small amounts of lumber:

1. All logs should be end-coated as soon as possible after felling to prevent end checking. Aluminum paint in a spar varnish base or asphalt roofing cement work well for several months. However, the sooner the log can be sawn, the better.

2. If the logs will not be sawn immediately, damage from insects, stain, and decay may result, especially during warm weather. To minimize this problem, check with your state forestry officials for their recommendations on use of insecticides and fungicides or keep logs submerged or continuously sprinkled with water in lieu of insecticides and fungicides.

3. Determine what lumber sizes you will need. As a general rule, the drying results will be best if the thickness is no greater than 2 in. If you need thicker material for turnings, it is better to saw 1 in. thick boards, dry them, and glue them back together into thicker pieces. Thicknesses less than 1 in. may lead to warping difficulty during drying. If you are going to use polyethylene glycol (PEG), frequently used for cross-section disks or carving stock, use it right after sawing and omit steps 4 through 9. [PEG is a chemical used by hobbyists to stabilize wood so it will not swell or shrink.]

4. Find a sawmill that can do the work needed. Again, state forestry officials may be of help. The more accurate the sawn thicknesses, the less wood wasted and the more uniform the drying job. If the sawn lumber is quite variable in thickness, one or both faces of the thicker material may be jointed or planed to bring it down to size.

5. Decide where you want to put your lumber for air drying—not too exposed to strong wind, but not too sheltered either. Avoid areas where grass or weeds might block air flow in the lower layers. Use bricks or cement blocks to keep the lowest layer off the ground.

6. Immediately after sawing, the lumber should be stacked in neat layers (with the thicker material on the bottom since it will be "done" last) with each layer consisting of only one thickness of lumber. Spacers, called stickers, running perpendicular to the board lengths and spaced every 12 to 18 in. along the lumber, separate each layer of lumber. Make certain stickers support the board ends. (With 12-in. spacing, 8-ft boards would require nine stickers per layer. If the pile is 4 ft wide, the stickers would be 4 ft long.) The purpose of the stickers is to permit air to move through the lumber pile and to keep the lumber flat.

7. At this point, it would be wise to check the ends of the thicker boards and make sure the end coatings are still intact; if not, use some more of the coating from step 1.

8. Lay another course of stickers on the top layer and cover the pile with a sheet of plywood or old boards to protect the top layers from the sun and repeated wetting from rain. If you feel that warping might be a problem, you can place a lot of weights, rocks, etc., on top of the pile cover.

9. In warm but not too humid weather, the 1-in. lumber will be fairly well air dried (15% to 20% moisture content) in 45 to 60 days (2-in. lumber, 60 to 90 days). In the winter, lumber may require twice as long to dry. Not much drying will occur after about 60 days of good drying weather. BUT IT IS NOT READY FOR USE INDOORS. For these applications, further drying is necessary. (For constructing unheated garages, barns, or outbuildings, air drying alone is adequate.)

10. If you can find a commercial kiln-drying operation, see if they can dry your lumber the rest of the way (6% to 8% moisture content for indoor use in most of the U.S.). Make sure you will get a stress-relieve period; no stress relief causes saw pinching when dried boards are ripped, as well as other problems.

11. Although some people have dried lumber in their attic, this procedure is not recommended as a substitute for kiln drying. However, a solar kiln—a small plastic-walled greenhouse with a fan to circulate air and a few holes in the wall to let out moisture—is a suitable substitute for commercial kiln drying. A month or longer during cold or cloudy weather in a solar kiln will finish drying most previously air-dried woods. If the food is not sufficiently dried when used *or* is allowed to pick up moisture by poor storage (i.e., not low enough humidity), you may experience shrinking, warping, or checking in use. Try to keep the temperature in the solar drying (on the average) about 15°F above the average outdoor temperature at the end of drying or during storage. You should be able to store lumber in the solar dryer indefinitely with this temperature difference. If you do your own drying, it is suggested that you measure the moisture content of wood so you can determine when the wood is dry enough to use. One approximate method is to saw a piece $1\frac{1}{2}$ to 2 ft long from several wider boards; the cut should be made at least 6 in. from any knot or other defect. From the freshly cut end of the board, cut off a section approximately 1 in. in length along the grain. Measure the width of this section (width of the board) to within $\frac{1}{64}$ in. and then place it near a radiator, hot air register, or a stove for at least a day. If no checks appear on the ends and no measurable shrinkage in width occurs, the wood is uniformly dry to a moisture content of about 7% or 8%.

12. If, at anytime, difficulty is experienced, check with a knowledgeable person—perhaps your State Forester's office can help, or your local library. You may also wish to write to the U.S. Forest Products Laboratory, P.O. Box 5130, Madison, WI 53705, for a needed report.

3 Woodworking Machines

Woodworking can be done successfully with hand tools only, but the use of machines makes the process much faster, and machines make it much easier to achieve professional looking results. Even the best woodworking machines, however, will not produce professional results unless a few basic precautions are observed.

WOOD PREPARATION

One of the more common problems is producing boards that are out of square, tapered, or otherwise not flat and true. Chipped or torn grain, machine burns, raised grain, and excessive mill marks are other common machining problems. These problems and their prevention will be discussed before proceeding to individual machines.

Squaring rough lumber. If rough boards are badly twisted or bowed, it is usually best to cut them to shorter lengths if possible, before attempting to square them. The procedure for squaring a rough, out-of-square board is as follows:

1. Run the face of the board across the jointer as described later in this chapter. This will get one face flat and straight.
2. Run the board through a surface planer to plane the second face parallel with the first.
3. Straighten one edge of the board on the jointer, making sure that the jointer fence is exactly square with the table and that the board is held tightly against the fence.
4. Cut the second edge parallel with the just planed edge using the table saw. This

cut should be made so that the board is cut to within about $\frac{1}{16}$ in. of the finished width of the board. The jointer can then be used to remove the saw marks from the sawn edge and bring the board down to final width.

5. Use either the radial arm saw or table saw with miter gage to cut the board to exact lengths.

If this procedure is followed carefully, the result will be a flat, true board with all surfaces square with adjacent surfaces.

Avoiding grain chipping and tearing. Grain chipping often seen on the surface of planed boards is caused by planing "against the grain." The grain direction is "read" on a surface adjacent to the surface to be planed. In other words, if you are running the edge of a board across the jointer, you look at the face of the board to determine grain direction. The proper direction is shown in Fig. 3–1. The reason for this is that the machine cutters act like wedges trying to split the wood when they hit the wood. The wood tends to split along the grain. In Fig. 3–1, the splits run back out to the edge of the board, but in Fig. 3–2 they tend to run into the wood, leaving a very rough surface. If the wood has visible medullary rays as those seen in red or white oak, the medullary rays determine which direction the board should be planed.

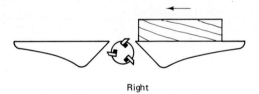

Right

Figure 3–1 Correct grain direction for planing edge of board on jointer.

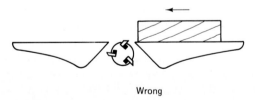

Wrong

Figure 3–2 Running board in this direction will cause grain chipping.

Occasionally, there will be boards in which the grain direction changes, and it will be necessary to plane part of the board against the grain. In this case, sharp cutters, light cuts, and slow feed speeds will help avoid chipping.

Avoiding machine burns. Machine burns are caused by dull cutters and by feed speeds that are too slow or by stopping the feed while cutters continue to run. Machine burns are very common with portable routers. Router cutters turn very fast and tend to burn the wood if the router is held in one place even momentarily, especially when the cutter is dull.

Woodworking cutters depend on contact with the wood to cool them. If they are not continually cutting in fresh cool wood, they will quickly overheat. The solution to the machine burn problem is to keep cutters sharp and make sure that the wood is kept moving past the cutters at a uniform rate. Keeping machine table tops and fences waxed helps a great deal in this regard.

Avoiding raised grain. Dull knives tend to compress the wood fibers rather than cut them off cleanly. The wood fibers then expand, causing the surface of the wood to be very uneven. Planing wet wood will also cause this problem. Again, the cure is sharp machine knives and cutters.

Avoiding mill marks. Mill marks are the result of the circular cutting motion of the knives on a planer, jointer, shaper, or router. These are shown in Fig. 3-3 These mill marks cannot be completely eliminated, but they can be reduced a great deal by running the board slowly. It is also very important that all the knives be set at exactly the same height in the cutter head. One knife higher than the rest will produce very bad mill marks.

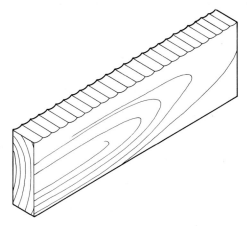

Figure 3-3 Mill marks on the edge of a board.

TABLE SAW

The table saw is probably the most useful and versatile machine in woodworking. Most table saws include a table with slots that run parallel with the blade, a rip fence, a miter gage, a control for setting blade height, and a control for setting the angle of the blade. They also have a blade guard, splitter, and antikickback device. On some machines, the splitter and antikickback device are incorporated in the guard. A typical table saw is shown in Fig. 3-4.

A properly set up table saw can be used for cutting dados, rabbets, miters, splines, tenons, tapers, coves, moldings, raised panels, box joints, dovetails, and for the conventional ripping and crosscutting of lumber and plywood. A good table saw is potentially a very accurate machine provided it is properly aligned and adjusted

Figure 3–4 Typical table saw (Powermatic, a division of Stanwich Industries, Inc.).

(see Chapter 7). The table surface and rip fence should be kept waxed with a hard paste wax to assist in feeding lumber and to prevent rusting.

Saw Blades

Using the correct saw blade also has a bearing on the quality of work. Because of the nature of the cell structure of wood, a saw blade requires a very differently shaped tooth for cutting across the grain (crosscutting) than for cutting with the grain (ripping) (Fig. 3–5). For the ultimate in efficiency and cut quality, it would be necessary to change saw blades each time you change from a ripping to a crosscutting operation. Fortunately, saw blade manufacturers have developed combination blades that either use groups of teeth with a rip tooth followed by either two or four crosscut teeth or use ripsaw teeth with the shape modified to allow crosscutting. Some of the better combination blades will do both jobs quite well. There are also special saw blades for cutting plywood, sheet plastics, and nonferrous metals.

Figure 3–5 Saw blades for different purposes: rip (left), combination (center), and crosscut (right) (DML, Inc.).

Woodworking Machines   Chap. 3

In addition to differences in tooth shape and size, all saw blades must have some method to provide side clearance, to keep the wood from pinching on the sides of the blade. On less expensive steel blades, this is accomplished by "setting" or bending the teeth to the side in alternate directions. On some more expensive steel blades, the sides of the saw blade are taper ground or hollow ground so that the blade thickness tapers away from the rim. Side clearance is achieved on carbide blades by virtue of the carbide tips being wider than the blade thickness.

Other Cutters

A dado head is a common accessory for a table (or radial arm) saw. They may be made up with two circular saw blades and chippers, or adjustable types are available (Fig. 3–6). Molding heads are also available. These usually consist of a steel head in which matched sets of molding cutters can be mounted (Fig. 3–7).

Figure 3–6 Adjustable dado head (Sears, Roebuck & Co.,).

Figure 3–7 Molding head for table saw.

Table Saw Safety

While the table saw is a very useful machine, it can be a potentially dangerous machine if not used properly. Most table saw accidents are caused by *kickbacks,* which are caused by the board either binding or pinching on the saw blade or binding between the rip fence and saw blade. The following are common causes of binding and kickbacks on table saws:

- Sawing boards that are badly twisted, warped, or cupped.
- "Free-hand" sawing without using a rip fence or miter gage as a guide.
- Rip fence not aligned with saw blade.
- Sawing wet wood, especially with a saw blade that has little set in the teeth.
- Ripping with a crosscut blade.
- Crosscutting using the ripping fence as a guide.
- Pitch or other foreign material on the fence or table that prevents the wood from sliding smoothly
- Using dull blades.

These conditions should always be avoided.

Several other precautions should be observed when using a table saw:

- The blade height should only be ⅛ to ¼ in. above the wood being cut.
- Use the guards provided by the manufacturer.
- When ripping, push the board past the *rear* of the blade before releasing it.
- Use a push stick such as the one shown in Fig. 3–8 when ripping narrow boards.
- Make sure that boards to be ripped have a *straight* edge to run against the rip fence.

Figure 3–8 Push stick used for ripping narrow boards on table saw.

Figure 3-9 Antikick back wheels help hold stock down and against rip fence (Western Commercial Products).

Several companies make antikickback feeder wheels that can be mounted on the rip fence. These are very helpful in many situations. One is shown in Fig. 3-9.

Using the Table Saw

A normal table saw ripping operation is performed as follows:

1. Set the rip fence for the desired width of cut. You will have to measure from the inside of the blade to the fence if your saw does not have an accurate scale.
2. Make sure that the fence is parallel with the blade. Many better quality saws are equipped with fences that automatically align themselves when locked down.
3. Stand to the *left* of the blade and use your left hand to hold the board against the fence and down on the table. Push the board with your right hand (Fig. 3-10).
4. Use a push stick to complete narrow cuts.
5. The procedure for starting a large board into the saw is shown in Fig. 3-11. To complete the cut, you need an off-bearing table behind the saw, or you can have someone support the board. In this case, make sure that he does not pull

Table Saw

Figure 3-10 Starting a board into the table saw.

Figure 3-11 Starting a long board into the table saw.

Woodworking Machines   Chap. 3

the board or move it from side to side. Another way to cut a long board is to cut halfway, shut the saw off, and remove the board. Then turn it end for end and complete the cut.

Crosscutting is done with the sliding miter gage. The location of the cut is usually marked on the board, which is then placed against the front surface of the miter gage (Fig. 3-12). Wider boards may be crosscut by reversing the miter gage, as shown in Fig. 3-13. The use of the miter gage is made easier by mounting a board on the face to increase the usable surface area. This helps in cutting larger boards.

Figure 3-12   Crosscutting a board using the miter gage.

Figure 3-13   Reversing the miter gage to cut a wide board. (The saw guard has been removed for clarity in showing this operation.)

Things can be improved even more by gluing a piece of fine abrasive paper to the miter gage facing board. This keeps the boards from "creeping," especially when cutting miters (Fig. 3–14). The board attached to the face of the miter gage also provides a convenient place to clamp stop blocks for cutting multiple lengths (Fig. 3–15).

Multiple lengths may also be cut using a stop block clamped to the rip fence. The fence should not be used for this purpose without the extra block because the cut off pieces will bind against the blade and kick back.

Figure 3–14 Board faced with sandpaper is attached to miter gage.

Figure 3–15 Stop block used with miter gage. (The saw guard has been removed for clarity in showing this operation.)

Woodworking Machines Chap. 3

Table Saw Operations

Cutting dados. Dados are usually cut with one of the dado heads described earlier. A conventional dado head consists of two outside saw blades and one or more chippers to achieve the desired thickness. A typical set consists of two outside saws (each $\frac{1}{8}$ in. thick), four chippers $\frac{1}{8}$ in. thick, and one chipper $\frac{1}{16}$ in. thick. Adjustments finer than $\frac{1}{16}$ in. are made with paper washers.

To set up such a dado, place one outside saw blade on the arbor. Then place the first chipper. On some carbide dado sets, the first chipper has to be placed against the outside blade in such a way that its teeth do not hit the teeth on the outside saw (Fig. 3–16). The remaining chippers are usually staggered so that they do not all come into contact with the wood at once (Fig. 3–17).

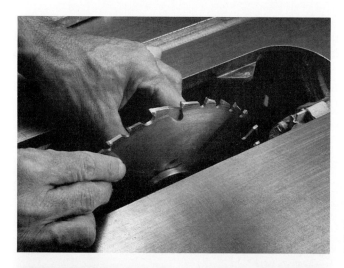

Figure 3–16 Placing the first dado chipper so that it does not contact the carbide teeth of the outside blade.

Figure 3–17 The chippers are staggered so they do not all contact the wood at the same time.

Some table saws have a very short arbor and require a special adapter to use a dado head. When the dado head is set up and tightened, a special throat plate with a wide slot is inserted in the table saw. Dados, rabbets, and grooves may then be cut using the same techniques described for ripping and crosscutting.

Cutting a blind dado. Since the dado head is covered by the board you are machining, it is difficult to cut a blind dado without a system of marking the location of the dado head. The following system can be used to cut a blind dado.

1. Set the dado head at the proper depth.
2. Slide a piece of scrap wood with a square end against the front edge of the dado as shown in Fig. 3-18. This represents the front point of the dado. This is marked on the rip fence.
3. Put a mark on the top side of the board where you want the dado to end. For instance, if you want the dado to stop ½ in. from the edge of the board, place a mark ½ in. from the back edge of the board (on the top side so you can see the mark).
4. Start the saw and run the board until the mark on the board lines up with the mark on the fence (Fig. 3-19.)
5. Stop the saw and remove the board.

Figure 3-18 Marking the rip fence for a blind dado.

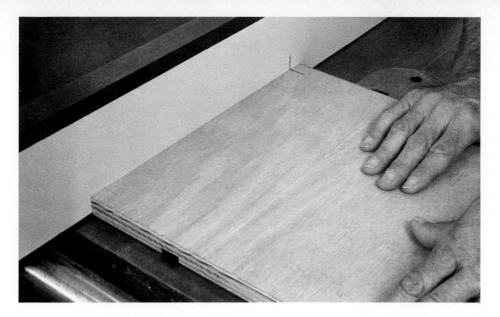

Figure 3-19 A mark on the board shows when to stop the blind dado cut.

If the dado needs to be blind from both sides, the process is similar, but a little more complicated. The rip fence is marked as before, but the rear of the dado must also be marked (Fig. 3-20). You will need marks on the top side of your board indicating where the dado is to start and stop. Then, follow these steps:

Figure 3-20 Marking the rip fence for the start of a blind dado cut.

Figure 3-21 The blind dado cut is started by aligning the mark on the board with the mark at the rear of the dado blade.

1. Make a note of the position of the blade-raising handle.
2. Crank the blade below the table, counting the number of turns.
3. Set the board on the table with the dado start mark aligned with the rear mark on the fence (Fig. 3-21).
4. Clamp a stop to the fence to keep your board from creeping forward when beginning the cut.
5. Start the saw and raise the blade to its original height by counting the number of turns. Be careful to hold the board down tightly while doing this. (*Note:* Never attempt to make this cut by lowering the board into the running saw.)
6. Complete the cut as described earlier.

It should be noted that some internal cutouts (such as for a drawer opening in a table rail) can be made in the same way.

Cutting rabbets.   The easiest and safest method of cutting rabbets with a dado head involves using a protective wood face clamped to the rip fence and then setting the fence against the dado head as shown in Fig. 3-22. If you have a number of rabbets of different widths to cut, set the dado head for the widest ones and cut those first. To cut the narrower ones, you can drop the dado head below the table and move the fence over the dado head until the desired width of cutter is exposed. Lock the fence in place and start the saw.

Figure 3–22 Cutting rabbets with the dado head against the rip fence. A piece of scrap wood is used to protect the fence.

Raise the dado head into the protective wood fence to the desired depth. For example, if the dado head is set up for a ¾-in.-wide cut and you want to cut a ½-in.-wide rabbet, just move the fence so that it covers ¼ in. of the dado head, leaving ½ in. exposed. This eliminates the necessity of stopping and changing the width of the dado set for each different rabbet width.

When cutting dados and rabbets in plywood, especially when cutting across the face grain of hardwood plywood with thin veneers, it is necessary to score the first ply before making the full depth cut. This is done by raising the dado set above the table by the thickness of the first veneer and making a slow cut. Then, without moving the rip fence, raise the blade to the full dado or rabbet depth and complete the cut.

If there are only a few rabbets to be cut, it is often faster to cut them with a regular saw blade than by setting up a dado head. To cut rabbets with a regular saw blade:

1. Set the saw blade height for the depth of the rabbets.
2. Set the rip fence for the width of the rabbet cut by measuring to the outside (left) of the blade.
3. Make the first cut.
4. The second cut is made with the board in the vertical position.
5. Set the rip fence for the thickness that will be left after the rabbet is cut (for a ½-in.-deep rabbet, cut in ¾-in.-thick material, set the rip fence at ¼ in.).

Figure 3-23 Completing a rabbet cut.

6. Make the second cut as shown in Fig. 3-23. This second cut should always be made so that the scrap piece of material falls to the outside (left) of the saw blade to prevent it from being trapped between the fence and the blade and then being kicked back.

Cutting miters. Very accurate miters can be made on the table saw if everything is properly set up. A facing board covered with fine abrasive paper should be attached to the miter gage to keep the boards from creeping during cutting. The miter gage is then set for the desired angle.

Forty-five degree angles required for typical miters can easily be set using a carpenter's framing square as shown in Fig. 3-24. The 12-in. mark on both legs of the square is aligned with the miter slot in the saw table.

A right-hand miter is cut as shown in Fig. 3-25, and a left-hand miter is shown in Fig. 3-26. While it is possible to make both the left- and right-hand cuts on flat miters with the same miter gage setting by turning the boards face down for the second cut, it is better to make the cuts as shown so that the boards are always cut face up. Most saws will chip the wood to a certain extent on the bottom side of the cut. If all cuts are made with the good or face side up, the face side will always be good.

The easiest way to cut a group of miters is to set the miter gage for one side, say the right-hand miters, and cut this miter on all boards. Then set it for the left-hand miters, measure and mark the desired length, and cut the left-hand miters.

Figure 3–24 Using a framing square to set the miter gage at 45°.

Figure 3–25 Cutting a right-hand miter with the miter gage. (The saw guard has been removed for clarity in showing this operation.)

Figure 3–26 Cutting a left-hand miter with the miter gage. (The saw guard has been removed for clarity in showing this operation.)

Before cutting the miters on the workpieces, a trial miter should be cut and checked with a combination square, as shown in Fig. 3–27. It is also a good idea to cut a second miter and put it together with the first one to make sure that the two make a perfect 90° by checking with a framing square.

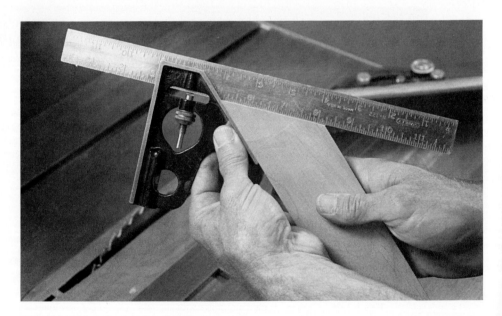

Figure 3–27 Checking a miter cut.

Edge miters are made by setting the miter gage at 0° (perpendicular to the saw blade) and tilting the saw blade to the desired angle (Fig. 3–28). Trial cuts should again be made. Most saws have an adjustable stop for setting the saw blade at 45°. This should be checked and adjusted if necessary.

Compound miters may be cut in one of two ways. One method requires cutting a piece of scrap wood that is beveled by an amount that matches the angle of the finished part. For example, to cut compound miters for a picture frame with sides at a 30° angle to the wall, you would cut a piece of scrap wood with a 30° bevel. This piece of wood is used to support the workpiece at the proper angle while the 45° miter is being cut, as shown in Fig. 3–29.

Figure 3–28 Cutting a flat miter by tilting the saw blade. (The saw guard has been removed for clarity in showing this operation.)

Figure 3–29 Cutting a compound miter. (The saw guard has been removed for clarity in showing this operation.)

Table Saw

Tilt of workpiece (degrees)	Blade tilt (degrees)	Miter gage angle (degrees)
5	44¾	85
10	44¼	80¼
15	43¼	75½
20	41¾	71¼
25	40	67
30	37¾	63½
35	35¼	60¼
40	32½	57¼
45	30	54¾
50	27	52½
55	24	50¾
60	21	49

Figure 3-30 Compound miter table.

The other method requires the use of a compound miter table such as the one in Fig. 3–30. In this case, the workpiece is flat on the table, and the saw blade and miter gage are angled to achieve the compound miter.

Cutting miters on large pieces such as pieces of plywood can be done by clamping a wood board on the rip fence and tilting the blade into the fence as shown in Fig. 3–31. There should be someone behind the saw to pull the narrow scrap piece from the saw so that it is not trapped against the blade and kicked out of the saw.

Figure 3-31 Cutting a miter on a large piece.

Cutting splines. Splines are often used to reinforce miter joints and butt joints. Splines may be cut in edge miters by placing the fence to the left of the blade (for saws that tilt to the right) and making the cut as shown in Figure 3–32. Splines may be cut in flat miters using the simple jig shown in Fig. 3–33.

Many carbide-tipped saw blades make a kerf $\frac{1}{8}$ in. wide. In this case, $\frac{1}{8}$-in. plywood or $\frac{1}{8}$-in. tempered hardboard can be used for hidden splines.

Figure 3–32 Cutting a spline for a miter.

Figure 3–33 Jig used for cutting a spline in a flat miter.

Figure 3-34 Cutting tenons with a dado head using the miter gage and rip fence as guides.

Cutting tenons.   Tenons are usually cut with a dado head and the miter gage using the rip fence as a guide, as shown in Fig. 3-34.

Cutting box joints.   Box joints may be cut on the table saw using a dado head and the miter gage. The pins and grooves must be equal in size, but they may be almost any width and depth. To make a box joint with ½-in.-wide pins and grooves, use the following procedure:

1. Attach a board to the face of the miter gage.
2. Set up the dado set for a ½-in.-wide cut (the depth of the cut will usually be equal to the thickness of the workpieces).
3. Make a cut through the miter gage board (see Fig. 3-35).
4. Remove the board from the face of the miter gage and move it *exactly* 1 in. to the left and make another cut (see Fig. 3-36).
5. Remount the board on the miter gage in its original position.

Figure 3-35 Making the first cut for a box joint jig.

Figure 3-36 Making the second cut for a box joint jig.

6. Place a ½-in.-square pin in the right-hand groove, as shown in Fig. 3–37.

7. Make the cuts for the joint by indexing the first part against the pin, cutting a groove, and then moving it to the right, indexing it against the pin each time (Fig. 3–38). The mating piece will be indexed one pin width to the left for the first cut. The rest of the cuts are the same. The completed box joint is shown in Fig. 3–39.

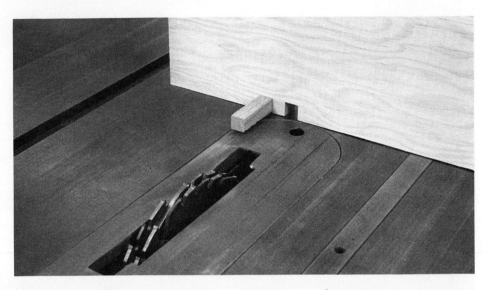

Figure 3–37   Guide pin for indexing cuts for making box joints.

Figure 3–38   Using the guide pin to index each cut on the box joint.

Figure 3-39 Finished box joint.

Cutting tapers.   Tapers may be safely cut on the table saw using a jig such as the one shown in Fig. 3-40. The jig is constructed by using a piece of ¾-in. plywood for a base and tacking on wood cleats at the desired angle. A pair of toggle clamps hold the wood in place so the operator's fingers do not need to be near the saw blade. An adjustable taper cutting jig such as the one shown in Fig. 3-41 may be used when the parts being cut are large enough to be held safely.

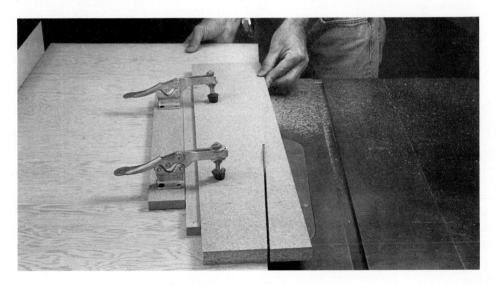

Figure 3-40 Jig for cutting tapers.

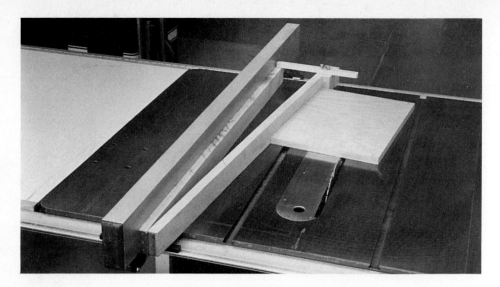

Figure 3-41 Adjustable taper cutting jig.

Tapers on large pieces such as plywood parts may be cut by clamping a wood guide under the sheet and running it along the edge of the saw table, as shown in Fig. 3-42. Make sure that the edge of the saw table is parallel with the blade when using this method.

Figure 3-42 Cutting a taper on a plywood sheet by clamping a guide under the sheet and running against the edge of the saw table.

Cutting coves. Coves may be cut on a table saw by running a board diagonally across the blade in a series of very light cuts. This technique is useful in making cove moldings, especially for coves of larger radius and, as we shall see shortly, for making very attractive raised panels. The radius of the cove is varied by the angle at which the board is run across the blade. The diameter of the blade will determine the maximum-radius cove that can be cut.

The basic process of cove cutting is quite simple. A straight board is used as a guide fence and is clamped to the saw table. The blade is raised just slightly above the table and the board to receive the cove is run over the saw. The blade is then raised slightly again and the board is run again. This is repeated until the cove reaches the desired depth. Figure 3–43 shows such a cove cut.

There is a procedure for determining in advance the depth and width of the cove. A simple parallelogram jig such as the one shown in Fig. 3–44 is required. The procedure for checking the cove width and depth is as follows:

1. Raise the saw blade to the desired final depth of the cove.
2. Adjust the parallelogram jig to the desired cove width.

Figure 3–43   Cutting a cove by running a board diagonally across the saw blade.

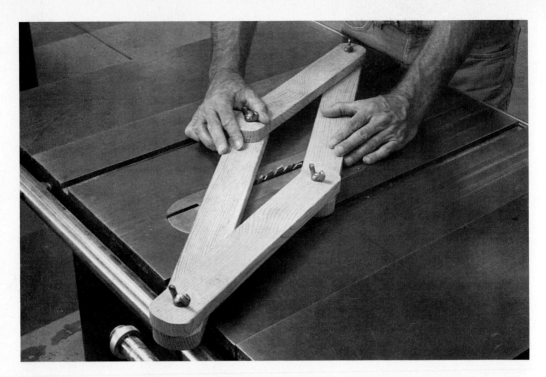

Figure 3-44 Parallelogram jig used to determine width of a cove cut.

3. Set the jig over the saw blade and rotate it until one side of the jig just touches the back of the blade and the opposite side just touches the front (Fig. 3-45).

4. Draw a pencil line on the saw table along the inside of the front edge of the jig as shown in Fig. 3-46. This line shows the angle to set the fence and shows the edge of the cove. If the cove is to be ½ in. from the edge of the board, you clamp the guide fence ½ in. from the line and parallel to the line.

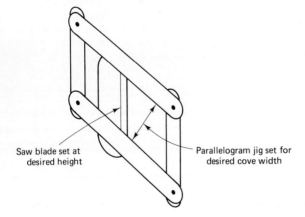

Saw blade set at
desired height

Parallelogram jig set for
desired cove width

Figure 3-45 Using the parallelogram jig to determine the angle for setting the guide fence.

Figure 3–46 Marking the angle for setting the guide fence.

5. Make a note of the position of the blade-elevation handle on the saw. This will be the position for the final cut. You are then ready to put the blade down to the position for the first cut and begin. The final cut should be a very light one and should be done very slowly to minimize the amount of sanding required.

Cutting raised panels. Raised panels are very popular for furniture and cabinet doors, as well as other furniture parts. Two of the most popular raised panel styles can be made on the table saw. The two popular methods of making raised panels are with the bevel and with the cove, as shown in Fig. 3–47.

The bevel-style panel is made by tilting the saw blade to the desired angle and making the first cut as shown in Fig. 3–48a. If the saw tilts to the right, the fence will have to be set on the left of the blade. The second cut for the small bevel is made as shown in Fig. 3–48b.

Figure 3–47 Two popular raised panel shapes are the bevel (left) and cove (right).

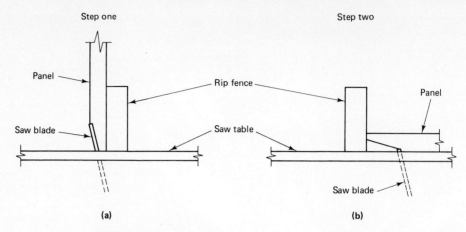

Figure 3-48 Cutting a beveled raised panel on the table saw.

The cove-style raised panels can be made using the previously described cove-cutting technique with the exception that the guide fence now covers half the blade. However, a better cove-style raised panel can be made by using a dado head rather than a saw blade. The difference is that the tongue on the edge of the panel is flat rather than tapered, so it will fit in a groove much better (Fig. 3–49). The backing cut shown in Fig. 3–50 makes sure that the tongue accurately fits the groove in the stiles and rails.

The setup for making this cove cut with a dado head is shown in Fig. 3–51. Very professional looking raised panels can be made using this method (Fig. 3–52). Once you have a setup that you like, mark the location of the guide fence on the saw table and save the guide fence. Write the setup information on the fence. It might read something like this: "Dado head set for ¾-in. cut. Blade height 3½ turns up with handle at 3 o'clock position." This will save you a great deal of time the next time you want to make raised panels.

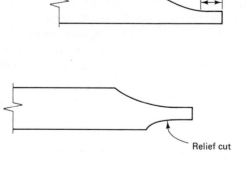

Figure 3-49 Cove cut made with dado head leaves a flat area for inserting panel into grooves in stiles and rails.

Figure 3-50 Relief cut on back of raised panel.

Figure 3–51 Setup for cutting a cove raised panel using a dado head.

Figure 3–52 Finished raised panel.

Cutting dovetail dados. While the dado part of a dovetail dado is usually cut with a router, the dovetail part is often cut with a table saw. Four cuts are required to make the dovetail, two shoulder cuts and two face cuts. The shoulder cuts are made as shown in Fig. 3–53 using the miter gage and the rip fence as a guide. The face cuts are then made with the board in the vertical position and the saw blade tilted 15° (see Fig. 3–54).

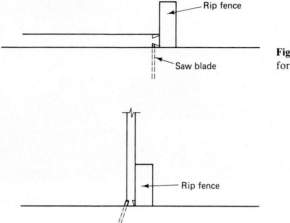

Figure 3–53 Making the shoulder cuts for a dovetail dado.

Figure 3–54 Making the face cuts for a dovetail dado.

Cutting moldings. A number of molding heads with interchangeable knives are available for table saws (Fig. 3–7). They are capable of producing good quality moldings, but they do have some limitations compared to a shaper or even a portable router. These molding heads are good for making long straight pieces of molding that might later be attached to a project. They are not particularly good, however, for molding the edge of a table top because, with most cutters, the table top would have to be run in a vertical position. Their most serious limitation is that it is nearly impossible to mold a curved edge such as the edge of an oval table top.

As long as these limitations are kept in mind, they can serve useful functions. When machining moldings on thin or narrow pieces, it is best to use feather boards or one of the available antikickback feeder wheels to keep the wood tight against the fence and the saw table.

Jigs and Fixtures for the Table Saw

There are a number of fixtures that you can build to make your table saw even more useful. If you are working with large boards or sheet material, an off-bearing table or cabinet behind the saw is one of the most useful accessories. It should be the same height as the saw table and should have a slick, hard surface, such as a plastic laminate or tempered hardboard. This table may be enclosed to form a storage cabinet.

A support rail to the left of the saw is very handy for cutting plywood and other sheet materials. Figure 2–39 shows a table saw with an off-bearing table and a support rail. With this setup, one person can cut a sheet of plywood into smaller parts.

The sliding crosscut jig shown in Fig. 3–55 is very handy for crosscutting boards to length, especially if a radial arm saw is not available. It is also much easier to use than a miter gage for crosscutting wide boards, such as a glued-up desk top. Plans for a sliding crosscut jig are shown in Chapter 8.

A sliding miter cutting fixture such as the one shown in Figure 3–56 is made in much the same way as the sliding crosscut jig. Plans are also shown in Chapter 8.

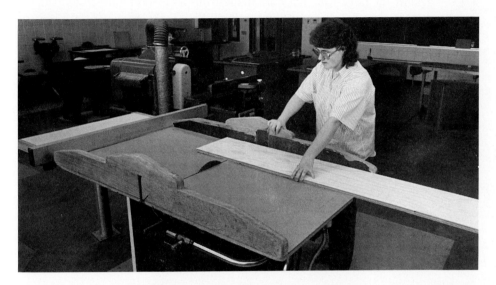

Figure 3–55 Sliding crosscut jig for crosscutting.

Figure 3–56 Miter cutting fixture.

Push sticks are very important for making narrow cuts on the table saw. The push-stick design shown in Fig. 3–8 can be used to hold the wood tightly against the table and the fence while pushing the wood through the saw. It should be made from ½- or ¾-in. plywood.

This push stick can also be used to make very narrow cuts by keeping it tightly against the saw fence and running it through the blade along with the stock being cut (Fig. 3–57). Make several push sticks and discard them after they get several saw cuts in them.

Feather boards are useful for holding stock tightly against the fence and down against the table top. They are made from hardwood lumber and can be made in various sizes for different applications (Fig. 3–58).

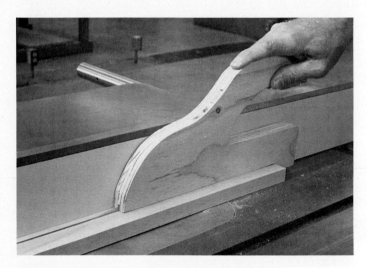

Figure 3-57 The push stick is run through the saw when making very narrow cuts.

Figure 3-58 Assortment of feather boards.

Figure 3-59 Typical radial arm saw (Black & Decker, Inc.).

RADIAL ARM SAW

The radial arm saw is also a very versatile machine and, in addition to normal cross-cutting and ripping operations, can be used to make dados, rabbets, miters, compound miters, and bevels and to shape moldings.

A typical radial arm saw is shown in Fig. 3–59. The saw and motor travel along a horizontal arm. The arm can be raised or lowered to vary the depth of cut. The arm can also be rotated at least 45° right and left (some machines go farther) for cutting miter joints. The motor and blade assembly can be rotated from the vertical position for bevel cuts and can be rotated horizontally so that the blade is parallel with the fence to make ripping cuts. On some machines, the motor can be rotated so the shaft is in the vertical position. This allows the machine to be used as a shaper.

Radial Arm Saw Safety

The radial arm saw cuts in the opposite direction compared with other circular saws (except when it is used for ripping). The rotation of the saw blade tends to pull the saw into the cut at an ever faster rate. (On the table saw, for example, the wood is fed against the rotation of the blade.) Therefore, one must always remember to keep a firm grip on the handle and control the rate of feed. This is especially true when using a dado head.

Other safety precautions include:

1. Make sure that the wood is held snugly against the fence and the table before starting the cut. Bowed boards should be blocked as shown in Fig. 3–60 to prevent pinching the blade when completing the cut.

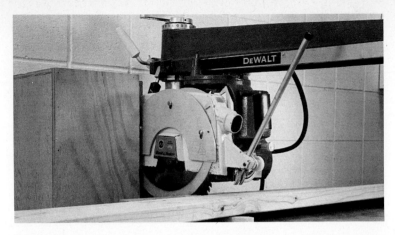

Figure 3-60 Blocking a bowed board to prevent it from pinching the blade as the cut is completed.

2. The saw should be all the way back against the column before starting the motor. The saw should be equipped with a return spring or counterweight so that it cannot inadvertently be started while in contact with the wood.

3. Make sure that the fence is continuous, with only a narrow slot for the blade to pass through. If part of the fence is cut away, it should be replaced.

4. If the saw is to be used for ripping, the cut must always be made against the direction of blade rotation. Make sure that the antikickback fingers are in place and are adjusted so that they are about ⅛ in. lower than the top surface of the stock being cut.

5. Check to see that the lower blade guards move up and down freely as they pass over the wood.

Radial Arm Saw Operations

Crosscutting with the radial arm saw. The board to be cut is placed flat on the table against the fence. The cut can be made with either the right or left hand. To make the cut with the right hand, hold the material down with the left hand on the left side of the blade. To make the cut with the left hand, hold the material down with the right hand on the right side of the blade. Draw the blade smoothly through the board until the cut is complete and then push the saw all the way back.

To measure and mark the location of cuts, hook a measuring tape on the end of the board and put a mark on the board at the desired location. Remember to cut on the outside edge of the mark. Most saw blades make a cut approximately ⅛ in. thick.

Making miter cuts. The arm is set at the desired angle and the cut is made using the same technique as for a crosscut. A trial cut should be made on scrap material and a protractor used to make sure that the angle is exact. A combination square can be used to check 45° angles.

Figure 3–61 Ripping using the "in-rip" position.

Making rip cuts.   The motor may be rotated 90° either direction for rip cuts. The blade may be facing the column or may face away from the column, depending on how wide the cut is to be.

The motor can then be moved along the arm until the desired width of cut is obtained. This is checked by measuring between the blade and the fence. Some saws have a measuring scale on the arm and a pointer on the saw carriage. This can be used if it is checked for accuracy.

The antikickback fingers are adjusted for height ($\frac{1}{8}$ in. below the top surface of the board being cut). The board is then fed against the blade rotation (Figs. 3–61 and 3–62).

Figure 3–62 Ripping using the "out-rip" position.

Radial Arm Saw

The series of photographs in Fig. 3–63a through e shows the radial arm saw being used for cutting bevels, dados, and rabbets, for shaping, and for cutting compound miters, respectively. The chart shown in Fig. 3–64 may be used to obtain the saw settings for compound miters.

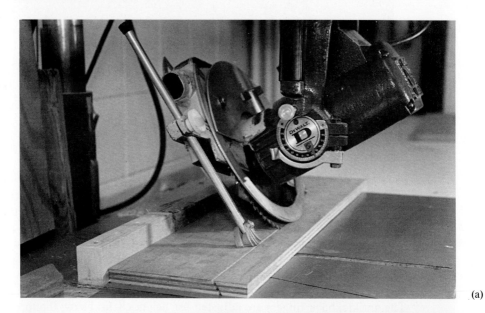

(a)

(b)

Figure 3–63 (a) Cutting a bevel; (b) cutting a dado; (c) cutting a rabbet; (d) shaping; (e) cutting a compound miter.

(c)

(d)

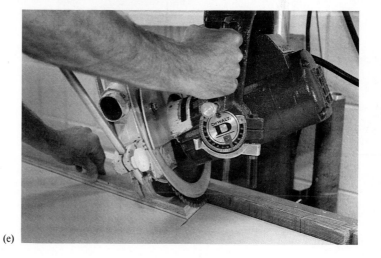

(e)

Tilt of workpiece (degrees)	Blade tilt (degrees)	Arm angle (degrees)
5	44¾	5
10	44¼	9¾
15	43¼	14½
20	41¾	18¾
25	40	23
30	37¾	26½
35	35¼	29¾
40	32½	32¾
45	30	35¼
50	27	37½
55	24	39¼
60	21	41

Figure 3-64 Compound miter chart for radial arm saw.

JOINTER

The jointer is another very valuable woodworking machine. It is used to establish a straight face or edge on boards and for planing saw marks from boards. It can also be used to make tapers, bevels, chamfers, and rabbets. Most jointers consist of a base, a cylindrical cutter head with three or four knives, an infeed table, an outfeed table, and a fence. The depth of cut is regulated by raising or lowering the infeed table and is indicated by a depth-of-cut scale.

Figure 3-65 Typical jointer (Delta Industrial Machinery Corp.).

The jointer size is designated by the length of the knives, which in turn dictates the maximum-width board that can be planed. Four-, six-, and eight-inch jointers are popular in home shops, while 16-in. and even larger jointers are not uncommon in industry. A typical jointer is shown in Fig. 3–65.

Alignment is very critical in a jointer. The infeed and outfeed table must be parallel with each other, and the outfeed table must be tangent with the cutting circle of the knives in order to obtain straight cuts. See Chapter 7 for more information on alignment and adjustment.

Jointer Safety

As with other machines, certain precautions must be observed when operating a jointer:

1. Do not run pieces shorter than 10 in. Shorter pieces have a tendency to tip down into the gap between the infeed and outfeed table and will be kicked back by the cutter head.
2. Use a push block when face jointing as shown in Fig. 3–66 or when edge jointing narrow boards. Never push a board by hooking your thumb or fingers behind the board to push it.
3. Check all boards for loose knots or other foreign material that could be kicked out of the machine.
4. Make sure that the knives are sharp. Dull knives are more likely to kick a board back, especially when face jointing.
5. Use a depth of cut appropriate for the operation being performed. A $\frac{1}{4}$-in. cut may be perfectly safe for edge jointing a large board, while $\frac{1}{32}$ in. would be the maximum for face jointing an 8-in.-wide piece of hardwood.
6. Make sure that the fence is securely locked in place and that the guard is working properly.

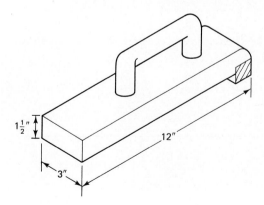

Figure 3-66 Push block for jointer.

Jointer Machine Operations

Face jointing. Boards are face jointed to remove twists, warp, or bow in preparation for planing with a surface planer. The jointer may also be used to smooth a previously sawn surface. A jointer alone, however, is not used to plane boards down to specified thickness, since there is no provision that the board will be uniform throughout in thickness. A surface planer must be used for this purpose.

The procedure for face jointing a board is as follows:

1. Set the desired depth of cut.
2. Make sure the fence is set back far enough to accommodate the board you are jointing.
3. Run the board as shown in Fig. 3–67, using a push block to complete the cut.

The jointer is capable of establishing a straight surface on a board that is badly twisted or bowed, but it will not just happen automatically by pushing the board through the machine! Once the cut has been started, the board must not be allowed to rock or twist in any way or the resulting cut will not be straight. For example, let us look at a common mistake in jointing bowed lumber. If a bowed board were

Figure 3–67 Face jointing a board.

to be jointed on the convex side, an inexperienced woodworker would probably push the leading end of the board down tightly on the table to start the cut and keep applying downward pressure over the infeed table to keep the jointer cutting as the board is fed through. This causes the jointer to "follow the curve." The jointer has taken a uniform amount of material from the entire length of the board, but it is still bowed!

The proper way to joint the board would be to apply the downward pressure near the middle of the board and then shift the pressure to the *outfeed* table as the board is fed to keep the newly planed surface flat on the table. The jointer will no doubt stop cutting before it gets to the end of the board, but a small flat surface will have been established. The next cut is made with this flat surface held firmly against the table. It may take several cuts until the entire surface is true, depending on how badly warped the board was.

A twisted board is a little more difficult. A board with a twist will tend to rock from side to side while it is being jointed. This must be prevented. Furthermore, to remove the least material when straightening a twisted board, the board must be balanced in "mid rock" (resting on diagonally opposite corners) for the first cut.

An example will help explain this. If you set a board with a $\frac{1}{4}$-in. twist on a flat table and push one end down, one corner on the opposite end will be raised $\frac{1}{4}$ in. off the table. It would require removing $\frac{1}{4}$ in. of material to get the surface flat if it were jointed in this position. However, if the high corner were pushed down halfway ($\frac{1}{8}$ in.), then the diagonally opposite corner would also be $\frac{1}{8}$ in. off the table. It now requires removing only $\frac{1}{8}$ in. of material to get the same surface flat. This is not as difficult as it sounds, and it becomes routine after a little practice.

Edge jointing. Edge jointing is done to establish a straight edge on a board, to remove saw marks, or to prepare for edge gluing. One objective of edge jointing is to get an edge of the board square with the face, so it is important that the fence be checked to see that it is square with the table. The procedure for edge jointing a board is shown in Fig. 2–17. Just as when face jointing, it is important that the board not be allowed to rock or twist while being jointed.

Edge jointing long boards. Many home shop jointers have relatively short tables, making it difficult to joint long boards. The following procedure can be used to straighten long boards on a short jointer:

1. Sight along the edge of the board to see which edge would be easiest to straighten. In this situation, it is usually best to do the convex edge.
2. To straighten the convex edge, start about one-third of the way from the end of the board, as shown in Fig. 3–68.
3. Start the cut with downward pressure on the infeed table, but keep your hands on the same location on the board as you move it across the cutters so that you are holding the newly jointed surface flat on the outfeed table (Fig. 3–69). This will establish a straight surface on part of the board, perhaps only the middle one-third of the board.

Figure 3-68 Starting a bowed board on the jointer. (The guard is being held back to show the board position.)

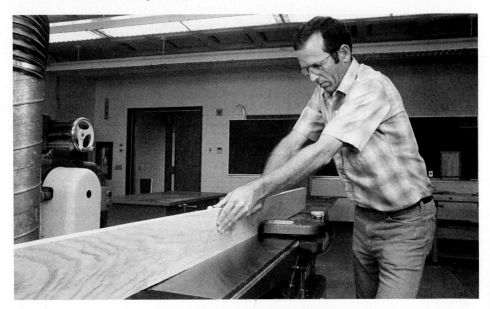

Figure 3-69 Finishing the first cut.

4. The second cut is made by starting with this flat surface on the infeed table (Fig. 3-70) and running the board, keeping the surface flat. The flat surface will now be longer.

5. This is repeated until the entire edge of the board is flat.

Figure 3-70 Starting the second cut.

Figure 3-71 Position for starting a long board into jointer.

6. It is best to have someone help support the board while doing this operation. If you must do it alone, start the board as shown in Fig. 3-71 and finish the cut as shown in Fig. 3-72.

7. The series of cuts necessary to get the board straight are shown in Fig. 3-73.

Figure 3-72 Position for finishing a cut on a long board.

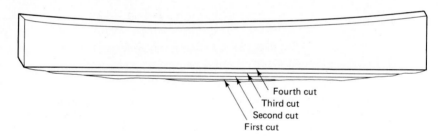

Fourth cut
Third cut
Second cut
First cut

Figure 3-73 Sequence of jointer cuts for establishing a straight edge from a convex surface.

Jointing plywood and end grain.   It is no longer common to routinely joint end grain or plywood edges since a good carbide saw blade of the proper type will produce a cut on plywood or end grain as smooth as that of a jointer. However, if it is necessary, precautions should be taken to prevent the bad chipping that almost always occurs on the trailing end of the cut. This can be done by starting the board into the jointer for about an inch and then removing the board and reversing it to make the cut as shown in Fig. 3-74. For safety reasons, boards narrower than 10 in. should not be run on end on the jointer.

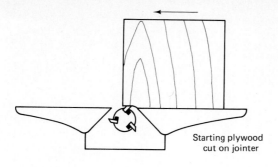

Starting plywood
cut on jointer

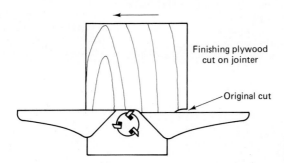

Finishing plywood
cut on jointer

Original cut

Figure 3–74 Procedure for planing plywood or end grain on a jointer.

Taper cuts. In many situations in woodworking, the ability to make taper cuts is very important. You can use this technique to make tapered legs for a table, chair, or desk. Another not uncommon situation is to find plywood pieces that were cut with a hand saw or portable saw and are not square. The jointer can be used to get two adjacent edges square on these parts so that they can be cut square on the circular saw. You may also want to intentionally make something out of square by tapering it. For instance, a pair of cabinet doors might have the proper gap at the top, but may touch each other at the bottom, so a tapered cut is necessary.

The procedure for making a taper cut on the jointer is as follows:

1. Determine where the taper is to start and how much taper is needed.
2. Set the depth of cut on the jointer equal to the amount of taper. (Large tapers must be made with several cuts.)
3. Start the cut by setting the board down on the outfeed table where the taper is to begin (Fig. 3–75). If the taper is longer than the infeed table on the jointer, the taper must be made in two or more cuts. For example, to make a 24-in.-long by $\frac{3}{8}$ in.-taper, set the jointer for a $\frac{3}{16}$-in. cut and start with a 12-in. taper. Then set the tapered surface flat on the infeed table and take another $\frac{3}{16}$-in. cut. Figure 3–76 shows an example of making taper cuts.

Figure 3-75 Starting a tapered cut on the jointer.

Figure 3-76 Making a tapered leg for a table leg.

Cutting a rabbet. A jointer with a rabbeting table (an extension of the table on the left side) may be used to cut rabbets. The guard must be removed and the fence set for the width of the rabbet. The infeed table is set to the depth of the cut (Fig. 3-77). (*Note:* If a jointer is to be used for rabbeting, the knives must extend slightly beyond the left end of the cutter head.)

Figure 3-77 Cutting a rabbet on the jointer.

Cutting bevels and chamfers. The fence on some jointers is designed to tilt to the right only (away from the operator) and some will tilt either way. In either case, bevels and chamfers may be cut. (Having a fence that tilts in either direction allows chamfering both edges of a board without running against the grain.) Figure 3-78 shows a chamfer being cut with the jointer.

Figure 3-78 Cutting a chamfer on the jointer.

BAND SAW

The band saw is designed to make curved and irregular cuts and is also useful for resawing (cutting thick boards into thin ones). A band saw is quite different from the circular saws previously described. The cutting blade is an endless steel band that runs on two (or occasionally three) wheels. A table through which the blade runs supports the work. This table on most machines can be titled to do bevel cutting. Guide wheels or guide blocks on both sides of the blade both above and below the table keep the blade from twisting. Blade-support bearings behind the blade prevent it being pushed off the wheels while cutting. A typical band saw is shown in Fig. 3–79.

Figure 3–79 Typical band saw (Delta Industrial Machinery Corp.).

Band saw size is designated by wheel diameter. A saw with 14-in.-diameter wheels is considered a 14-in. saw. Some band saws are equipped with a rip fence and miter gage similar to those found on a table saw.

Band saw blades are available in widths from $\frac{1}{8}$ to 1 in., although not all machines will accommodate the wider blades. Some manufacturers make band resaws that look somewhat like an ordinary band saw, but have a very wide ($2\frac{1}{2}$ to 3 in.) blade. They are designed to saw boards from small logs or to saw boards from thick planks. The blade width determines the minimum radius that can be cut. A $\frac{1}{8}$-in.-wide blade, for example, will cut a much smaller radius turn than will a $\frac{1}{2}$-in. blade. On the other hand, the $\frac{1}{8}$-in. blade is much more susceptible to flexing and will not make as straight a cut as the $\frac{1}{2}$-in. blade. A large-radius turn will be smoother with a wider blade. The very narrow blades also tend to break easier.

Band saw blades are available with different tooth sizes and shapes. Tooth size is designated in teeth per inch. In general, the more teeth per inch, the smoother the cut will be, but the slower the saw will cut. Skip tooth blades with wide spaces between teeth are popular for woodworking. The wide spaces between teeth help carry the sawdust from the cut.

Band Saw Safety

1. Make sure that the blade is correct for the type of cut being made and that it has the proper tension.
2. Set the upper guide assembly close to the top of the board being cut. This helps keep the blade from twisting and covers most of the otherwise exposed blade.
3. Plan your cuts so that you do not have to back out of a curved cut. Backing out of curved cuts tends to pull the blade off the wheels.
4. Never push with your hands in line with the blade.

Band Saw Machine Operations

Curved cuts. The method for making curved cuts on the band saw is as follows:

1. Draw the desired pattern on the board.
2. Set the adjustable upper guide assembly just slightly above the top of the board to be cut (Fig. 3–80).
3. Hold the stock with both hands and guide it through the cut as shown in Fig. 3–81. It is necessary to anticipate the turns by starting to turn the wood just slightly before the saw actually gets to the turn.

If there are tight-radius curves to be cut, a series of relief cuts should be made on the scrap side of the line, as shown in Fig. 3–82. As the curve cut is made these pieces will fall away from the blade, rather than causing it to bind.

Figure 3-80 Setting the guide assembly just above the top surface of the board to be cut.

Figure 3-81 Making a curved cut.

Figure 3-82 Relief cuts aid in making tight radius turns.

Many patterns require a series of cuts. In this case, the sequence of cuts should be planned to avoid backing out of curved cuts or long cuts. Make short cuts before long ones and straight cuts before curved ones. See the example for cutting out the push stick shown in Fig. 3-83. To make a rectangular cutout on the edge of a board, the cutting sequence would be as shown in Fig. 3-84.

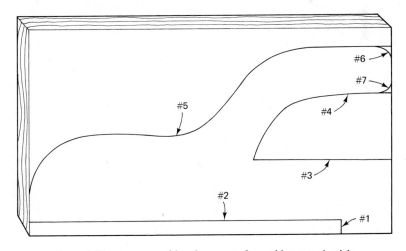

Figure 3-83 Sequence of band saw cuts for making a push stick.

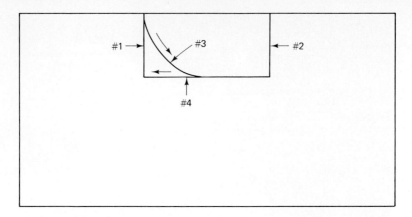

Figure 3-84 Sequence of band saw cuts for making a rectangular cutout.

If constant-radius curves are part of the pattern, they can sometimes be made more neatly by boring holes of the desired radius in the appropriate location and then sawing tangent to the hole. This technique could be used to make the barrel rest for a gun cabinet, as shown in Fig. 3–85.

Figure 3-85 Bored holes are used for the radius cuts.

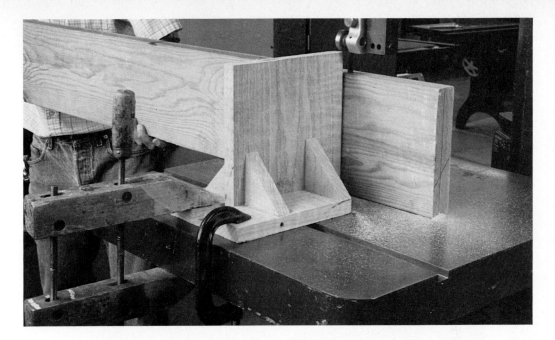

Figure 3-86   Resawing using a pivot block as a guide.

Resawing.   If the boards to be resawn are very wide, it is best to use the widest blade that the band saw will accommodate. A skip tooth blade is best for this. There are two ways to guide the wood for resawing. One is to use a rip fence much like the one for a table saw. The other is to use a pivot block, as shown in Fig. 3-86. The pivot block method is preferred since it allows the board to be pivoted slightly to compensate for the blade's tendency to wander from side to side.

Cutting compound curves.   Compounds curves such as those found in cabriole legs can be cut on the band saw. The pattern is drawn on two adjacent sides of the stock as shown in Fig. 3-87. After the first side is cut, the scrap pieces are

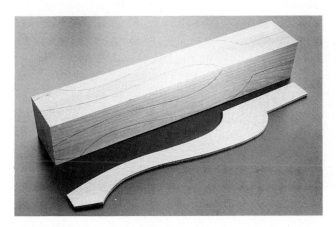

Figure 3-87   A pattern for a cabriole leg is traced on two adjacent sides of the stock.

Figure 3–88 Cutting the second side of a cabriole leg after the scrap material from the first side was tacked back in place.

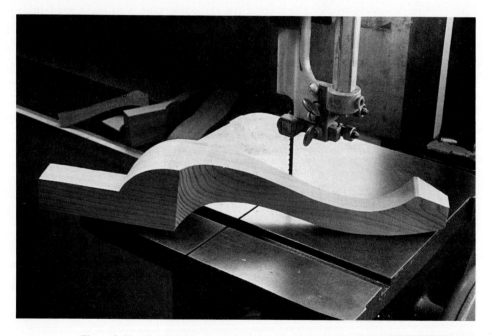

Figure 3–89 Finished leg. Final shaping and sanding are done by hand.

Woodworking Machines Chap. 3

Figure 3-90 Example of compound curves cut on a band saw.

tacked back into place by driving nails on the scrap side of the line, and the part is turned one-quarter turn and the second side is cut (Fig. 3-88). The finished leg is shown in Fig. 3-89. The handle and arrow rest area for the archery bow in Fig. 3-90 were cut this way and then filed and sanded to shape.

Cutting circles. When there are several circles of the same size to the cut, a circle cutting jig such as the one shown in Fig. 3-91 can be used. The jig is a piece of ¾-in. plywood with a cleat attached to the underside that slides in the miter slot on the table. The jig is slid onto the saw table until the line on it is lined up with the front edge of the blade as shown.

The radius of the curve is then measured along the line from the blade, and a finish nail is driven on the line. The head of the nail is filed sharp so that it can be used for a pivot in cutting the circle (Fig. 3-92).

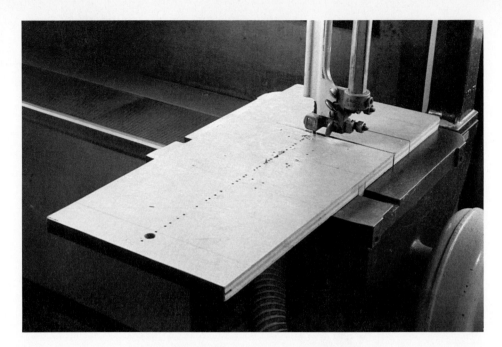

Figure 3–91 Circle-cutting jig for the band saw.

Figure 3–92 Using the circle-cutting jig.

Sanding with the band saw.   Some saw manufacturers have designed their band saws so that the blade can be replaced with a narrow sanding belt. The blade guides are replaced by a platen to support the belt.

Coiling a band saw blade.   Band saw blades are much easier to store if they are coiled into three loops. A procedure for coiling a blade is shown in Fig. 3–93a through e.

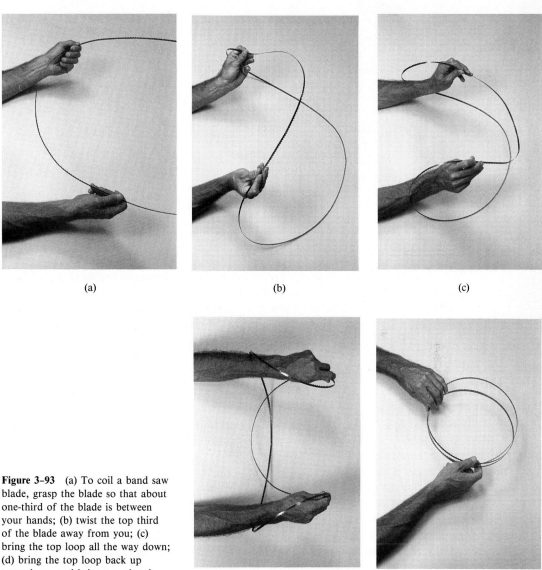

(a)

(b)

(c)

(d)

(e)

Figure 3-93   (a) To coil a band saw blade, grasp the blade so that about one-third of the blade is between your hands; (b) twist the top third of the blade away from you; (c) bring the top loop all the way down; (d) bring the top loop back up toward you and bring your hands together; (e) this completes the coil.

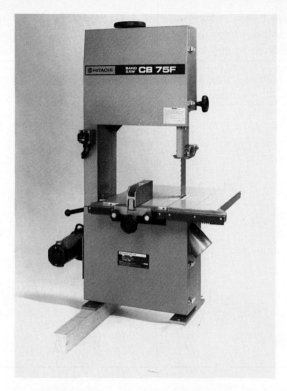

Figure 3–94 Band resaw (Hitachi Power Tools USA, Ltd.).

Band resaws. Several manufacturers are making band resaws (Fig. 3–94) for the woodworker who is interested in cutting his or her own lumber. Rather than the usual ¼- to ½-in.-wide blade, these machines are designed to accept a 2½- to 3-in.-wide blade. This wide blade remains very stable even when cutting very wide boards, making it ideal for resawing or sawing boards from small logs or branches.

SURFACE PLANER

The surface planer is used to smooth rough boards and to plane boards to uniform thickness. The planer, by itself, will not straighten crooked boards, but, rather, it planes one face of a board parallel to the opposite face. The first face must be straightened with a jointer.

Most planers consist of a table for sliding the wood and a cylindrical cutter head above the table. There is usually a power-driven infeed roll in front of the cutter head above the table and a power-driven outfeed roll behind the cutter. Between the infeed roll and the cutter is a chip breaker, and behind the cutter head is a pressure bar to hold the wood down. Idle feed rollers are usually mounted in the table also.

The controls consist of a handle to raise and lower the bed, a handle to control the feed speed if it is a variable-speed model, and a handle to adjust the bed rolls on some machines.

Planer size is designated by the length of the cutter head, which determines the maximum-width board that can be planed. Twelve-inch planers are typical for home shops, and 16- to 24-in. machines are often found in cabinet shops.

A typical planer is shown in Fig. 3–95a, and a smaller home shop type of planer is shown in Fig. 3–95b.

(a)

(b)

Figure 3–95 (a) Typical planer (Powermatic, a Division of Stanwich Industries, Inc.); (b) small home shop planer (Ryobi America Corp.).

Surface Planer

Planer Safety

Most planers are quite well guarded and are not considered particularly dangerous machines. However, several important safety precautions must be observed:

1. Unless you have an industrial model with segmented infeed roll and chip breaker, do not feed more than one piece at a time. If the pieces are not equal in thickness, the thicker one will lift up the spring-loaded feed roll and chip breaker, allowing the cutter head to kick the thinner piece back.
2. Do not bend down and look directly into the cutter area when the machine is running. Loose knots or other foreign material could be kicked out the front.
3. Do not plane boards shorter than the distance between the centers of the feed rolls.
4. Do not plane boards with loose knots or other foreign material.
5. Do not stand directly behind the board being planed.

Surface Planer Machine Operations

Planing boards. The general procedure for planing a board is as follows:

1. Measure the thickness of the board.
2. Set the machine to remove the desired amount of material within the limits of the machine. A small 12-in. model might be stressed to remove $\frac{1}{32}$ in. on a 12-in.-wide board, but could remove $\frac{1}{8}$ in. on a narrower board.
3. Check the grain direction of the board.
4. Start the machine and feed in the board. Remember to put the flat (jointed) face down, assuming a top head planer.

If it is necessary to plane a crooked board that was too wide to be face jointed first on the jointer, a reasonably flat surface can be made by clamping the board to a bench and planing the high spots with a hand plane or portable power plane. Turn the board over on a flat surface and check to see if it sets flat. If not, mark the points on which the board rocks and continue to plane those down. When the board sets flat, run it through the planer with the flat side down. Then you can turn the board over and plane your rough hand planing marks off!

Planing thin stock. Most planers have a built-in stop to prevent the table being brought too close to the cutter. This would ordinarily prevent one from planing thin stock (usually less than $\frac{1}{4}$ in.). However, a board with a cleat attached, such as the one shown in Fig. 3–96, can be inserted on the planer table and will allow planing of thin stock. The board should have a hard, slick surface and should be as long as the planer table. Don't forget to add the thickness of this board to your thickness setting.

Figure 3-96 Fixture to allow planing of thin stock.

Making beveled moldings.   A simple jig similar to the one described for planing thin stock can be used for making beveled moldings. The jig has a beveled groove
cut in it to hold the wood at the desired angle (Fig. 3-97). Some planers are also
designed to accept molding knives and can be used to manufacture a variety of wood
moldings.

Figure 3-97 Fixture for making beveled moldings on the planer.

Surface Planer

WIDE BELT SANDERS AND ABRASIVE PLANERS

Wide belt sanders and abrasive planers are prohibitively expensive for a home shop, but they are becoming quite common in cabinet and custom woodworking shops. They are good to know about when you have a glued-up board that is too wide for your planer (or maybe you don't have a planer), or when you have a special piece of bird's-eye maple or other wavy grain wood that wants to chip no matter how you plane it.

A wide belt sander (Fig. 3–98) works much like a planer except that the material is removed with a wide sanding belt rather than knives. These sanders will not cause chipping regardless of grain direction, and they are often wider than planers; 36- and 48-in.-wide machines are not unusual. They can be used with very coarse belts for stock removal, down to very fine belts requiring only a light, final finish sanding. Expect the hourly rates to be quite high when boards are run for you because of the high cost of the machine and belts, but remember how long it would have taken you to do the same job by hand!

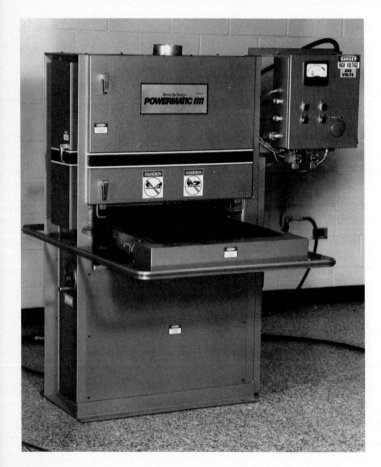

Figure 3–98 Wide belt sander (Powermatic, a division of Stanwich Industries, Inc.).

SHAPER

The basic shaper is a fairly simple machine consisting of a vertical spindle protruding from a table. Various cutters are mounted on the spindle to make moldings and certain joints. The work is guided either by a fence or, in the case of stock with curved edges, by a bearing on the spindle. The spindle adjusts up or down to regulate the depth of cut and can be tilted on some machines. On many shapers, the spindle rotation is reversible. The fence usually consists of two independently adjustable sections, one for the infeed side and one for the outfeed side. A typical shaper is shown in Fig. 3–99.

Shapers were not much used for many years, but in recent years they have enjoyed great resurgence of popularity. Part of this is due to the increasing use of more ornate woodwork with molded surfaces. Cutter manufacturers have responded with an impressive array of high-quality, carbide-tipped shaper cutters. Unfortunately for the small shop or home shop owner, many of these cutters are very expensive and require a large, industrial-type shaper to safely run them. There are, however, many high-quality smaller cutters that can be safely used on smaller machines.

Figure 3–99 Typical shaper (Delta International Machinery Corp.).

Shaper Safety

The shaper is potentially one of the more dangerous woodworking machines. There are several reasons for this. Most shapers are reversible; so if the stock is fed the wrong direction, it will be kicked out of the machine. It is a difficult machine to guard completely and it runs at very high speed. The following precautions must be observed:

1. Always check the spindle rotation direction; make sure the cutter is mounted in the proper direction, and feed the stock against the cutter rotation.
2. Make sure the shaper is sturdy enough to handle the cutter. Some larger cutters require a large shaper with a 1- or 1¼-in. spindle. Don't put a bushing in one of these cutters and run it on a ½-in. spindle. Along the same line, check to see what the maximum safe speed of the cutter is. Most newer cutters have the maximum speed marked on the cutter or on the packaging box. Many smaller shapers run in the 10,000-rpm range.

Figure 3–100 Shaping should be done on the underside of the board whenever possible.

3. Try to set up the cutter so it is cutting on the underside of the stock, making the stock act as a guard over the cutters (Fig. 3–100). There is an added advantage to doing the cutting on the underside of the stock. If the shaping were being done on the top side of the stock and the stock were allowed to raise off the table for any reason, the cutters would cut a gouge in that spot and ruin the part. If the stock were allowed to raise while shaping on the bottom, one merely has to run the part through again to complete the cut.

4. When using the fence, make sure it is positioned properly and securely locked in place.

5. Make sure there are no loose knots, splits, or other defects in the wood.

6. Use feather boards or spring hold-downs when shaping narrow pieces.

7. When shaping curved edges, always start against a guide pin.

8. Never run stock shorter than 10 in.

Shaper Cutters

The most common cutter for the smaller shaper is the three-wing cutter shown in Fig. 3–101. Shaper cutters are available in many patterns, as shown in Fig. 3–102. Some of these are larger cutters that require heavy-duty shapers.

Figure 3–101 Typical small shaper cutter.

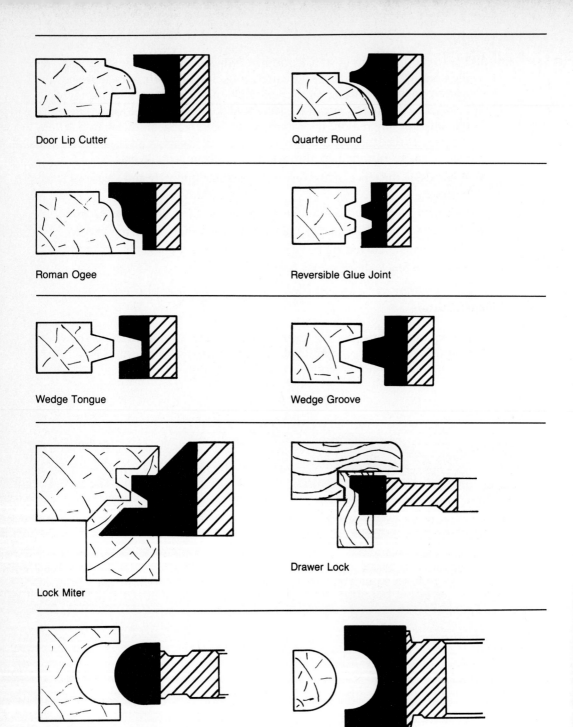

Figure 3–102 Some of the many shaper cutters available (Frued USA, Inc.).

Door Lip Cutter

Quarter Round

Roman Ogee

Reversible Glue Joint

Wedge Tongue

Wedge Groove

Lock Miter

Drawer Lock

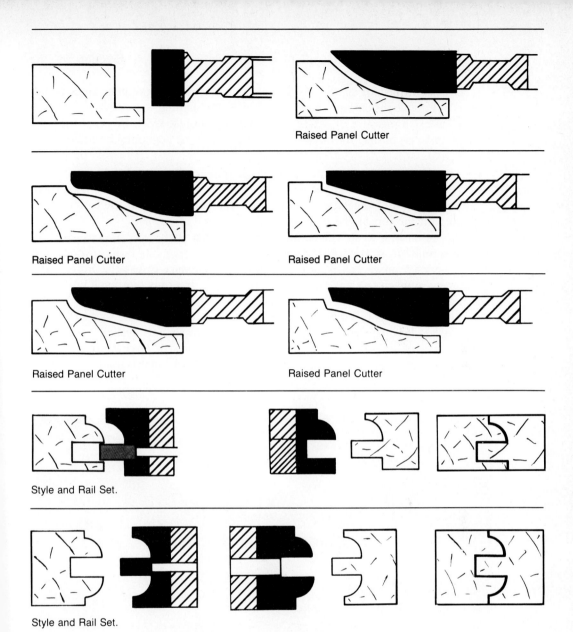

Raised Panel Cutter

Raised Panel Cutter

Raised Panel Cutter

Raised Panel Cutter

Raised Panel Cutter

Style and Rail Set.

Style and Rail Set.

Figure 3-102 (continued).

Shaper Operation

After the cutter has been selected, it is mounted on the machine. If the shaper is reversible, care must be taken to see that the cutter is mounted in the proper direction. On reversible machines, it is generally best to mount the cutter so that it cuts on the underside of the stock. This will then determine the rotation direction for the operation.

If an assortment of depth collars is available, it is good to mount an appropriately sized one above the cutter. These are designed for shaping curved edges, but they provide an extra measure of safety when shaping straight stock by preventing the stock from being pushed too deeply into the cutter at the beginning or end of a cut (Fig. 3–103).

After the cutter has been mounted on the spindle, the cutter height is adjusted. This is done by sighting along the table top to see how much of the cutter is exposed. If the entire width of the cutter is to be used, the bottom edge of the cutter would be flush with the top of the table surface.

It is often best to set the cutter for a somewhat shallower first cut and then make a second cut to the finish depth. In fact, very large cuts in hardwoods may have to be made in several passes. It is also not necessary to use the entire width of a cutter. Some cutters have fairly complex shapes, but only one small portion of the cutter might be used for a particular operation.

The next step is to set the fence for the desired cut (assuming that stock with straight edges is to be shaped). Setting the fence is largely an "eyeball" operation. The cutter is rotated until it is at the point of maximum cut, and the fence is then adjusted to expose the desired portion of cutter. If a depth collar is used as described in mounting the cutter, the fence can be aligned with the depth collar.

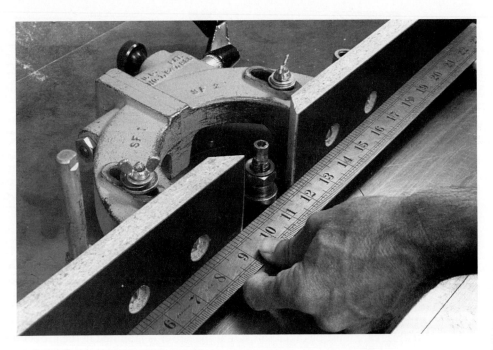

Figure 3-103 Aligning the shaper fence with a depth collar.

Figure 3–104 The outfeed table is adjusted to compensate for the amount of material removed.

The front and rear halves of the shaper fence are independently adjustable. If the entire edge of the stock is being cut away by the shaper (in other words, if the board is being made narrower), then the outfeed fence must be adjusted inward by an amount equal to the depth of the cut. For example, if $\frac{1}{16}$ in. of material is being removed, then the outfeed fence must be adjusted inward $\frac{1}{16}$ in. (Fig. 3–104).

If part of the original edge of the stock remains after the cut, then the two halves of the fence must be in line. Make sure that the fence is securely locked down.

If the stock to be shaped is thin or narrow, either feather boards, as shown in Fig. 3–105, or spring hold-downs should be used to keep the stock from chattering or being kicked back and to keep the operators fingers away from the cutting area.

When a large part, such as a table top, is to be shaped on all four edges, the cuts across the end grain should always be made first. The reason for this is that when end grain is shaped some chipping almost always occurs on the trailing end of the cut. This chipping will usually be machined away by the subsequent cut along the edge of the board. However, if the edge cut were made first, the end-grain chipping would ruin the first cut.

If the wood being shaped is prone to chipping, it may be necessary to use a backup block as shown in Fig. 3–106 to prevent end-grain chipping. This backup block must be large enough to be safely machined on the shaper. A better way to avoid the chipping problem is to make the board wider than the finish width to start with, say 1 in. over width. Then do the shaping on the end grain, and then trim the board to final width before shaping the edge grain.

Shaper

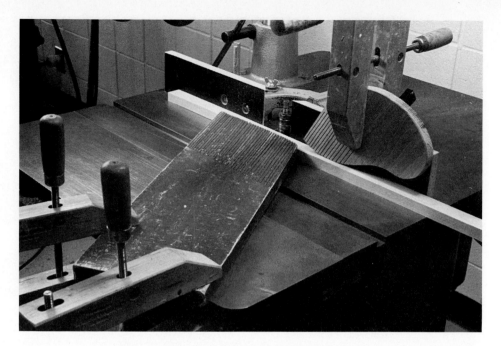

Figure 3–105 Using feather boards to shape thin stock.

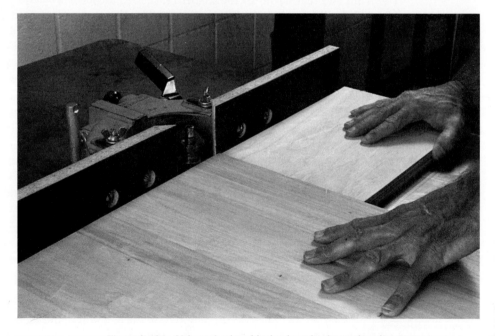

Figure 3–106 Using a backup block when shaping end grain.

Figure 3–107 Depth collars for shaping curved edges.

Shaping curved edges.   The cutter is mounted on the spindle as previously described, but there *must* be a depth collar or spindle guide bearing (Fig. 3–107). Depth collars come in various outside diameters. The wood rides against the depth collar during the cut, so the diameter of the depth collar determines the depth of the cut.

A starting pin is also necessary when shaping curved edges. The stock is held against the starting pin (Fig. 3–108) and then fed into the cutter until it contacts the

Figure 3–108   Using a starting pin and depth collar to shape a curved edge.

Shaper

depth collar. It can then be pulled away from the starting pin and fed against the depth collar. This operation should be done using a series of light cuts, rather than one deep cut.

Shaping with a pattern. If a number of identical parts are to be made, it is often worthwhile to make a pattern and mount the stock on the pattern. The pattern is run against the depth collar as previously described for shaping curved edges The parts do not have to be accurately cut to size, since the shaper will cut them to match the contour of the pattern. The part may be mounted on the pattern with nails, screws, or toggle clamps if there is one side that is not shaped.

Making stiles and rails. One reason for the renewal of interest in the shaper is the fact that it lends itself well to making the popular frame and panel or stile and rail doors. A matched set of stile and rail cutters is needed for this operation. A typical stile and rail shaper cutter set is shown in Fig. 2-28. Some cutters are accurately ground to match each other; others are designed so that the thickness of the tenon can be adjusted by placing shims between sections of the cope cutter. The stiles are run as shown in Fig. 3-109. A jig such as the one shown in Fig. 3-110 can be made to allow the ends of the rails to be safely run against the fence.

Figure 3-109 Shaping a stile for a stile and rail assembly.

Figure 3-110 Jig for shaping the cope cut for a stile and rail assembly.

Making raised panels.   The shaper is the best machine to use for making raised panels, provided that it is sturdy enough to safely run the raised panel cutters. Some of them are quite large and require very heavy duty shapers. A typical raised panel cutter is shown in Fig. 2–33. The actual setup and running of the panel is very much like shaping an edge on any other part. The end-grain cuts should be made first.

Raised panels with a cathedral or arched top, such as the one shown in Fig. 3–111, can be made using the procedure previously described for shaping curved edges.

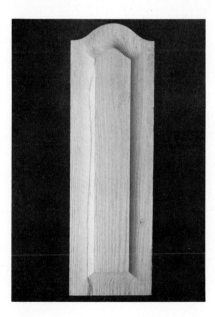

Figure 3-111 Raised panel with an arched top.

A depth collar, preferably with a ball bearing, is necessary. Rather than starting against a guide pin, it is best to put the fence in place and start the arched cut on each of the panels to be made; then remove the fence and complete the cut.

Making lock miter joints.   There is a single cutter that will make both halves of a lock miter joint (Fig. 3-112). One part is run flat on the table in the normal manner, and the mating part is run in a vertical position against the fence.

Figure 3-112 Shaper cutter for making a lock miter.

SANDERS

The most popular sanders for woodworking are the disc sander, belt sander (these two are often combined in one machine), and spindle sander. A combination belt and disc sander is shown in Fig. 3-113. These are generally considered to be quite

Figure 3-113 Combination belt and disc sander (Delta International Machinery Corp.).

safe machines when used with common sense. However, the work table should be adjusted so that the gap between it and the sanding surface is very small. Getting a dowel caught between the table and a sanding belt can be guaranteed to break the belt. Getting your fingers caught there is even worse!

Sanding discs are available with an adhesive backing, or plain discs can be mounted with either a paste or liquid adhesive. The disc sander is used primarily for sanding end grain and for doing some reshaping of the wood.

The belt sander is somewhat more versatile; in addition to the above operations, it can be used for sanding edges and faces of small parts. Many belt sanders can be set up in either a vertical or horizontal position, as shown. On some machines, the guard over the idle pulley can be removed and concave surfaces can be sanded on the idle pulley (Fig. 3–114).

Oscillating spindle sanders (Fig. 3–115) are very handy for sanding scroll cuts and curved edges. Abrasive sleeves of various diameters are available for these spindle sanders. Spindle sanders are quite expensive, but, fortunately, many of the same

Figure 3–114 Using the top drum of a belt sander for sanding a curved edge.

Sanders

Figure 3–115 Oscillating spindle sander.

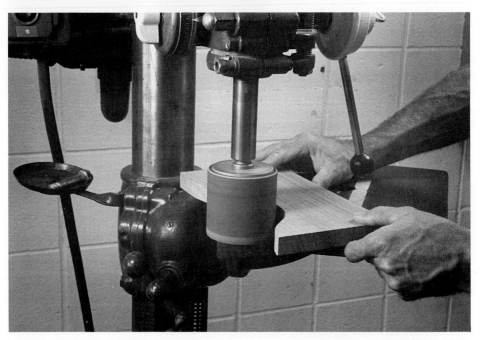

Figure 3–116 Using a drill press for spindle sanding.

Figure 3–117 Using a lathe for spindle sanding.

operations can be performed on a drill press or even a wood lathe with a sanding spindle. These operations are shown in Figs. 3–116 and 3–117.

Two other specialty sanders can be useful for sanding irregular surfaces. One is the flap wheel sander shown in Fig. 3–118. It can be attached directly to the shaft of a motor, and the work is held free hand. The other is the wood sanding wheel.

Figure 3–118 Flap wheel sander.

Sanders

Figure 3-119 Scotch-Brite™ woodworking wheel used to sand moldings (3-M Company).

It is used on a machine similar to a shaper (Fig. 3–119). This could easily be a home-made machine. These wood wheels are used when it is necessary to sand many feet of the same molding. The wheel is shaped to the contour of the molding by gluing abrasive paper to a sample of the molding and running it against the revolving wheel. After the wheel has been shaped, it will maintain that shape throughout the life of the wheel.

DRILL PRESS

A typical drill press is shown in Fig. 3–120.

Drill Press Safety

The primary safety precautions to observe when using a drill press include:

1. Clamp small stock and sheet metal when drilling.
2. Make sure that the drill press speed is appropriate for the material being machined and for the cutting tool being used.
3. Make sure that long hair is tied back or covered to prevent it from being caught in the revolving spindle.

Drill Press Accessories

Drill bits.   There are many types of drill bits that can be used for drilling wood. The conventional twist drill bit used to drill metal, plastics, and other materials will also drill wood, although other special wood bits are better for this purpose.

Figure 3-120 Typical drill press (Delta Industrial Machinery Corp.).

A twist drill bit tends to leave a ragged edge around the parameter of the hole. Woodworkng bits usually have sharp spurs on the circumference of the bit to score the wood fibers around the edge of the hole. Some of these bits are shown in Fig. 3-121. Flat spade-type bits such as those shown in Fig. 3-122, are less expensive and will do an acceptable job in many woods.

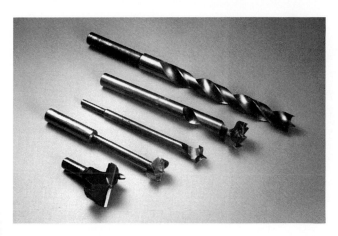

Figure 3-121 Special bits for drilling wood.

Drill Press

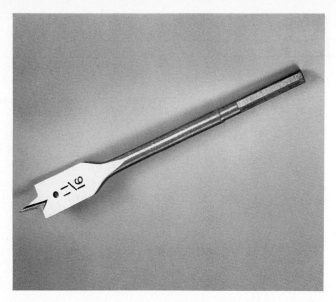

Figure 3-122 Spade bit.

Circle cutters and hole saws. Large holes may be made in wood using either an adjustable circle cutter, as shown in Fig. 3-123, or a hole saw. In either case, the drill press is run at a low speed and the workpiece should be clamped to the table. The cut is made by drilling approximately halfway through the board from one side, turning the board over and finishing from the back. This will prevent the chipping that otherwise would occur on the back side of the cut, and it makes it much easier to remove the round plug cutout from the cutter.

Figure 3-123 Adjustable circle cutter.

Figure 3-124 Making wood plugs with a plug cutter.

Plug cutters.   Plug cutters are usually available in ⅛-in. and sometimes ¹⁄₁₆-in. increments. They are especially useful for making wood plugs to cover screw heads. An easy way to make plugs is to make a series of cuts on the edge of a board, as shown in Fig. 3-124, and then make a cut on the band saw to cut the plugs free. The plug cutter should not be run completely through the stock being used for plugs.

Countersink bit.   A number of manufactures make special bits for drilling pilot holes and countersink holes for wood screws. Some of these are adjustable for different lengths for a given screw size. In other words, a number 10 countersink bit could be used for number 10 screws of any length. These bits drill a small hole for the screw threads, a larger hole for the screw shank, and a countersink hole for setting the screw head flush with the surface, or a counterbore hole for recessing the screw head below the surface (Fig. 3-125). This is done in one operation rather than three, so they can be real time savers.

Figure 3-125 Countersink bit for installing wood screws.

Drill Press Operations

Using the drill press.   Many drill press operations are quite simple and merely require marking the location of a hole, installing an appropriate bit, and drilling. If a number of holes are to be drilled in a straight line, a fence can be clamped to the drill press table to serve as a guide.

If the holes are to be spaced on regular intervals, a long fence with small holes, such as the one shown in Fig. 3–126, can be used. A stop pin is put in one hole at a time to index the workpiece for each hole to be drilled. A pattern with predrilled holes can also be placed over the workpiece to locate holes. (One-quarter-inch tempered pegboard with holes on 1-in. centers makes a good pattern for drilling holes in cabinet sides for adjustable shelf supports.)

Sanding with the drill press.   Sanding drums available in several diameters (Fig. 3–116) allow the drill press to be used for spindle sanding. When used for this kind of sanding, do not push the stock against the side of the sanding spindle with very much force, since drill press bearings are designed for thrust rather than radial (side) loads.

For sanding small-radius curves, a simple, small-diameter sander can be made by using a half-inch dowel as a spindle. Make a cut approximately 1 in. long from one end of the dowel as shown in Fig. 3–127. Then take a 1-in.-wide piece of sanding cloth or paper and insert one end of it in the saw cut and wrap it around the dowel

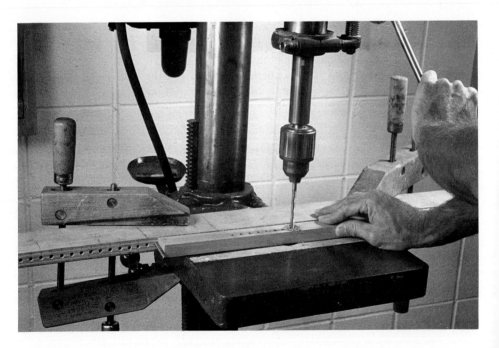

Figure 3-126   Using a guide fence with holes and a pin to index the drilling of holes.

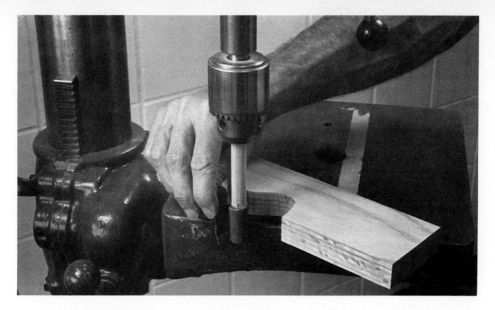

Figure 3-127 Using a dowel wrapped with sandpaper as a sanding spindle.

so that it will tighten on the dowel as it rotates in the drill press. Mount the dowel in the drill press and bring the workpiece lightly against the abrasive paper to hold it in place before starting the drill press. Start the drill press and complete the sanding. A piece of steel or aluminum round stock can be used in place of the wood dowel if a more permanent spindle is needed. Flap wheels can also be used for sanding irregular shapes.

Drilling holes at an angle. The tables on most drill presses can be tilted; but they usually do not have degree scales, so the actual tilt must be measured with a protractor (Fig. 3-128) or with a sliding T-bevel that has been set using a protractor. The workpiece must be clamped to the table when drilling at an angle.

Figure 3-128 Setting the drill press table at an angle with a sliding T-bevel.

A speed bore bit with a long brad point, as shown in Fig. 3-121, is good for starting holes on an angle, since the brad point helps keep the bit from creeping down the slope of the wood. A Foerstner bit will also work.

When drilling completely through a board, it is best to have a backup board to drill into. This will minimize the chipping that would otherwise occur.

SCROLL SAW

Scroll saws are used primarily for cutting curves. Their cutting speed is generally much slower than that of a band saw, because the blade cuts with an up-and-down motion and therefore spends half its time on the noncutting up stroke. The scroll saw (sometimes called a jig saw) is better suited than that band saw for making very tight radius curves because of the very narrow blades that can be used. The scroll saw is capable of making internal cutouts in the center of a board that would be impossible with an ordinary band saw.

Two basic types of scroll saws are manufactured. A conventional scroll saw is shown in Fig. 3-129. The lower chuck is driven by the motor and moves the blade up and down. The upper chuck is spring loaded and keeps the blade in constant tension while moving up and down with the blade.

Figure 3-129 Conventional scroll saw (Delta Industrial Machinery Corp.).

Figure 3–130 Parallel-arm scroll saw (Delta Industrial Machinery Corp.).

A parallel arm scroll saw is shown in Fig. 3–130. The top and bottom arms both pivot at the back of the machine, and both move up and down to move the blade.

Scroll Saw Safety

The scroll saw is not considered to be a particularly dangerous machine. The main precautions to observe are the following:

1. Make sure the blade is mounted with the teeth pointing downward, and the hold-down foot should be adjusted with the proper tension to hold the wood securely on the table.
2. The tension on the upper chuck must be adjusted so that it keeps the blade taut at the top of the cutting stroke. The drive pulley should be rotated by hand to verify this.

Blade Selection

Scroll saw blades are available in many widths and with many tooth shapes and sizes. In general, a wider blade will be better for large-radius curves, and a narrow blade will be better for small-radius curves. It is also generally true that the more teeth per inch on the blade, the smoother the cut (but also the slower the cut). A large

Scroll Saw

tooth blade cuts faster, but generally leaves a rougher cut. In any case, at least two teeth should always be in contact with the work at all times. This means, for example, that $\frac{1}{16}$-in.-thick stock should *not* be cut with a blade with teeth $\frac{1}{8}$ in. apart.

Installing the Blade

The correct installation of the blade is critical on a scroll saw, both to minimize blade breakage and to obtain good cuts. To install a blade in a conventional saw, follow these steps:

1. Remove the throat plate.
2. Clamp the blade in the lower chuck with the teeth pointing down.
3. Clamp the blade in the upper chuck and adjust the blade tension. The tension on most machines can be adjusted by rotating the pulley by hand until the blade is at the top of the cutting stroke. The upper-tension cylinder clamp is loosened, and the upper cylinder is adjusted so that 1 in. of the square shaft that holds the upper chuck is showing (Fig. 3–131).
4. The blade guide should then be adjusted. Many saws have a metal disc with various-size slots cut in from the parameters that serve as blade guides. In this case, a slot that matches the blade width (minus tooth depth) is selected. If there

Figure 3–131 Adjusting the blade tension.

is a backup roller to support the blade, it should be adjusted to just touch the back of the blade.

5. Rotate the saw through one full stroke to make sure that the blade moves freely.

6. Adjust the spring hold-down to keep the workpiece securely on the table.

Scroll Saw Machine Operations

Making cuts.   The pattern to be cut should be drawn on the wood and the sequence of cuts planned to avoid having to back out of long cuts. The saw is started and the workpiece is brought into contact with the blade. The pressure against the blade should be light, giving the saw a chance to cut freely. The pressure must be applied directly against the front of the saw blade, avoiding any sideways pressure that would cause the blade to bend. This is especially important when making curved cuts.

Internal cuts.   Internal cuts can be made by drilling a hole in the center of the workpiece so that the blade can be inserted. The blade is released from the top chuck and the guide assembly temporarily moved up out of the way. The blade is inserted through the hole and then remounted in the top chuck as described earlier (Fig. 3–132). The guide assembly must then be readjusted. The cut is completed and

Figure 3–132   Inserting a blade for an internal cutout.

Figure 3-133 Sanding with a scroll saw.

the blade removed. Saber saw blades that mount in the bottom chuck only can be used to make internal cuts if no sharp curves are required.

Sanding with a scroll saw. Small sanding sleeve holders, such as the one shown in Fig. 3-133, can be used for sanding curved edges.

WOOD LATHE

The wood lathe has an interesting history that can be traced back much farther than other woodworking machines. Of course, the power source has changed over the years and has included wind, water, the operator (using a foot treadle or a bow and string), and even slaves.

Wood may be mounted in the lathe between centers, referred to as spindle turning, or mounted to a face plate. Spindle turning is used for long, cylindrical shapes (spindles) such as lamps and table or chair legs and rungs. Face plate turning is usually used for shallow, round objects such as bowls and platters.

A typical wood lathe is shown in Fig. 3-134. The major parts include the bed, the head stock, which holds the driven spur center or face plate, tail stock, and tool rest.

Figure 3-134 Typical wood lathe (Delta Industrial Machinery Corp.).

Lathe Safety

The following safety rules should be observed when using the wood lathe:

1. Carefully check the wood for flaws such as splits that might allow it to fly apart at speed. Check any glue joints to be sure that they are sound.
2. Run the lathe at a safe speed for the conditions (see Fig. 3-135). Rough turning should be done at low speeds until the stock is completely rounded. Larger-diameter workpieces must be turned at lower speed than small ones.

Diameter of work (in.)	Roughing (rpm)	General cutting (rpm)	Finishing (rpm)
Under 2	1520	3000	3000
2–4	760	1600	2480
4–6	510	1080	1650
6–8	380	810	1240
8–10	300	650	1000
10–12	255	540	830
12–14	220	460	710

Figure 3-135 Lathe speed table.

Wood Lathe

Figure 3-136 Lathe guard.

3. The tool rest should be kept close to the work.

4. The tool rest should be removed when sanding to avoid any possibility of catching fingers between the tool rest and the workpiece.

5. A lathe guard, such as the one shown in Fig. 3-136, should be used.

6. Avoid wearing loose clothing or jewelry.

Turning Tools

A typical set of turning tools is shown in Fig. 3-137. The gouge is used for rough cutting stock to a cylindrical shape and for cove cuts. The skew is used for making smooth finish cuts on a cylinder and for making V-cuts.

The parting tool is used for cutting grooves and square shoulders. The roundnose is used for scraping coves and other concave surfaces, and the diamond point is used for scraping V's and for finishing shoulder and corner cuts. The correct angle for sharpening these tools is also shown in Fig. 3-137.

Turning is accomplished by either cutting as the stock rotates or scraping. The gouge, skew, and parting tool are considered cutting tools. The roundnose and diamond point are scraping tools.

The cutting tools are used as shown in Fig. 3-138. They cut a shaving off the wood and result in a smoother finish. However, they are somewhat harder to use than scraping tools.

Scraping tools are held in a horizontal position as shown in Fig. 3-139. They scrape wood fibers off the surface. They are slower, but easier to use than cutting tools. Cutting tools are also occasionally used for scraping. Face plate turning is always done using the scraping method because of the end-grain problem.

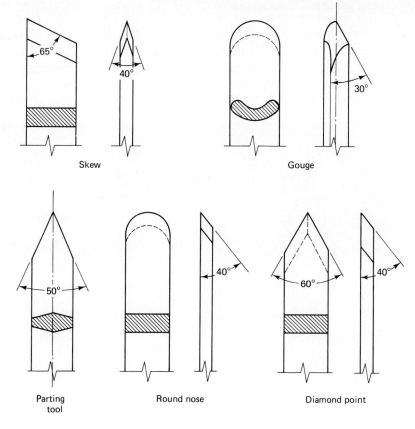

Figure 3-137 Typical set of lathe tools.

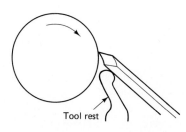

Figure 3-138 Lathe cutting tools are held at an angle with the handle down.

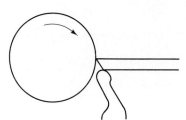

Figure 3-139 Lathe scraping tools are held horizontally.

Wood Lathe

Lathe Machine Operations

Spindle turning.   In spindle turning, the stock is mounted between the drive center (or spur centers) in the head stock and the tail stock center, as shown in Fig. 3-140. Small stock can be mounted by locating the center of each end and driving the spur center into one end, as shown in Fig. 3-141. For larger stock, especially a hardwood, diagonal cuts should be made with either a band saw or handsaw (Fig.

Figure 3-140   Stock mounted in the lathe for spindle turning.

Figure 3-141   Driving the spur center into the wood.

3–142). This will help ensure that the spur center is properly set in the end of the workpiece.

The spur center and workpiece are then mounted in the lathe by pushing the tapered spur center into the tapered seat on the head stock. The tail stock is then brought up near the other end of the workpiece and locked to the table. The tail stock center is then adjusted against the center of the workpiece, as shown in

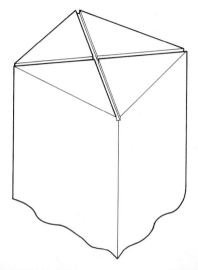

Figure 3–142 Diagonal cuts on end of workpiece for mounting spur center.

Figure 3–143 Mounting the tail stock center in the wood.

Wood Lathe

Fig. 3-143. If the tail stock center has a "dead" center (does not have a bearing allowing it to rotate with the wood), it should be set very firmly, backed off slightly, and then lubricated with oil or wax.

The tool rest should be set close to the work and at about the center height. The lathe should be run at a low speed until the workpiece is turned round.

A gouge is used first to turn the stock to a cylinder and to get it close to finished size. The correct position for holding the gouge is shown in Fig. 3-144. Note that the handle is lower and the tool is rolled slightly.

Finish cuts can be made with a skew, as shown in Fig. 3-145. The heel of the skew is set on the tool rest, and the toe is rotated upward about 30°. The cutting is done with the lower one-third of the tool.

Shoulder cuts and grooves are cut with the parting tool. The tool is set on its edge, as shown in Fig. 3-146, so that it cuts near the top of the stock. The handle is dropped so that the cutting edge cuts rather than scrapes. The tool is then pushed into the rotating stock until the desired diameter is reached. The diameter can be checked with a caliper (Fig. 3-147).

Figure 3-144 Position for holding the gouge.

Figure 3-145 Finish cut with a skew.

Figure 3-146 Using a parting tool to cut a groove.

Figure 3–147 Checking the diameter with a caliper.

Making a V-cut. A V-cut may be made with a diamond point tool (scraping method), as shown in Fig. 3–148. The cutting should only be done on one side of the tool at a time. If the diamond point is forced into the wood so that both edges are cutting, it will tend to catch in the wood.

Figure 3–148 Using a diamond-point tool to cut a V-groove.

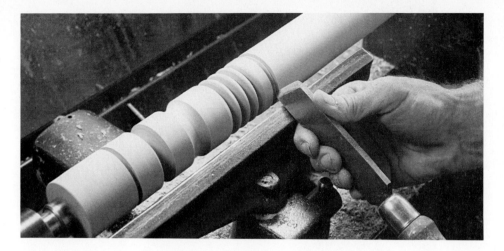

Figure 3-149 Using the skew to cut a V-groove.

A V-cut may also be made with a skew using the tip of the chisel to make the center of the V; then turn the skew over and cut the V with the heel of the chisel (Fig. 3–149). Cutting V's with a skew requires a great deal of practice, but will give smooth results.

Cutting coves.   Coves can be made with the scraping method using a round-nose tool. The tool is forced into the wood and pivoted back and forth on the tool rest to shape the cove (Fig. 3–150). Coves can also be cut with a gouge using much the same method, except that the handle end of the tool is dropped to produce a cutting action, and the tool is rotated when cutting the edge of the coves.

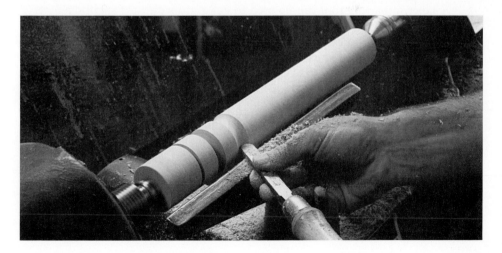

Figure 3-150   Using the round-nose tool to cut a cove.

Figure 3-151 Cutting beads with a diamond-point tool.

Cutting beads.   Beads may also be cut with either the scraping method or the cutting method. If there is a space between the beads, it is cut with a parting tool. The beads are then scraped with a diamond-point tool as shown in Fig. 3-151.

Beads may also be cut with a skew. Although this is much more difficult to learn, the result will be a smoother cut. The heel of the tool is used in much the same way as when making V-cuts.

Cutting tapers.   After the stock has been turned to the large diameter of the taper, a parting tool can be used to cut a groove to the small diameter at the end of the taper. Several intermediate grooves should also be cut as reference points (Fig. 3-152). A gouge can then be used to remove the stock to the reference grooves, leaving the taper just slightly oversize. The skew is used to make the final cut.

Figure 3-152   A series of grooves is used as references for cutting a taper.

Face plate turning. Face plate turning is used for bowls, platters, trays, and other shallow, circular objects. The workpiece can be mounted directly to the face plate using wood screws. If the screw holes are undesirable in the workpiece, a block of scrap wood can be temporarily glued to the bottom of the workpiece with a piece of paper in the glue joint. The face plate is then mounted on the scrap piece for turning the part. When the work is completed, a wood chisel is inserted in the joint and tapped lightly. The paper will split, causing the joint to separate.

If the item to be turned is large, the stock should be cut round, but slightly oversize, on the band saw. This will minimize the normal out-of-balance conditions when starting to turn rough stock, and it will save time in getting the stock round.

The outside edge of the stock is turned first to get the stock round and in balance. The tool rest is set close to the edge of the stock. The lathe should be run at its lowest speed until the stock is round. The tool rest is then mounted across the face of the workpiece. The cut is started at the center and moved out toward the outside. The tool rest must be set so that the cutting edge of the tool is at exactly the center height for this operation.

Wood lathe duplicating. A number of duplicating attachments for wood lathes make it easy to turn multiple identical parts (Fig. 3–153). Most of these allow

Figure 3–153 Lathe duplicating attachment shown with a turned pattern (top) and a band-sawn pattern (bottom) (Toolmark Co.).

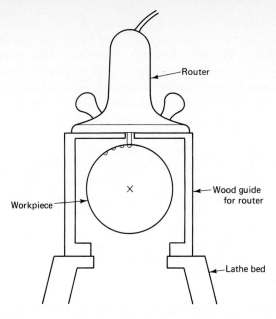

Figure 3-154 Homemade jig for making flute cuts on the lathe with a router.

Labels on figure: Router, Wood guide for router, Workpiece, Lathe bed

the use of an existing turning or a band sawn template for a pattern. A metal stylus follows the pattern, allowing the shape to be reproduced on the workpiece. The main difficulty encountered in setting up a duplicating attachment is that a different cutting tool is required for cutting square shoulders and V's, as opposed to simple cylinders and coves. The stock is cut to size first with a round-nose tool. All shaping that can be done with the round-nose tool is done next. The special-purpose tools for cutting V's for shoulders are then installed. These tools must be carefully indexed in the machine to maintain the desired diameter of the workpiece. These duplicators save a lot of time on multiple turnings.

Cutting flutes.   Some lathes have an indexing feature on the head stock that allows the workpiece to be locked into position for other machining operations, such as cutting flutes. The indexing head allows the 360° of one rotation to be divided into various equal increments. Thus the workpiece could be locked into place every 90°, for example, to allow cutting four equally special flutes or every 45° for eight cuts, and so on. A wooden jig mounted on the lathe bed allows the use of a portable router for cutting the flute (Fig. 3-154).

Drum sanding.   The lathe can be used to sand curved edges, as shown in Fig. 3-117, using an appropriate sanding drum.

PORTABLE POWER TOOLS

Portable power tools are less expensive than stationary tools and are better for certain operations. However, in most cases, it requires more skill and practice to obtain comparable quality work with a portable power tool.

Portable Power Tool Safety

Portable power tools have some safety requirements that differ from stationary power tools. The following safety rules should be observed when operating portable power tools:

1. Be sure that the tool is properly grounded electrically.
2. Be sure that the workpiece is securely clamped down.
3. Make sure that the cutter is up to speed before starting a cut.
4. Wear eye protection.
5. Make sure that cutters are sharp and are appropriate for the material being cut.

Router

The portable router is certainly one of the most versatile of the portable power tools. It can be used for making moldings, dados, rabbets, mortise and tenon joints, dovetail joints, dovetail dados, box joints, splines, hinge mortises, and many other operations. A typical router is shown in Fig. 3–155.

Router bits. One reason for the popularity of routers is the great number of router bits available. Some of these bits are shown in Fig. 3–156. The bit may be made of high-speed steel or may have carbide cutting tips. The carbide-tipped bits are more expensive, but will stay sharp much longer, especially when cutting through the glue line on plywood or cutting particle board or plastic laminate.

Figure 3–155 Typical portable router (Porter Cable Corp.).

ROUTER BITS

Choose The Bit That's Right For You

High Speed Steel Bits
All specially heat treated to retain their precision ground cutting edges over longer periods of operation.

Carbide Tipped Bits
Recommended for production cutting operations or when working with tough, more abrasive materials such as flake board, plastic laminates, plywood and composition materials.

STRAIGHT BITS

STRAIGHT CUTTER BITS
SINGLE FLUTE
High Speed Steel, Carbide Tipped
& Solid Carbide

Designed for roughing operations and general stock removal, grooving, rabbeting.

HIGH SPEED STEEL

Bit. No.	A Cut Width	B Flute Length	C Shank Diameter	D Shank Length
43004	1/16″	3/16″	1/4″	1-1/4″
43607	1/8″	3/8″	1/4″	1-1/4″
43009	5/32″	1/2″	1/4″	1-1/4″
43608	3/16″	3/4″	1/4″	1-1/4″
43609	1/4″	3/4″	1/4″	1-1/4″
43010	7/32″	3/4″	1/4″	1-1/4″

CARBIDE TIPPED

Bit. No.	A Cut Width	B Flute Length	C Shank Diameter	D Shank Length
43717	1/4″	7/8″	1/4″	1-1/4″
43049	1/2″	1-1/2″	1/2″	1-1/2″

SOLID CARBIDE

Bit. No.	A Cut Width	B Flute Length	C Shank Diameter	D Shank Length
43206	1/8″	9/32″	1/4″	1-1/16″

STRAIGHT CUTTER BITS
DOUBLE FLUTE
High Speed Steel & Carbide-Tipped

Designed for through-template cuts where guiding with a ball bearing is desired.
Used with Porter-Cable's 5009 MorTen, Mortise & Tenon Jig

HIGH SPEED STEEL

Bit. No.	A Cut Width	B Flute Length	C Shank Diameter	D Shank Length
43450	5/16″	3/4″	1/4″	1″

CARBIDE TIPPED

Bit. No.	A Cut Width	B Flute Length	C Shank Diameter	D Shank Length
43451	5/16″	3/4″	1/4″	1″

STRAIGHT CUTTER BITS
DOUBLE FLUTE
High Speed Steel & Carbide Tipped

Designed for roughing operations and general stock removal, grooving, rabbeting.

HIGH SPEED STEEL

Bit. No.	A Cut Width	B Flute Length	C Shank Diameter	D Shank Length
43610	1/4″	5/8″	1/4″	1-1/4″
43611	1/4″	3/4″	1/4″	1-1/4″
43612	1/4″	1″	1/4″	1-1/4″
43303	5/16″	3/4″	1/4″	1-1/4″
43309	3/8″	1″	1/4″	1-1/4″
43321	1/2″	1″	1/4″	1-1/4″
43614	1/2″	1-1/2″	1/2″	1-1/2″
43615	1/2″	2″	1/2″	1-1/2″
43330	5/8″	3/4″	1/4″	1-1/4″
43336	3/4″	1″	1/4″	1-1/4″
43616	3/4″	1-1/4″	1/2″	1-1/2″
43618	1″	1-1/4″	1/2″	1-1/2″

CARBIDE TIPPED

Bit. No.	A Cut Width	B Flute Length	C Shank Diameter	D Shank Length
43051	3/16″	1/2″	1/4″	1-1/4″
43718	1/4″	7/8″	1/4″	1-1/4″
43207	1/4″	7/8″	1/2″	1-1/2″
43742	1/4″	1″	1/4″	1-1/4″
43300	5/16″	1″	1/4″	1-1/4″
43312	3/8″	1″	1/4″	1-1/4″
43719	3/8″	1″	1/2″	1-1/2″
43318	1/2″	1″	1/4″	1-1/4″
43057	1/2″	1″	1/2″	1-1/2″
43058	1/2″	1-1/4″	1/2″	1-1/2″
43720	1/2″	1-1/2″	1/2″	1-1/2″
43721	1/2″	2″	1/2″	2″
43327	9/16″	1″	1/4″	1-1/4″
43722	3/4″	1-1/4″	1/2″	1-1/2″
43333	5/8″	1″	1/4″	1-1/4″
43062	7/8″	1-1/4″	1/2″	1-1/2″
43208	11/16″	1″	1/4″	1-1/4″
43052	3/4″	1″	1/4″	1-1/4″
43209	13/16″	1″	1/4″	1-1/4″
43063	1″	1-1/4″	1/2″	1-1/2″

Figure 3–156   Typical router bits (Porter Cable Corp.).

PORTER·CABLE

STRAIGHT CUTTERS, SCREW TYPE

DOUBLE FLUTE
Carbide Tipped

Designed for roughing operations
and general stock removal,
grooving, rabbeting.

All cutters fit 1/4-28 threaded arbor.

No. 43274 3/8"arbor
No. 43736 1/4"arbor
No. 43737 1/2"arbor

	CARBIDE TIPPED	
43703	3/4"	17/32"
43700	13/16"	17/32"
43701	7/8"	17/32"
43702	15/16"	17/32"
43704	1"	17/32"
43699	1-1/8"	17/32"
43745	1-1/4"	17/32"

STAGGER TOOTH BITS

Carbide Tipped

For fast plunge cutting and
cut-out work. Staggered cutting
flutes give 2 flute balance with
single flute speed of cut.
Excellent chip clearance.

Bit. No.	A Cut Width	B Flute Length	C Shank Diameter	D Shank Length
43723	3/8"	1-1/4"	1/2"	1-3/4"
43724	1/2"	2-1/8"	1/2"	2"

STRAIGHT SPIRAL DOWN BITS

High Speed Steel

For through cutting plastics
and non-ferrous metals,
pushes chips down from
the cut.

Bit. No.	A Cut Width	B Flute Length	C Shank Diameter	D Shank Length
43601	1/4"	3/4"	1/4"	2"

DRYWALL CUTOUT BIT

For through-cutting of
Drywall or panelling for
outlet, ducting, and window
cutouts, etc.

Bit. No.	A Cut Width	B Flute Length	C Shank Diameter	D Shank Length
43218	3/16"	1-3/4"	3/16"	1-1/2"

STRAIGHT SPIRAL UP BITS

High Speed Steel

For slotting and mortising
operations, particularly in
non-ferrous metals such as
aluminum door jambs. Pulls
chips up and out of the cut.

Bit. No.	A Cut Width	B Flute Length	C Shank Diameter	D Shank Length
43604	1/4"	3/4"	1/4"	2"

T SLOT CUTTING BITS

2 FLUTE
High Speed Steel

For boring hole and routing
to make a T slot for plaques,
pictures, etc., where wall
mount and a nail or screw
is required. Hole diameter
is 3/8" with a neck
cutting width 3/16".

Bit. No.	A Cut Width	AA Neck Cut Width	B Flute Length	C Shank Diameter
43219	3/8"	3/16"	5/16"	1/4"

PILOT PANEL BITS

PILOT PANEL BITS

Pilot panel Spiral down bits with Plunge
point High Speed Steel

For cutting aluminum sheet, wall
panels, plywood, chipboards,
insulation sheeting and other
synthetic boards.

- Pushes chips down while cutting to
  eliminate chip build-up and clogging.
- Eliminates chipping and upward
  tearing of material.
- Eliminates vibration and extends
  bit life.
- Gives very smooth cut.

Bit. No.	A Cut Width	B Flute Length	C Shank Diameter	D Shank Length
43488	1/4"	3/4"	1/4"	1-3/16"

Figure 3–156 (continued).

Portable Power Tools

↓ ROUTER BITS

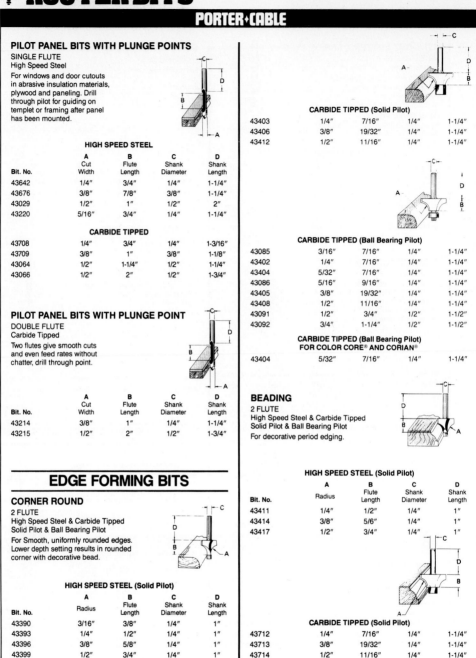

PILOT PANEL BITS WITH PLUNGE POINTS

SINGLE FLUTE
High Speed Steel

For windows and door cutouts in abrasive insulation materials, plywood and paneling. Drill through pilot for guiding on templet or framing after panel has been mounted.

HIGH SPEED STEEL

Bit. No.	A Cut Width	B Flute Length	C Shank Diameter	D Shank Length
43642	1/4″	3/4″	1/4″	1-1/4″
43676	3/8″	7/8″	3/8″	1-1/4″
43029	1/2″	1″	1/2″	2″
43220	5/16″	3/4″	1/4″	1-1/4″

CARBIDE TIPPED

43708	1/4″	3/4″	1/4″	1-3/16″
43709	3/8″	1″	3/8″	1-1/8″
43064	1/2″	1-1/4″	1/2″	1-1/4″
43066	1/2″	2″	1/2″	1-3/4″

PILOT PANEL BITS WITH PLUNGE POINT

DOUBLE FLUTE
Carbide Tipped

Two flutes give smooth cuts and even feed rates without chatter, drill through point.

Bit. No.	A Cut Width	B Flute Length	C Shank Diameter	D Shank Length
43214	3/8″	1″	1/4″	1-1/4″
43215	1/2″	2″	1/2″	1-3/4″

EDGE FORMING BITS

CORNER ROUND

2 FLUTE
High Speed Steel & Carbide Tipped
Solid Pilot & Ball Bearing Pilot

For Smooth, uniformly rounded edges. Lower depth setting results in rounded corner with decorative bead.

HIGH SPEED STEEL (Solid Pilot)

Bit. No.	A Radius	B Flute Length	C Shank Diameter	D Shank Length
43390	3/16″	3/8″	1/4″	1″
43393	1/4″	1/2″	1/4″	1″
43396	3/8″	5/8″	1/4″	1″
43399	1/2″	3/4″	1/4″	1″

CARBIDE TIPPED (Solid Pilot)

43403	1/4″	7/16″	1/4″	1-1/4″
43406	3/8″	19/32″	1/4″	1-1/4″
43412	1/2″	11/16″	1/4″	1-1/4″

CARBIDE TIPPED (Ball Bearing Pilot)

43085	3/16″	7/16″	1/4″	1-1/4″
43402	1/4″	7/16″	1/4″	1-1/4″
43404	5/32″	7/16″	1/4″	1-1/4″
43086	5/16″	9/16″	1/4″	1-1/4″
43405	3/8″	19/32″	1/4″	1-1/4″
43408	1/2″	11/16″	1/4″	1-1/4″
43091	1/2″	3/4″	1/2″	1-1/2″
43092	3/4″	1-1/4″	1/2″	1-1/2″

CARBIDE TIPPED (Ball Bearing Pilot) FOR COLOR CORE® AND CORIAN®

43404	5/32″	7/16″	1/4″	1-1/4″

BEADING

2 FLUTE
High Speed Steel & Carbide Tipped
Solid Pilot & Ball Bearing Pilot

For decorative period edging.

HIGH SPEED STEEL (Solid Pilot)

Bit. No.	A Radius	B Flute Length	C Shank Diameter	D Shank Length
43411	1/4″	1/2″	1/4″	1″
43414	3/8″	5/6″	1/4″	1″
43417	1/2″	3/4″	1/4″	1″

CARBIDE TIPPED (Solid Pilot)

43712	1/4″	7/16″	1/4″	1-1/4″
43713	3/8″	19/32″	1/4″	1-1/4″
43714	1/2″	11/16″	1/4″	1-1/4″

Figure 3–156 (continued).

ROUTER BITS ↓

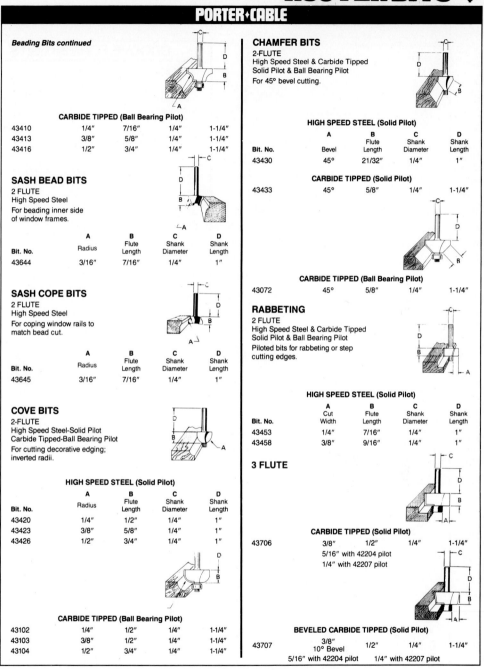

Beading Bits continued

CARBIDE TIPPED (Ball Bearing Pilot)

43410	1/4″	7/16″	1/4″	1-1/4″
43413	3/8″	5/8″	1/4″	1-1/4″
43416	1/2″	3/4″	1/4″	1-1/4″

SASH BEAD BITS
2 FLUTE
High Speed Steel
For beading inner side
of window frames.

Bit. No.	A Radius	B Flute Length	C Shank Diameter	D Shank Length
43644	3/16″	7/16″	1/4″	1″

SASH COPE BITS
2 FLUTE
High Speed Steel
For coping window rails to
match bead cut.

Bit. No.	A Radius	B Flute Length	C Shank Diameter	D Shank Length
43645	3/16″	7/16″	1/4″	1″

COVE BITS
2-FLUTE
High Speed Steel-Solid Pilot
Carbide Tipped-Ball Bearing Pilot
For cutting decorative edging;
inverted radii.

HIGH SPEED STEEL (Solid Pilot)

Bit. No.	A Radius	B Flute Length	C Shank Diameter	D Shank Length
43420	1/4″	1/2″	1/4″	1″
43423	3/8″	5/8″	1/4″	1″
43426	1/2″	3/4″	1/4″	1″

CARBIDE TIPPED (Ball Bearing Pilot)

43102	1/4″	1/2″	1/4″	1-1/4″
43103	3/8″	1/2″	1/4″	1-1/4″
43104	1/2″	3/4″	1/4″	1-1/4″

CHAMFER BITS
2-FLUTE
High Speed Steel & Carbide Tipped
Solid Pilot & Ball Bearing Pilot
For 45° bevel cutting.

HIGH SPEED STEEL (Solid Pilot)

Bit. No.	A Bevel	B Flute Length	C Shank Diameter	D Shank Length
43430	45°	21/32″	1/4″	1″

CARBIDE TIPPED (Solid Pilot)

43433	45°	5/8″	1/4″	1-1/4″

CARBIDE TIPPED (Ball Bearing Pilot)

43072	45°	5/8″	1/4″	1-1/4″

RABBETING
2 FLUTE
High Speed Steel & Carbide Tipped
Solid Pilot & Ball Bearing Pilot
Piloted bits for rabbeting or step
cutting edges.

HIGH SPEED STEEL (Solid Pilot)

Bit. No.	A Cut Width	B Flute Length	C Shank Diameter	D Shank Length
43453	1/4″	7/16″	1/4″	1″
43458	3/8″	9/16″	1/4″	1″

3 FLUTE

CARBIDE TIPPED (Solid Pilot)

43706	3/8″	1/2″	1/4″	1-1/4″
	5/16″ with 42204 pilot			
	1/4″ with 42207 pilot			

BEVELED CARBIDE TIPPED (Solid Pilot)

43707	3/8″ 10° Bevel	1/2″	1/4″	1-1/4″
	5/16″ with 42204 pilot		1/4″ with 42207 pilot	

Figure 3–156 (continued).

PORTER·CABLE

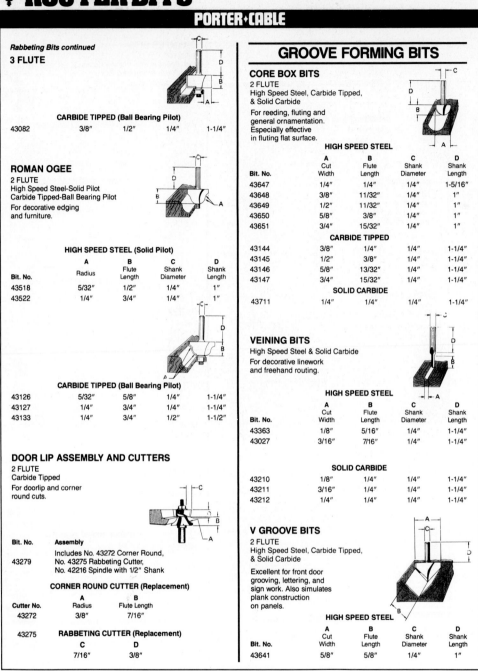

Rabbeting Bits continued

3 FLUTE

CARBIDE TIPPED (Ball Bearing Pilot)

| 43082 | 3/8″ | 1/2″ | 1/4″ | 1-1/4″ |

ROMAN OGEE

2 FLUTE
High Speed Steel-Solid Pilot
Carbide Tipped-Ball Bearing Pilot
For decorative edging
and furniture.

HIGH SPEED STEEL (Solid Pilot)

Bit. No.	A Radius	B Flute Length	C Shank Diameter	D Shank Length
43518	5/32″	1/2″	1/4″	1″
43522	1/4″	3/4″	1/4″	1″

CARBIDE TIPPED (Ball Bearing Pilot)

43126	5/32″	5/8″	1/4″	1-1/4″
43127	1/4″	3/4″	1/4″	1-1/4″
43133	1/4″	3/4″	1/2″	1-1/2″

DOOR LIP ASSEMBLY AND CUTTERS

2 FLUTE
Carbide Tipped
For doorlip and corner
round cuts.

Bit. No.	Assembly
43279	Includes No. 43272 Corner Round, No. 43275 Rabbeting Cutter, No. 42216 Spindle with 1/2″ Shank

CORNER ROUND CUTTER (Replacement)

Cutter No.	A Radius	B Flute Length
43272	3/8″	7/16″

RABBETING CUTTER (Replacement)

43275	C	D
	7/16″	3/8″

GROOVE FORMING BITS

CORE BOX BITS

2 FLUTE
High Speed Steel, Carbide Tipped,
& Solid Carbide

For reeding, fluting and
general ornamentation.
Especially effective
in fluting flat surface.

HIGH SPEED STEEL

Bit. No.	A Cut Width	B Flute Length	C Shank Diameter	D Shank Length
43647	1/4″	1/4″	1/4″	1-5/16″
43648	3/8″	11/32″	1/4″	1″
43649	1/2″	11/32″	1/4″	1″
43650	5/8″	3/8″	1/4″	1″
43651	3/4″	15/32″	1/4″	1″
CARBIDE TIPPED				
43144	3/8″	1/4″	1/4″	1-1/4″
43145	1/2″	3/8″	1/4″	1-1/4″
43146	5/8″	13/32″	1/4″	1-1/4″
43147	3/4″	15/32″	1/4″	1-1/4″
SOLID CARBIDE				
43711	1/4″	1/4″	1/4″	1-1/4″

VEINING BITS

High Speed Steel & Solid Carbide
For decorative linework
and freehand routing.

HIGH SPEED STEEL

Bit. No.	A Cut Width	B Flute Length	C Shank Diameter	D Shank Length
43363	1/8″	5/16″	1/4″	1-1/4″
43027	3/16″	7/16″	1/4″	1-1/4″
SOLID CARBIDE				
43210	1/8″	1/4″	1/4″	1-1/4″
43211	3/16″	1/4″	1/4″	1-1/4″
43212	1/4″	1/4″	1/4″	1-1/4″

V GROOVE BITS

2 FLUTE
High Speed Steel, Carbide Tipped,
& Solid Carbide

Excellent for front door
grooving, lettering, and
sign work. Also simulates
plank construction
on panels.

HIGH SPEED STEEL

Bit. No.	A Cut Width	B Flute Length	C Shank Diameter	D Shank Length
43641	5/8″	5/8″	1/4″	1″

Figure 3–156 (continued).

V Groove Bits continued

CARBIDE TIPPED

43725	1/2"	1/2"	1/4"	1"
43213	3/8"	1/2"	1/4"	1-1/4"
43077	3/4"	5/8"	1/2"	1-1/2"
43078	1"	5/8"	1/2"	1-1/2"

SOLID CARBIDE

43074	1/4"	5/16"	1/4"	1-1/16"

DOVETAIL BITS

2-FLUTE
High Speed Steel & Carbide Tipped

For smooth dovetail joints. Use with dovetail template.

HIGH SPEED STEEL

Bit. No.	A Cut Width	B Flute Length	C Shank Diameter	D Shank Length
43639	1/4"	3/8"	1/4"	1-1/4"
43640	1/2"	1/2"	1/4"	1-1/4"

CARBIDE TIPPED

43705	1/2"	7/16"	1/4"	1-1/4"

TRADITIONAL BITS

2-FLUTE
Carbide Tipped

Excellent where a wide, shallow cut is desired. Flat bottom gives a raised effect to panels. Also recommended for edge forming.

Bit. No.	A Cut Width	B Flute Length	C Shank Diameter	D Shank Length
43161	1/2"	3/8"	1/4"	1-1/2"
43162	3/4"	7/16"	1/4"	1-1/2"
43163	3/4"	7/16"	1/2"	2-1/4"

CLASSICAL BITS

2-FLUTE
Carbide Tipped

For beautiful bead and groove combination effect. Also excellent for edge forming.

Bit. No.	A Cut Width	B Flute Length	C Shank Diameter	D Shank Length
43166	1/2"	3/8"	1/4"	1-1/2"
43167	3/4"	1/2"	1/4"	1-1/2"
43168	3/4"	1/2"	1/2"	2-1/4"
43169	1"	5/8"	1/2"	2-1/4"

OGEE BITS

2-FLUTE
Carbide Tipped

Beautiful, symmetrical grooving bit. Also excellent for edge work.

Bit. No.	A Cut Width	B Flute Length	C Shank Diameter	D Shank Length
43157	3/8"	3/8"	1/4"	1-1/2"
43158	1/2"	13/32"	1/4"	1-1/2"
43159	3/4"	7/16"	1/4"	1-1/2"
43160	3/4"	7/16"	1/2"	2-1/4"

RAISED PANEL BITS

2-FLUTE
Carbide Tipped

Wide, shallow cutting bit for easy raised panel effect. Can also be used for edge forming.

Bit. No.	A Cut Width	B Flute Length	C Shank Diameter	D Shank Length
43154	1-1/8"	7/16"	1/2"	2-1/4"

MORTISING BITS

2-FLUTE
High Speed Steel & Carbide Tipped

For stock removal, dados, rabbets, hinge butt mortising.

HIGH SPEED STEEL

Bit. No.	A Cut Width	B Flute Length	C Shank Diameter	D Shank Length
43446	1/2"	9/16"	1/4"	1-1/2"
43449	5/8"	9/16"	1/4"	1-1/2"

Figure 3–156 (continued).

↓ ROUTER BITS

Hinge Butt Mortising Bits continued

CARBIDE TIPPED

43437	1/2"	9/16"	1/4"	1-1/2"
43440	5/8"	9/16"	1/4"	1-1/2"
43443	3/4"	9/16"	1/4"	1-1/2"
43442	1-1/4"	9/16"	1/4"	1-1/2"

STAIR ROUTER CUTTER
2-FLUTE, SCREW TYPE
High Speed Steel
Cuts dovetail-like joint for locking stair treads and risers into stair stringers.
NOTE: Fits 43274 or 43737 Arbors.

Cutter No.	A Cut Width	B Flute Length
43506	11/16"	1/2"

LAMINATE TRIMMING BITS

FLUSH CUT TRIMMING BITS
Solid Carbide
Self Pilot
Makes self-trim flush cut.

Bit. No.	Bevel	B Flute Length	C Shank Diameter	D Shank Length
43509	Flush	1/4"	1/4"	1"
43216	Flush	3/8"	1/4"	1-5/8"

FLUSH/BEVEL TRIMMING BITS
Solid Carbide
Makes flush or bevel cuts.

Bit. No.	Bevel	B Flute Length	C Shank Diameter	D Shank Length
43515	Flush & 10°	1/4"	1/4"	1-1/8"

BEVEL TRIMMING BITS
Solid Carbide
Self Pilot
Makes piloted bevel trim cuts.

Bit. No.	Bevel	B Flute Length	C Shank Diameter	D Shank Length
43512	7°	1/4"	1/4"	1"

BORING & FLUSH TRIM BITS
Solid Carbide
For penetrating laminate surface and then flush trimming pre-cut opening.

Bit. No.	A Cut Width	B Flute Length	C Shank Diameter	D Shank Length
43231	1/4"	1/4"	1/4"	7/8"

COMBINATION FLUSH/BEVEL TRIMMER BITS
SINGLE FLUTE
Carbide Tipped
Ball Bearing Pilot
Can be used for flush or 22° bevel trim edges.

Bit. No.	Bevel	B Flute Length	C Shank Diameter	D Shank Length
43277	Flush & 22°	3/8"	1/4"	1-1/4"

2-WING BEVEL TRIMMING BITS
DOUBLE FLUTE
Carbide Tipped
Ball Bearing Pilot
For fast, accurate bevel trim cuts.

Bit. No.	Bevel	B Flute Length	C Shank Diameter	D Shank Length
43253	25°	1/4"	1/4"	1-1/4"

Figure 3–156 (continued).

PORTER·CABLE

FLUSH LAMINATE TRIM BITS
2-FLUTE
Carbide Tipped
Ball Bearing Pilot

For fast flush trimming with smooth ball bearing action.

Bit. No.	Type	B Flute Length	C Shank Diameter	D Shank Length
43252	Flush	1/2″	1/4″	1″
43731	Flush	1″	1/4″	1″
43730	Flush	1″	1/2″	1-1/2″

FLUSH/BEVEL BITS
2-FLUTE
Carbide Tipped

Combines 22° bevel trim and flush trim cuts in one bit.
(Bevel: Flush & 22°)

Bit. No.	A Cut Width	B Flute Length	C Shank Diameter	D Shank Length
44858	3/8″	1/4″ Flush 1/4″ Bevel	1/4″	1-1/4″

3-WING TRIMMER ASSEMBLIES & CUTTERS
Flush Cut
Carbide Tipped
Ball Bearing Pilot

For extra smooth production trimming. Includes No. 43741 ¼″ or No. 43738 ½″ Spindle and No. 43740 Ball Bearing Guide.

ASSEMBLIES, FLUSH CUT

Bit. No.	B Flute Length	C Shank Diameter	D Shank Length
43268	3/8″	1/4″	13/16″
43271	3/8″	1/2″	15/16″

3 WING REPLACEMENT CUTTERS, FLUSH CUT

Bit. No.	B
43732	3/8″

3 WING TRIMMER ASSEMBLIES & CUTTERS
Bevel Cut
Carbide Tipped
Ball Bearing Pilot

For extra smooth production trimming. Includes No. 43741 ¼″ Spindle and No. 43740 Ball Bearing Pilot.

ASSEMBLIES, BEVEL CUT

Bit. No.	Bevel	B Flute Length	C Shank Diameter	D Shank Length
43270	10°	1/4″	1/4″	1-1/8″
43257	25°	1/4″	1/4″	13/16″

3 WING REPLACEMENT CUTTERS, BEVEL CUT

Bit. No.	Bevel	B Flute Length
43733	10°	1/4″
43734	25°	1/4″

SLOTTING CUTTERS

Used to make slots for "T" molding and weather stripping

2 WING SLOTTING CUTTERS
Carbide Tipped

Cutter No.	Cutter Diameter	Arbor Hole	A Depth of Cut	B Cut Thickness
43726	1-7/8″	5/16″	1/2″	1/16″
43727	1-7/8″	5/16″	1/2″	5/64″
43728	1-7/8″	5/16″	1/2″	3/32″
43234	1-7/8″	5/16″	1/2″	1/8″
43729	1-7/8″	5/16″	1/2″	1/4″
43235	1-7/8″	5/16″	1/2″	3/16″

3 WING SLOTTING CUTTERS
Carbide Tipped

Cutter No.	Cutter Diameter	Arbor Hole	A Depth of Cut	B Cut Thickness
43247	1-7/8″	5/16″	1/2″	1/16″
43249	1-7/8″	5/16″	1/2″	5/64″
43250	1-7/8″	5/16″	1/2″	3/32″
43255	1-7/8″	5/16″	1/2″	1/8″
43256	1-7/8″	5/16″	1/2″	3/16″
43258	1-7/8″	5/16″	1/2″	1/4″

Figure 3–156 (continued).

Cutters, Arbors, & Spindles

	1/4" Shank		3/8" Shank	1/2" Shank	
Arbor/ Spindle	Trim Spindle **43741**	Slotting Spindle **42195** **42196** W/Collar W/Ball Bearing	Slotting Spindle **43032** **42197** W/Collar W/Ball Bearing	Trim Spindle **43738**	Door Lip Spindle **42216**
Shank Diameter	1/4"	1/4"	3/8"	1/2"	1/2"
Shank Length	13/16"	1-3/8"	1-7/16"	15/16"	29/32"
Thread Length	5/16"	9/16"	3/16"	5/16"	1-3/8"
Spindle Capacity	1-1/8"	3/4"	3/4"	1-1/8"	2-1/4"
Arbor Diameter	5/16"	5/16"	5/16"	5/16"	5/16"
Total Length	2-5/32"	2-9/16"	2-9/16"	2-1/16"	3-21/64"
Collar Diameter	7/8"	7/8"	7/8"	7/8"	N/A
Nut Size	5/16-24	5/16-24	5/16-24	5/16-24	5/16-24
Item	**Use Correct Part Number**				
Flush Trim Laminate Cutters	3 wing 43732			3 wing 43732	
Bevel Trim Laminate Cutters	3 wing 43733 43734			3 wing 43733 43734	
2-Wing Slotting Cutters		43726 43727 43728 43234 43235 43729	43726 43727 43728 43234 43235 43729		
3-Wing Cutters		43247 43249 43250 43255 43256 43258	43247 43249 43250 43255 43256 43258		
Corner Round Cutter					43272
Rabbeting Cutter					43275
Bearing	Regular 7/8" O.D. 43740	Regular 7/8" O.D. 43740 Oversized 1-1/16" O.D. 43217	Regular 7/8" O.D. 43740 Oversized 1-1/16" O.D. 43217	Regular 7/8" O.D. 43740	

Figure 3-156 (continued).

Many router bits have a self-guiding pilot that guides the router along the edge of the board being machined. This may be a solid steel pilot, or it may be a small ball bearing mounted on the tip of the bit (Fig. 3–157). The ball-bearing guides are more expensive, but much easier to use and much less likely to burn the wood.

The router is sometimes used for freehand work, but it is usually guided in one of four ways:

1. The previously mentioned pilot guide bearing may be used to guide the router along straight or curved edges (Fig. 3–158).

Figure 3–157   Router bit with a ball-bearing pilot.

Figure 3–158   The ball-bearing pilot guide is used to guide the router along the edge of the wood.

Figure 3-159 A board clamped to the workpiece is used as a guide for the router.

2. A straight-edge guide clamped to the wood may be used as a guide for the base of the router (Fig. 3-159). This is especially useful for cutting dados and grooves.

3. An accessory edge guide can be mounted to the base of the router to guide the router parallel with the edge of the board (Fig. 3-160). These guides are usually made so that they can be reversed, with one edge being designed for straight edges and the other being used for curved edges.

Figure 3-160 Accessory guide fence for a router (Porter Cable Corp.).

Figure 3–161 Guide collar for the router.

4. The fourth method of guiding the router requires a template and a template guide collar mounted in the base of the router (Fig. 3–161). This guide collar is run against a template, which can be band sawn from hardboard (Fig. 3–162). These collars are also used in conjunction with dovetail cutting jigs and for hinge-butt routing jigs.

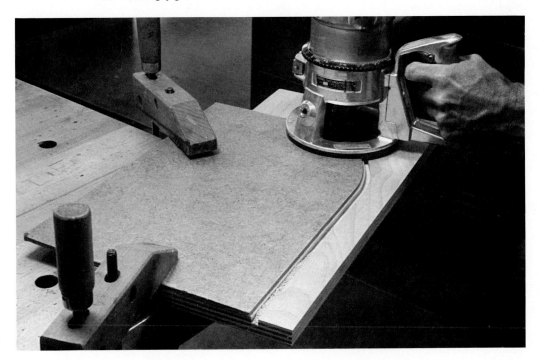

Figure 3–162 Using the guide collar with a hardboard template.

Portable Power Tools

Cutting a molding.   Select the bit to cut the desired molding pattern and mount the bit in the router. On many routers, it is easier to completely remove the motor from the base to mount the bit in the collar. The router base is then adjusted to obtain the desired depth of cut. When using molding cutters, the depth of cut is determined by sighting across the base of the router to see how much of the bit is exposed for cutting. It is often best to make a molding cut in two passes, with the first cut being fairly heavy to remove most of the material, and then a second, lighter cut to produce a smooth surface. If the molding cut is to run across the end grain of the wood, the end-grain cuts should always be made first so that any chipping that may occur at the end of the cross-grain cut will be removed when making the cut with the grain.

The actual cut is made by setting the router flat on the stock, making sure that the cutter is not in contact with the stock. The router is then started and moved into the stock until the guide bearing makes contact with the edge of the stock. The router is then moved from left to right as you face the edge of the workpiece. The router must be kept moving at a uniform pace. Any stop or hesitation will result in a machine burn on the wood. If the wood grain runs in the wrong direction and tends to chip while being machined, the router may be run in the other direction (right to left). The router is harder to control when feeding in this direction so a series of lighter cuts should be made.

Figure 3–163   Plunge cut router
(Makita USA, Inc.).

Cutting a dado.   Dado cuts are usually made with a straight cutting bit and a straight-edge guide clamped to the workpiece. The location of the guide in relation to the required cut can easily be determined by clamping the straight-edge guide to a scrap piece of wood, making a trial cut, and then measuring the resulting distance from the cut to the guide.

Blind dados may be cut by starting the router in a tilted position, with the edge of the base against the guide, and carefully lowering the cutter into the wood. Some manufacturers make plunge routers (Fig. 3–163) that make cutting blind dados much easier.

Cutting rabbets.   There are two common methods of cutting rabbets with the router. One method involves the use of the router guide fence and a straight cutting bit. In the absence of a router guide fence, a wood board with a straight edge may be clamped to the base of the router to guide the rabbet cut. The wood board will need to have a notch cut in its edge to accommodate the router bit (Fig. 3–164).

The other method is to use a rabbet-cutting bit with a pilot bearing, as shown in Fig. 3–157. This system is very easy to use and is essential for cutting a glass rabbet in assembled door frames. This bit also allows easy cutting of curved rabbets, such as those used for installing oval mirrors or glass in doors with arched tops.

Figure 3–164   Wood guide used for cutting rabbets.

Cutting dovetails. Several dovetail cutting fixtures are available that allow quick and accurate cutting of dovetail joints. The fixture shown in Fig. 3–165 is used for cutting a blind dovetail. This is an excellent method for joining drawer sides to drawer fronts and backs.

Unequal dovetails can be cut with the fixture shown in Fig. 3–166. These are through dovetails (they show from both sides), and they make excellent joints for joining the corners of cases.

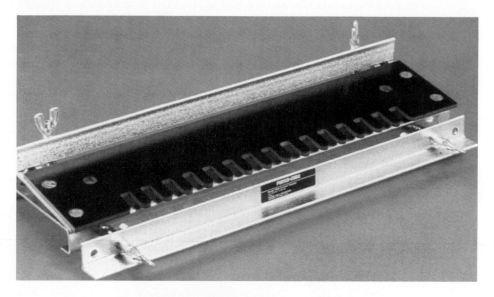

Figure 3–165 Dovetail cutting jig (Porter Cable Corp.).

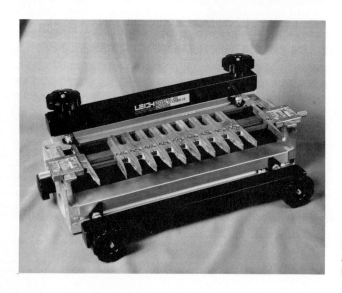

Figure 3–166 Dovetail cutting jig that allows cutting unequally spaced dovetails. (Leigh Industries.)

Figure 3-167   Cutting a dovetail dado.

Cutting dovetail dados.   The dovetail dado is often used for joining drawer sides to drawer fronts when the drawer front must extend beyond the drawer sides. It is also sometimes used to join shelves to cabinet sides. A dovetail bit is used, and the cut is made in the same way as for the dado cut (Fig. 3-167). The dovetail part of the joint can be cut with the table saw, as described in the section on the table saw.

Cutting box joints.   The setup for cutting box joints described in the table saw section is easier than the one about to be described for the router, especially if you are not planning on making very many joints or if you will be needing to make joints with pins of different widths.

However, if you are planning on using a lot of box joints with pins of the same width, the jig shown here will be worth making. It is essentially a box to hold the parts that are to receive the box joint. The parts are stacked in the box and indexed against one side, as shown in Fig. 3-168. Note that half of the boards must be offset by one pin width. A slotted guide board is then attached to the top with flat head screws (Fig. 3-169). The router is used with a guide collar around the straight cutting bit.

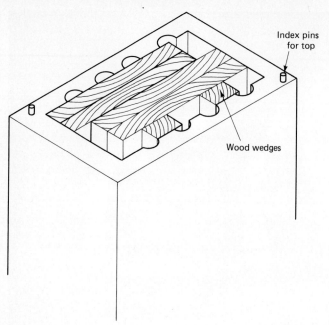

Index pins
for top

Wood wedges

Figure 3–168 Jig for cutting box joints
with the router.

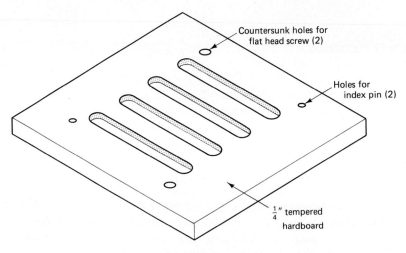

Countersunk holes for
flat head screw (2)

Holes for
index pin (2)

$\frac{1}{4}''$ tempered
hardboard

Figure 3–169 Router guide for cutting box joints.

Mortising for butt hinges.   Routers are very handy for cutting the recess or
"gain" required for setting butt hinges. For small, cabinet-door-size hinges, the outline of the hinge is drawn on the wood. The router can be used free hand to cut close
to the line and remove most of the material. The final cut to the line is done with
a sharp chisel.

Setting larger butt hinges for entry doors is easiest if a hinge routing jig is used. This jig can be tacked to the door to cut the hinge mortises and then tacked to the door frame to make the cuts for the mating hinge leafs.

Cutting mortises. A straight cutting bit and a guide clamped to the router base are used to make a mortise, as shown in Fig. 3–170. The round ends of the mortise will need to be cut square with a chisel.

Using a router table. A router mounted upside down in a table will do many of the operations of a shaper. Router tables are available from some router manufacturers or they may be homemade. They are especially handy for cutting moldings and rabbets (Fig. 3–171).

Figure 3–170 Cutting a mortise with the router.

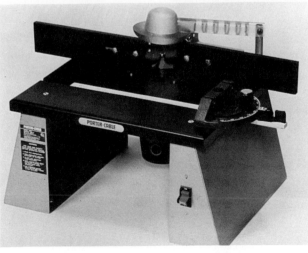

Figure 3–171 Router table (Porter Cable Corp.).

Figure 3-172 Groove-cutting bit for cutting splines.

Cutting splines. Groove-cutting bits, such as the one shown in Fig. 3-172, work well for cutting splines. This bit can be used when it is necessary to edge glue two pieces of plywood for a large cabinet or anywhere a splined joint is needed.

Saber Saw

The saber saw shown in Fig. 3-173 (also known as a jig saw) is used primarily for making curved cuts and is especially useful for making internal cuts. Blades are avail-

Figure 3-173 Typical saber saw (also known as a jig saw) (Skil Power Tool Co.).

able in a variety of tooth sizes. Larger teeth will usually cut faster, but leave a rougher edge. There are also taper-ground or hollow-ground blades that will make smoother cuts. Metal-cutting blades are also available. The saber saw cuts on the upstroke, so the pattern should be drawn on the back side of the part whenever possible to avoid chipping on the face side.

Some of these saws are designed so that the blade can rotate, which allows the saw to continue cutting when pulled sideways or even backward. This feature is handy when it is necessary to cut in confined areas where it may not be possible to rotate the entire saw to make a curved cut.

A pilot hole is usually drilled in the stock to insert the blade for making internal cuts. It is important that the saber saw be held down tightly against the stock while cutting.

Portable Circular Saws

Portable circular saws are not used a great deal for cabinet and furniture work, but they can be very handy for cutting large sheets of plywood to manageable sizes if the table saw is not large enough and, of course, they are very useful for building construction work.

There are two basic portable circular saw designs. The worm drive saw (Fig. 3–174) gets its name from the worm gear used to change the drive shaft direction 90° with respect to the motor. The direct drive saw is shown in Fig. 3–175. Worm drive saws are usually heavy-duty, industrial models, while the direct drive models range from inexpensive consumer models to heavy-duty industrial models. Many carpenters prefer the worm drive model because the blade is on the left, making it easy to follow a cutting line. Others prefer the direct drive models.

Safety is a very important consideration when using a portable circular saw. The blade guard should be checked to make sure it snaps back into place as soon as a cut is completed. The blade should be sharp and of the proper type for the material

Skilsaw model #77
7 ¼" worm drive saw

Figure 3–174   Worm drive portable circular saw (Skil Power Tool Co.).

Skilsaw model # 5650 (553)
7 ¼'' circular saw

Figure 3–175 Direct drive portable circular saw (Skil Power Tool Co.).

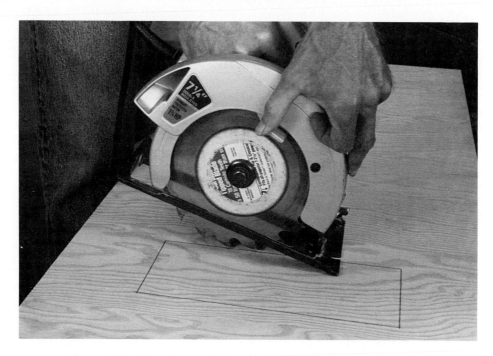

Figure 3–176 Using the portable circular saw to make an internal cutout.

being cut. A cut should never be made between two supports. This will cause the material to sag as the cut is being completed and will cause the material to pinch on the blade, causing the saw to kick back.

The blade assortment available for portable circular saws is quite similar to that available for table saws or radial arm saws. There are rip blades, crosscut blades, combination blades, and blades for cutting plastics, metals, and masonry.

As with the saber saw, the cut should be made with the good face of the material down, since chipping is most likely to occur on the top side of the cut as the blade teeth break through the surface of the material.

The saw may be used freehand to follow a line drawn on the material, or a straight edge may be clamped to the material as a cutting guide. The saw can usually be tilted to 45° for bevel cuts. The saw can also be used to make internal cutouts as shown in Fig. 3–176.

Power Planes

Portable power planes (Fig. 3–177) perform the same function as hand planes, but they do the job with less effort and are faster. They are often used for trimming doors to fit, planing cabinet scribe strips to fit a wall, and other on-the-job fitting operations.

Drills and Doweling Jigs

Portable drills are used for many woodworking operations. They are usually designated as $\frac{1}{4}$, $\frac{3}{8}$, or $\frac{1}{2}$ in., depending on the capacity of the drill chuck. A typical $\frac{3}{8}$-in. drill is shown in Fig. 3–178.

SKIL model # 96 plane

Figure 3–177 Portable power plane (Skil Power Tool Co.).

Skil model #6520
3/8″ VSR drill

Figure 3–178 Portable drill (Skil Power Tool Co.).

Portable drills can use any of the bits described in the section on the drill press, provided the chuck is large enough and the drill has enough power. Many drills have variable-speed control and are reversible. This feature makes them useful as power screw drivers.

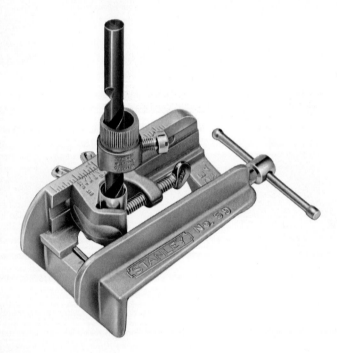

Figure 3–179 Adjustable dowel jig (photograph courtesy of Stanley Tools, division of the Stanley Works, New Britain, CT 06050).

A major use of portable drills in woodworking is drilling dowel holes for making dowel joints. A number of dowel jigs are available for this purpose. They differ in some of their features, but they all are designed to clamp on the wood and provide an accurate guide hole for drilling a dowel hole.

Two popular dowel jigs are shown in Figs. 3–179 and 3–180. Most dowel jigs require locating marks on the wood parts. This is done by putting the wood parts together in the position in which they will be doweled and making marks across the joint where the dowels are to be located (Fig. 3–181).

Figure 3–180 Self-centering dowel jig.

Figure 3–181 Marking the location of dowel holes.

Figure 3-182 Drilling the dowel holes.

The dowel jig has an alignment mark that must be aligned with the mark on the wood when the dowel jig is clamped to the wood. Some dowel jigs then require the hole guide to be centered on the board at this point. The drill is then used with either a conventional twist bit or a brad-point twist bit to drill the hole to the desired depth (Fig. 3-182). A drill bit stop may be used to indicate when the proper depth has been achieved, or a piece of masking tape can be put on the bit for this purpose.

Sanders

Two types of portable sanders are used extensively in woodworking, the belt sander (Fig. 3-183) and the finish sander (Fig. 3-184). Disc sanders are also sometimes used for rapid stock removal. The portable belt sander is one of the more difficult portable power tools to use successfully. It takes great skill and concentration to sand a flat surface without putting small dips in the surface when changing directions with the sander. The sander should be used with long forward and backward strokes, while gradually working it sideways across the surface. Sanding belts come in a variety of grits, from very coarse for very rapid stock removal to very fine for all but the final finish sanding.

Figure 3–183 Portable belt sander (Porter Cable Corp.).

Figure 3–184 Orbital finishing sander (Makita USA, Inc.).

Finish sanders are much easier to use and may have an orbital motion or a straight-line motion. Some finish sanders can run either way. Finish sanders vary a great deal in size. Some of the larger ones use one-half of a standard 9 by 11 in. sandpaper sheet, while smaller palm-size sanders may use one-fourth of a sheet or even smaller sizes. Orbital sanders cut faster than straight-line sanders, but they leave small, circular sanding marks in the wood that should be removed with a final hand sanding.

Air-powered, dual-action sanders, such as the one shown in Fig. 3–185, are also often used for woodworking. Some can be used as a disc sander for fast material removal or as an orbital sander for finish sanding. They are usually much faster than electrically powered sanders, but they require a fairly large air compressor.

Portable Power Tools

No. 590—Orbital Disc Air Finish Sander

Figure 3–185 Dual action, orbital disc air finish sander (Sioux Tools, Inc.).

Wafer Jointing Machines

Wafer jointing machines (Fig. 3–186) were developed in Europe and eliminate the need for cutting dado, rabbet, and dowel joints in many applications. The wafer jointing system is based on the use of small, football-shaped wood wafers that are used much like splines to reinforce wood joints. The wood wafers are compressed in manufacturing. They are installed in a snug-fitting slot with a special water-based glue, which causes the compressed wood to expand, making a very tight joint. They work very well using butt joints to join parts of cabinets or furniture together. They can also be used to reinforce miter joints.

The machine used to cut the slots for installing the wafers has a small-diameter saw blade of the proper thickness. It makes a semielliptical slot in the wood to accept the wafer. Some applications are shown in Fig. 3–187.

Figure 3–186 Wafer jointing machine (Colonial Saw).

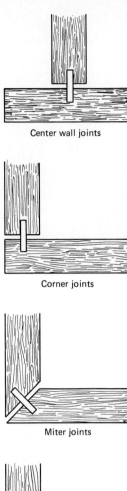

Center wall joints

Corner joints

Miter joints

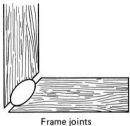

Frame joints

Figure 3–187 Typical wafer joint applications (Colonial Saw).

Chop Saw

The chop saw (Fig. 3–188) or motorized miter box has become quite popular in woodworking. It can be used for cutting accurate left- or right-hand miters, as well as for cutting stock to length. It is usually used with a fairly fine tooth crosscutting blade. A homemade table extension can be helpful for cutting long boards, and it can provide a convenient place to clamp a stop block for cutting multiple lengths.

Figure 3-188   Chop saw or motorized miter box (Ryobi America Corp.).

HAND TOOLS

Saws

The grain structure of wood makes it necessary to use saws with different tooth shapes for cutting with the grain (ripping) or cutting across the grain (crosscutting). Handsaws are either ripsaws or crosscut saws. The ripsaw tooth is shown in Fig. 3–189 and the crosscut tooth is shown in Fig. 3–190.

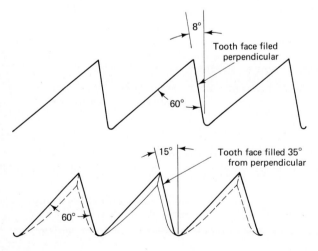

8°
Tooth face filed
perpendicular
60°

Figure 3-189   Ripsaw tooth shape.

15°
Tooth face filled 35°
from perpendicular
60°

Figure 3-190   Crosscut tooth shape.

Saw teeth are made in various sizes and are designated by the number of points per inch. The ripsaw usually has larger teeth, with five points per inch being quite common. Crosscut saws are often found in 8-point sizes for construction work and 10 or 11 points per inch for finish work.

There are many special-purpose saws, such as back saws and dovetail saws for cutting joints and keyhole saws, compass saws, and coping saws for curved work. These are shown in Figs. 3–191 through 3–196.

Figure 3–191   Hand ripsaw. (Disston Co.)

Figure 3–192   Hand crosscut saw. The ripsaw and the crosscut saw are the same except for the shape of the teeth. (Disston Co.)

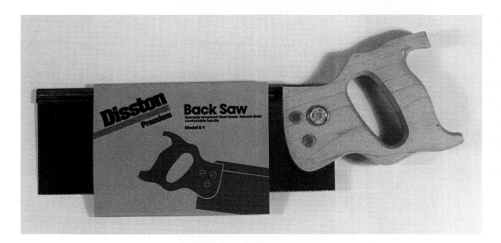

Figure 3–193   Back saw. (Disston Co.)

Figure 3–194 Dovetail saw. (Disston Co.)

Figure 3–195 Compass saw. (Disston Co.)

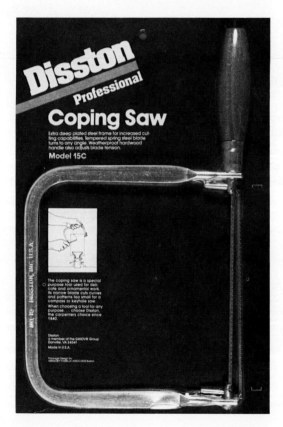

Figure 3–196 Coping saw. (Disston Co.)

The previously described saws all cut on the push stroke. Some woodworkers, however, prefer Japanese saws, which cut on the pull stroke. This allows a much thinner blade since the blade does not have to be thick to resist bowing on the push stroke.

Planes

Many types of hand planes are available for woodworking. The planes with the longer beds are used to true up crooked boards, while short-bed planes are used for fine, accurate fitting of parts. Rabbet planes are very useful because of their ability to plane right up to an adjacent surface.

Most commercially manufactured planes are made of metal, but some woodworkers prefer wood planes because of their light weight and lack of friction when sliding over another wood surface. Some of the more popular planes are shown in Figs. 3–197 through 3–201.

Figure 3–197   Jack plane (photograph courtesy of Stanley Tools, Division of the Stanley Works, New Britain, CT 06050).

Figure 3–198   Block plane (photograph courtesy of Stanley Tools, Division of the Stanley Works, New Britain, CT 06050).

Figure 3–199 Rabbet plane (photograph courtesy of Stanley Tools, Division of the Stanley Works, New Britain, CT 06050).

Figure 3–200 Spoke shave (photograph courtesy of Stanley Tools, Division of the Stanley Works, New Britain, CT 06050).

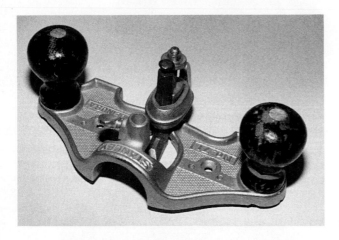

Figure 3–201 Router plane.

Drilling and Boring Tools

The main hand tools for drilling holes in wood are the hand drill (Fig. 3–202), the push drill (Fig. 3–203), and the auger brace (Fig. 3–204). The hand drill uses ordinary twist drill bits, the push drill uses special bits with two straight cutting flutes, and the auger brace uses auger bits, expansion bits, countersink bits, and screwdriver bits. The auger bit is shown in Fig. 3–205 and the expansion bit in Fig. 3–206.

Figure 3–202 Hand drill (photograph courtesy of Stanley Tools, Division of the Stanley Works, New Britain, CT 06050).

Figure 3–203 Push drill (photograph courtesy of Stanley Tools, Division of the Stanley Works, New Britain, CT 06050).

Figure 3–204 Auger brace (photograph courtesy of Stanley Tools, Division of the Stanley Works, New Britain, CT 06050).

Figure 3-205 Auger bit (photograph courtesy of Stanley Tools, Division of the Stanley Works, New Britain, CT 06050).

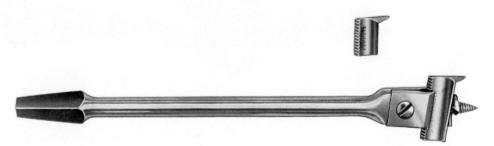

Figure 3-206 Expansion bit (photograph courtesy of Stanley Tools, Division of the Stanley Works, New Britain, CT 06050).

Measuring and Layout Tools

The most commonly used measuring and layout tools include the steel tape, the framing square, the try square, the combination square, the bevel square or sliding T-bevel, the marking gage, and the dividers. These are shown in Figs. 3–207 through 3–213.

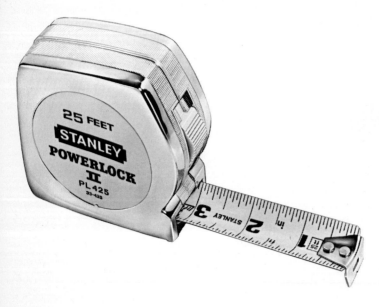

Figure 3-207 Steel measuring tape (photograph courtesy of Stanley Tools, Division of the Stanley Works, New Britain, CT 06050).

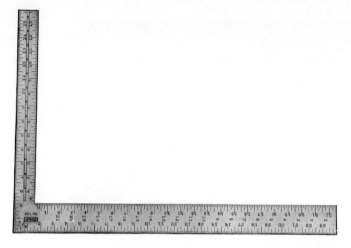

Figure 3–208 Framing or carpenter's square (photograph courtesy of Stanley Tools, Division of the Stanley Works, New Britain, CT 06050).

Figure 3–209 Combination square (photograph courtesy of Stanley Tools, Division of the Stanley Works, New Britain, CT 06050).

Figure 3–210 Try square (photograph courtesy of Stanley Tools, Division of the Stanley Works, New Britain, CT 06050).

Hand Tools

Figure 3–211 Bevel square or sliding T-bevel (photograph courtesy of Stanley Tools, Division of the Stanley Works, New Britain, CT 06050).

Figure 3–212 Marking gage (photograph courtesy of Stanley Tools, Division of the Stanley Works, New Britain, CT 06050).

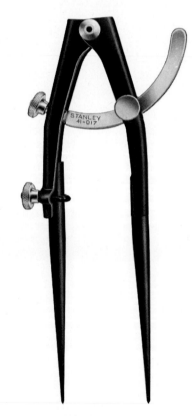

Figure 3–213 Dividers (photograph courtesy of Stanley Tools, Division of the Stanley Works, New Britain, CT 06050).

4 Adhesives, Abrasives, and Hardware

ADHESIVES

Modern adhesives have made woodworking much easier by allowing relatively easy joining of wood parts and the development of plywoods, particle boards, and other sheet material.

How Adhesives Work

In theory, if two surfaces to be joined could be made perfectly flat so that all the molecules of one surface were in contact with the other surface, the two surfaces could be joined by natural molecular attraction without the use of an adhesive. In practice, this is impossible, as even highly polished metal surfaces have very large hills and valleys compared to the size of the molecules.

Liquids, however, are capable of filling these valleys and making good molecular contact with the surface. If this liquid then hardens and has a good cohesive bond between its own molecules, it will cause the two surfaces to adhere. In addition, on porous surfaces such as wood, the adhesive penetrates into cell cavities and hardens, forming interlocking fingers that create a mechanical bond. A number of adhesives have been developed especially for joining wood parts.

Characteristics of Woodworking Adhesives

While most woodworking adhesives will produce a joint stronger than the wood under proper conditions, they do vary in a number of important characteristics. The moisture resistance of the cured glue joint can vary from almost nonexistent to completely waterproof. Woodworking adhesives are generally classified for moisture resistance in one of three categories: low moisture resistant, moisture resistant, and waterproof.

There are no requirements for the low-moisture-resistant category. Adhesives in the moisture-resistant category must pass a number of rather stringent tests, including a number of soaking and drying cycles. These adhesives are usually satisfactory for exterior furniture and other applications where they are not constantly submerged in water. To be rated as waterproof, an adhesive must pass very stringent tests and, in fact, the wood must deteriorate and fail before the glue line fails.

Adhesives also vary a great deal in their setting time. The required clamping time may vary from 30 minutes at room temperature to over 12 hours. All the conventional woodworking adhesives require that the wood parts be clamped tightly together while the adhesive is setting to obtain optimum strength.

Adhesives also vary in their maximum *open* time, that is, the time from beginning to spread the adhesive on the wood until the parts must be securely clamped. If the adhesive starts to set before the parts are clamped in place, the inevitable movement between parts when tightening clamps will break the initial bond and result in a weaker glue joint. An adhesive with a short open time can make it very difficult to assemble a complex project.

Adhesives also vary on their gap-filling properties. The best glue joints are obtained when the mating parts fit accurately with as much wood-to-wood contact as possible. Some adhesives will tolerate a certain amount of looseness between parts without seriously weakening the glue joint.

Some adhesives are ready to use; others require mixing with water or a catalyst.

Potential Gluing Problems

Several conditions that can affect the strength of a glue joint are discussed next.

Moisture content of the wood.   If the wood has too much moisture, it tends to dilute the glue and weaken it, and as the wet wood dries and shrinks, it also tends to put stress on the glue joint. If the wood is too dry, it tends to draw moisture from the glue joint. The wood will also swell from the moisture in the glue, and if it is planed before the moisture has left the wood, the area around the glue joint will shrink as the wood dries, leaving a depressed area around the joint.

Temperature.   Most woodworking adhesives work best at room temperature or slightly above. The setting time increases rapidly as temperatures dip below 70 °F. The setting time decreases with elevated temperatures. Some adhesives set twice as fast as 90 °F as they do at 70 °F. The open time also decreases with increased heat.

Oily woods.   Some tropical hardwoods are very oily. This prevents the adhesive from wetting the surface properly. Some adhesives are better for this than others. Washing the wood surface with a solvent such as lacquer thinner before gluing helps.

End grain.   It was mentioned earlier that most woodworking adhesives produce a glue joint stronger than the wood under the right conditions. This is true when gluing boards edge to edge or face to face with the grain running in the same direction. End-grain surfaces do not glue well. The tubular wood cells tend to draw adhesive away from the joint, and they do not provide much surface area for bonding. End-grain gluing almost always requires some kind of reinforcement, such as an interlocking joint design, dowels, splines, or metal fasteners such as nails, screws, or bolts.

Common Woodworking Adhesives

The following paragraphs give descriptions, typical uses, and same advantages and disadvantages of some of the more popular woodworking adhesives.

Aliphatic resin.   This cream-colored adhesive comes ready to use. It is probably the most popular all-around woodworking adhesive. It is used a great deal for cabinet and furniture assembly. Several properties make this an ideal adhesive for many applications. It has a very fast setting time, only requiring a clamping time of 30 minutes to 1 hour at room temperature.

Aliphatic resin has excellent gap-filling properties, and it remains tough rather than getting brittle when dry. It does not get soft from the heat generated by sanding as some adhesives do, so it will not load up sanding belts. It is also resistant to all the normal solvents used in wood finishes.

The major disadvantages are that it is not water resistant, and its short open time can make it difficult to assemble complex projects before it starts to set. This open time can be as little as 3 minutes at room temperature and even less than that at warmer temperatures.

Polyvinyl resin.   This is a pure white, multipurpose adhesive that is often used for woodworking and comes ready to use. It can be used for just about any gluing situation that does not require water or heat resistance. It has good gap-filling properties. The required clamping time is about 1 hour at room temperature, and the open time is about twice that of aliphatic resin glues, which can make assembling a complex project somewhat easier. Its disadvantages include low water resistance and low heat resistance. It tends to plug sanding belts if it has to be sanded from a surface.

Liquid hide glue.   This is a brown colored, ready-to-use glue made from animal hides and various other parts. Some woodworkers like it because of its slow drying time, which permits a long open time. This gives the woodworker time to get clamps positioned on a complex project and to get everything pulled into place before the glue starts setting. It also has good gap-filling properties. The main disadvantages include low water resistance, long clamping time (at least 12 hours), and that it is sticky and somewhat unpleasant to use.

Powdered plastic resin.   This adhesive comes in powder form and is mixed with water prior to using. It is highly water resistant and is most often used for exterior applications, although it is sometimes used for interior work when a slow setting time is desired. Setting takes about 12 to 14 hours at room temperature with

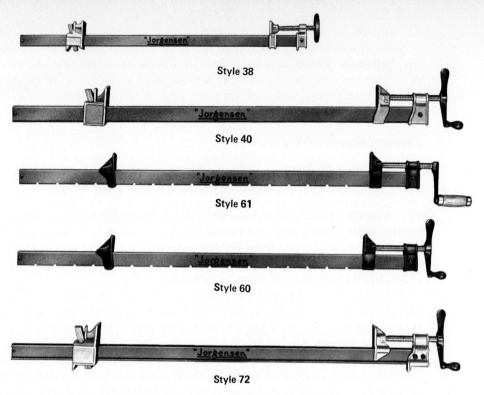

Style 38

Style 40

Style 61

Style 60

Style 72

Figure 4–1 Bar clamps (Adjustable Clamp Co.).

a 15-minute open time permitted. Disadvantages include slow setting time, poor gap-filling properties, and the inconveniences associated with having to mix glue before each use.

Casein glue.   This glue also comes in powder form and is mixed with water for each use. It has fair gap-filling properties, low water resistance, and a slow setting time. It has two properties that are useful in special situations. It is good for gluing oily woods, and it will set (albeit slowly) at temperatures down to freezing. Disadvantages include slow setting time, low moisture resistance, and having to mix it before use.

Resorcinol resin.   This is a two-part adhesive made by mixing a liquid resin and a powdered catalyst prior to use. It is totally waterproof and has good gap-filing properties and thus has become a very popular adhesive for boat building. It is quite slow in curing, requiring 8 to 12 hours clamping at room temperature. Two disadvantages that keep it from being a popular all-around woodworking glue are its high cost and the fact that it leaves a very dark brown glue line.

Contact cement.   This is not a general-purpose woodworking adhesive, but it is sometimes used to apply edge banding to the edges of plywood, to apply wood veneers, and, of course, plastic laminates. The main advantage of contact cement

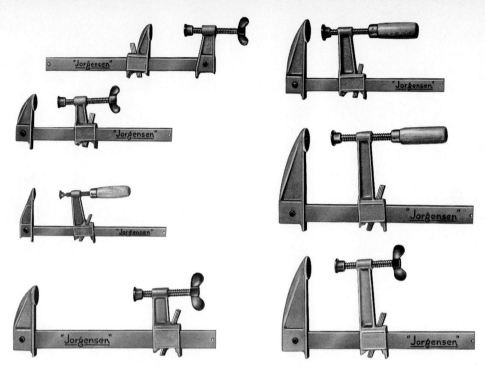

Figure 4-2 High-speed clamps (Adjustable Clamp Co.).

is that it does not need to be clamped. The two parts to be joined are coated with contact cement and allowed to dry before being joined by pressing them tightly together. The drying time can vary from 10 to 15 minutes for some of the fast-dry cements to over 1 hour for some of the water- or latex-base cements.

Hot melt adhesives. These adhesives are not used for general woodworking, but they are very handy for making repairs or gluing objects that cannot be clamped easily. The adhesive comes in sticks that are melted by an applicator gun. It sets as soon as it cools.

Clamps

All the previously mentioned adhesives, with the exception of contact cement and hot melt glue, require clamping of the parts during curing of the glue. A variety of clamps are available for this purpose. Most clamps will mar smooth wood surfaces, so blocks of scrap wood should be used under the jaws of clamps.

Bar clamp. Some bar clamps are shown in Fig. 4-1. They are long clamps (2 ft to 8 ft or more) and are used to clamp boards edge to edge, to assemble cabinet face frames, and to assemble furniture and cabinets.

A variation of the bar clamp, sometimes called a high-speed clamp, is shown in Fig. 4-2. It allows pressure to be applied up to 5 in. in from the edge of the workpiece. It is available in 6- to 36-in. grip sizes.

Adhesives

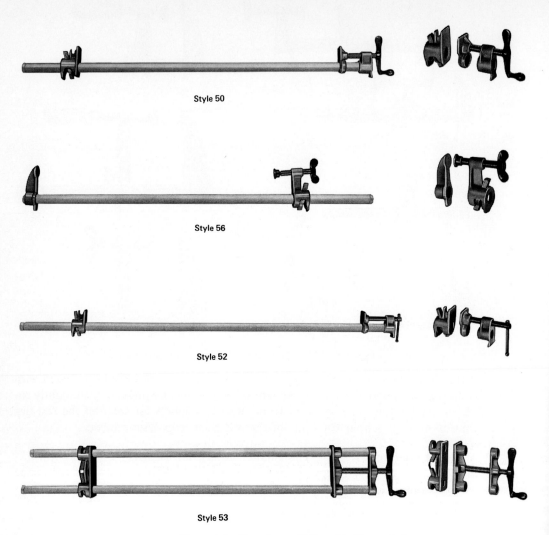

Style 50

Style 56

Style 52

Style 53

Figure 4-3 Pipe clamps (Adjustable Clamp Co.).

The pipe clamp (Fig. 4–3) is very similar to the bar clamp and is used for the same purposes. It can be mounted on steel pipe of any length and is less expensive than bar clamps.

Handscrew clamp. These wood-jawed clamps are shown in Fig. 4–4. They are one of the most widely used woodworking clamps and come in sizes that range from a 2-in. opening between jaws to 17 in. They are used for clamping boards face to face, for many repair operations, for furniture assembly, for holding parts in place on a benchtop for sanding, routing, or other work, and for many other purposes. One application is shown in Fig. 4–5.

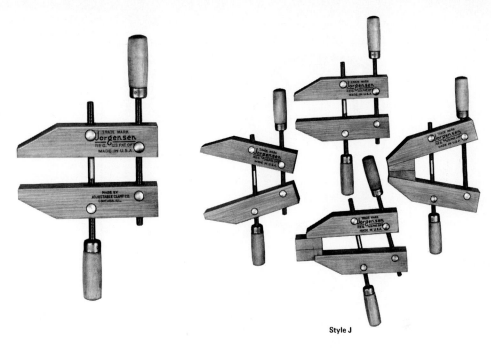

Style J

Figure 4-4 Handscrew clamps (Adjustable Clamp Co.).

Figure 4-5 Using handscrew clamps to hold a plywood shelf for edge banding.

Adhesives

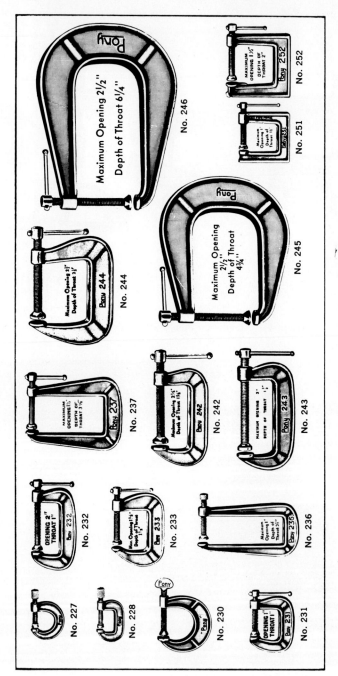

Figure 4–6 C-clamps (Adjustable Clamp Co.).

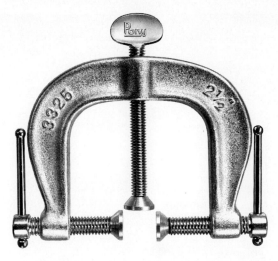

Figure 4-7 Three-way edging clamp (Adjustable Clamp Co.).

C-clamps.   These clamps (Fig. 4-6) are used for some of the same operations as hand screw clamps, although they are slower to use and not quite as versatile for woodworking. Edging clamps (Fig. 4-7) are an interesting variation of a C-clamp that permits easy clamping of edge-banding material.

Band clamp.   Band clamps (Fig. 4-8) are used to assemble chairs, hex- and octagonal-shaped objects, and other difficult shapes.

Figure 4-8 Band clamp (Adjustable Clamp Co.).

Figure 4-9 Miter clamp.

Miter clamps. Miter clamps (Fig. 4-9) are used for gluing miter joints for frames.

Gluing and Clamping Techniques

Since most popular woodworking glues set quite fast, it is important to have everything ready before starting to spread glue. This includes all the clamps that will be necessary, along with blocks of scrap wood to protect the project surface from the clamp jaws.

It is always best to assemble the project "dry" once to make sure everything fits before applying glue. You don't want any surprises after you have applied glue to the project! This also gets all the clamps set in advance so you can work faster when doing the real clamping.

Edge gluing. Edge gluing is one of the first gluing operations on many woodworking projects. This procedure is described in detail in Chapter 2.

Face gluing. Face gluing of boards is often done to obtain the necessary thickness for table legs, bowls, and other parts. It is sometimes more difficult than edge gluing because of the larger gluing surface areas and the difficulty in getting enough uniform clamping pressure. Handscrew clamps, C-clamps, and high-speed bar clamps are used.

Project assembly. It is often advantageous to make several subassemblies and then assemble them into a finished project, rather than trying to assemble a complex project in one operation.

When assembling a project, it is especially important to keep from getting excess glue on surfaces to be finished or from having excess glue squeeze from joints. As the project is clamped, it should be checked for squareness. Any out of squareness caused by clamping can usually be corrected by loosening the clamps and changing the clamping angle.

Check all glue joints to be sure that they are tightly clamped. Use as many clamps as necessary to get all joints closed tightly. The clamps should be left in place until the glue cures. Any excess glue that does get on the project should be carefully scraped or cut from the wood surface *after* it has dried. Wiping wet glue forces it into the wood pores and will show when the wood is finished.

ABRASIVES

Coated abrasives are used to smooth wood surfaces in preparation for finishing and for smoothing finishes between coats. They come in a wide range of grit sizes and types.

The grit size is designated by the smallest screen size through which the grip will pass. A 60-grit abrasive, for example, will just pass through a screen with 60 openings per linear inch, a 220-grit abrasive will just pass through a screen with 220 openings per linear inch, and so on.

These abrasives may be glued to either a paper or cloth backing. Papers used for sanding are designated as A (very light) through D weight (a thick, heavy paper). There are also X and J weights for cloth backings, with X being heavier.

The lighter-weight papers are usually used for finer grits and heavy paper for coarser grits. It is, however, possible to get a fine grit on a heavy paper, which can be useful for machine sanding. Cloth backings are usually used for sanding belts to be used on machines. Some belts are also made from synthetics such as polyester or Mylar.

Coated abrasives are further designated open coat or closed coat. Closed-coat abrasives have the entire surface covered with abrasive grit. They will give a very smooth finish on hardwoods, but they tend to fill easily. Open-coat abrasives have less abrasive grit on a sheet, leaving more space between abrasive grits to carry sanding dust away from the surface. They are more popular than closed coat.

Abrasive Materials

Several materials are used for woodworking abrasives. They vary in hardness sharpness, and cost.

Flint. This is the least expensive of the woodworking abrasives, but also the least satisfactory for most purposes. It is relatively soft, so it breaks down quickly,

Abrasives **225**

and it does not have very sharp edges. It is best used for sanding soft, resinous woods that tend to plug abrasive paper before it is worn out or for removing old finishes.

Garnet. This is a much harder abrasive. It is a reddish-brown abrasive that fractures with very sharp edges. It is very good for hand sanding.

Aluminum oxide. This is a tan to brown abrasive. It is a by-product of the aluminum manufacturing industry. It is extremely hard and is excellent for machine sanding as well as hand sanding.

Silicon carbide. This is a black abrasive, although it sometimes appears white on sanding sheets because of the adhesive used to bond it to the sheet. It is used for hand sanding and light machine sanding with finish sanders, and it is used on water-proof paper for wet sanding between coats of finish.

Sanding

Sanding on raw wood should be done with sandpaper wrapped over a hard-rubber or softwood sanding block. The sanding strokes should be parallel with the wood grain. The starting grit requirement will vary depending on how smooth the final machining or scraping operation was.

Paper with 120 grit or even finer could be used for the first sanding on a board that was planed with a planer or jointer with sharp cutters and then had been scraped. Successive sanding should be done with finer grits. A typical schedule could start with 120-grit paper, 150 grit, 180 grit, and finish with 220 grit.

HARDWARE

Hardware for woodworking can include fasteners such as nails and screws, a wide range of hardware for mounting moving parts such as doors and drawers, and decorative hardware. We will consider the various fasteners first.

Fasteners

Fasteners may be used to join wood parts or they may be used as a reinforcement in a wood joint.

Nails. There are many types of nails for various purposes. The general-purpose nails used for the assembly of wood parts include common, box, finish, and casing nails. These are shown in Fig. 4–10. Nail lengths are designated by penny size, as shown in Fig. 4–11.

Common nails are thicker than box nails of the same penny size. There are also special-purpose nails for roofing, siding, floor underlayment, and many other applications. In addition, several cement and vinyl coatings are designed to make the nails hold better. Some of these nails are available galvanized for exterior use.

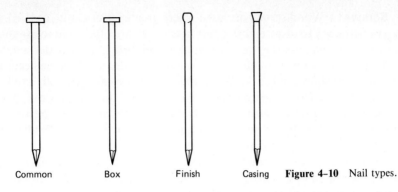

Common   Box   Finish   Casing   **Figure 4–10**   Nail types.

Penny size	Length (in.)
2d	1
3d	$1\frac{1}{4}$
4d	$1\frac{1}{2}$
5d	$1\frac{3}{4}$
6d	2
8d	$2\frac{1}{2}$
10d	3
16d	$3\frac{1}{2}$

Figure 4–11   Nail sizes.

The use of nails is limited to nonexposed surfaces on high-quality furniture, if they are used at all. On other types of woodwork, it may be considered acceptable to use finish nails if they are countersunk and the nail holes filled.

To obtain the maximum holding power from nails, they should be driven at an angle, as shown in Fig. 4–12. Care must be taken not to split the wood. Blunting the point of the nail will help prevent splitting when nailing near the end of a board. It may be necessary to drill pilot holes for nails driven near the end of a board, especially on hardwoods. The pilot hole should be slightly smaller than the nail diameter.

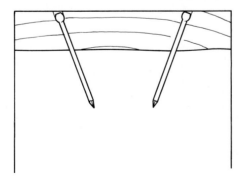

Figure 4–12   Driving nails at an angle increases their holding power.

Hardware

Screws.   Wood screws are used where greater strength is required or where it may be necessary to disassemble a part later. They are often used to assemble wood furniture, in which case they may be countersunk and hidden under a wood plug.

Wood screws are available with a round head, flat head, bugle head, and oval head. These are shown in Fig. 4–13. Round-head screws are generally used when the heads are exposed. The bugle-head screw was developed for drywall work, but is rapidly replacing conventional flat-head screws for woodworking. They are very hard and have sharp threads with a ''fast'' thread pitch and have either a Phillips or square slot, making them easy to drive with power drivers.

Oval-head screws are used with a decorative finish washer in exposed applications. The screws and matching washers are available in several hardware finishes, including chromium plated, flat black, and antique brass.

Wood screw size is designated by gage size for thickness and inches and fractions for length. The length is measured from under the shoulder of a round head and from the top of the head for bugle- and flat-head screws.

Installing wood screws normally requires drilling pilot holes and sometimes counterbore holes. The hole for the threaded portion of the screw should be drilled with a bit of the same diameter as the inside diameter of the threads. The hole for the shank should be drilled slightly larger than the shank diameter.

Holes for flat-head screws should be countersunk so that the screw head is flush with the surface or counterbored to receive a wood plug. Special drill bits are available to drill the pilot hole for the threads, the hole for the shank, and countersink or counterbore all in one operation. A typical pilot hole for a flat-head screw is shown in Fig. 4–14.

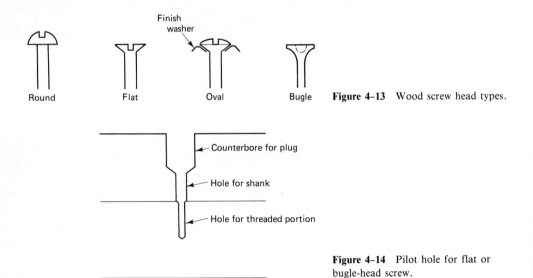

Figure 4–13   Wood screw head types.

Figure 4–14   Pilot hole for flat or bugle-head screw.

Lag screws (Fig. 4–15) are similar to wood screws except for having a square or hex head, allowing them to be driven with a wrench. They are usually available in larger sizes and are used in heavier construction.

Figure 4–15 Lag screw.

Bolts.   Bolts are used in situations requiring greater strength than can be obtained with screws or in situations where it is necessary to be able to disassemble a project. The carriage bolt (Fig. 4–16) is designed especially for woodworking. The square shoulder under the head keeps it from turning as the nut is tightened. Conventional machine bolt and cap screws are also used in woodworking.

Figure 4–16 Carriage bolt.

Threaded inserts and tee nuts.   If wood screws are removed and reinstalled very many times, the wood threads soon strip out. In situations where it is necessary to frequently disassemble work fastened with wood screws, it is best to use either threaded inserts or tee nuts. The threaded insert is a steel insert that is threaded into the wood and is left there. It in turn has a threaded hole that will accept a conventional cap screw or machine screw.

Tee nuts are used when a hole can be drilled all the way through both parts to be joined. The tee nut is driven into the hole from the back, which provides permanent threads for a machine screw. A threaded insert and a tee nut are shown in Fig. 4–17.

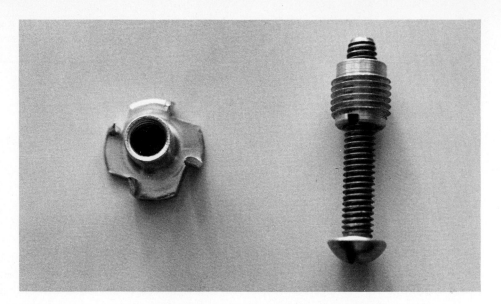

Figure 4–17 Tee nut (left) and threaded insert.

Joint fasteners. Joint fasteners may be used to reinforce glued wood joints or they may be used for parts that will need to be disassembled. The Tite Joint Fastener shown in Fig. 4–18 requires boring two $\frac{7}{8}$-in.-diameter holes in the wood for the ends and a smaller hole in the edges of the two pieces to be joined. The draw bolt requires routing a recess in the back side of the part to be joined.

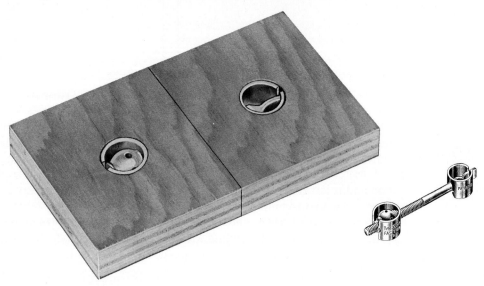

Figure 4–18 Tite-joint fastener (Knape & Vogt Mfg. Co.).

Adhesives, Abrasives, and Hardware   Chap. 4

Hinges

To the casual observer, it must appear that there is an endless variety of hinges from which to choose, and it is true that there are many types and styles of hinges. However, the type of door being used will limit the number of hinges available. The various types of doors are described in Chapter 2. Each type of door has different hinge requirements.

Semiconcealed hinge.   These hinges generally mount on a cabinet face frame with one leaf and to the back of the door with the other. They are available for ⅜-in. inset as well as for overlay doors, as shown in Fig. 4–19. They are usually self-closing.

Wrap-around hinges.   These hinges are similar to the semiconcealed hinge except that the face frame leaf wraps around behind the door leaf, as shown in Fig. 4–20. Several variations are available to fit both overlay and ⅜-in.-inset doors.

Figure 4-19   Semiconcealed hinges.

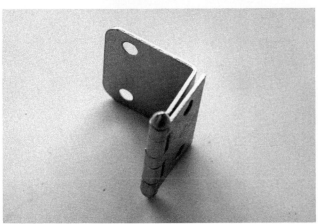

Figure 4-20   Wrap-around hinge.

Figure 4-21 Pivot hinge.

Pivot hinges.   These hinges require machining a slot in the edge of the door for the pivoting portion of the hinge. They are adjustable vertically and horizontally and are inconspicuous when installed. They usually are used for overlay doors on cabinets with no face frame, but a version is available for ⅜-in.-inset (lip) doors. A pivot hinge is shown in Fig. 4-21.

European hinges.   These hinges (Fig. 4-22) offer many attractive features and have become very popular. They are completely hidden when the door is closed, and they allow the door to be adjusted up or down, sideways, and in or out in relation

Figure 4-22 European-style hinge (Julius Blum, Inc.).

to the face of the cabinet. Most of them require boring a 35-mm hole in the back of the door. They are usually used for overlay doors on cabinets without face frames, although they are also made for flush doors. They are available as either self-closing or free swinging.

Other. Other hinges used in woodworking include butt hinges (Fig. 4–23), H hinges (Fig. 4–24), double-acting hinges (Fig. 4–25), and lid support hinges (Fig. 4–26).

Figure 4-23 Butt hinge.

Figure 4-24 H-hinge.

Hardware

Figure 4-25 Double-acting hinge.

Figure 4-26 Lid support hinge.

Catches

Non-self-closing hinges usually require the use of a catch to keep the door closed. Some of the more popular ones include magnetic (Fig. 4–27), roller (Fig. 4–28), friction (Fig. 4–29), elbow catch (Fig. 4–30), and bullet catch (Fig. 4–31). The touch latch (Fig. 4–32) is sometimes used for flush doors or overlay doors and eliminates the need for a door pull.

Figure 4-27 Magnetic catch.

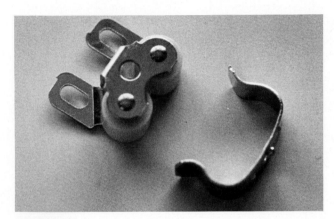

Figure 4-28 Roller catch.

Figure 4-29 Friction catch.

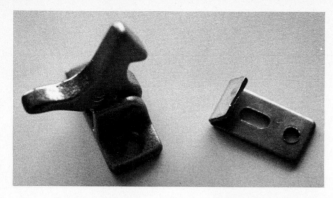

Figure 4–30   Elbow catch.

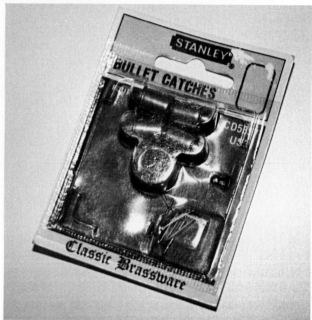

Figure 4–31   Bullet catch.

Figure 4–32   Touch latch.

Pulls and Knobs

Pulls and knobs for doors and drawers are available in many types, styles, materials, and finishes. They may be made of metal, plastic, ceramic, or wood.

Shelf Hardware

Shelves are often designed to be adjustable for height. This can be done by drilling holes in the side of the cabinet and installing pegs or clips, such as the one shown in Fig. 4–33. Adjustable shelf pilasters or standards such as those shown in Fig. 4–34

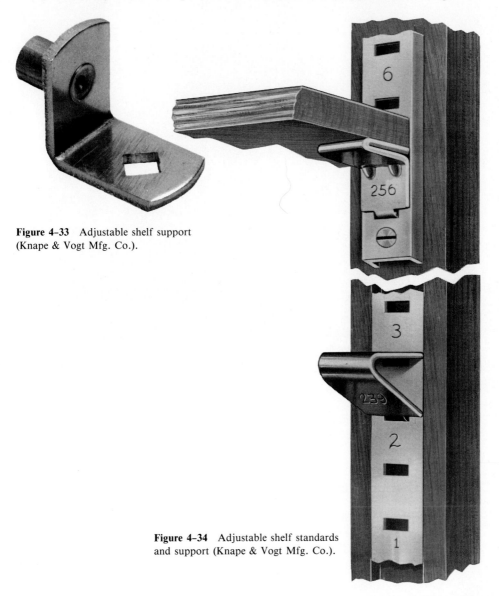

Figure 4-33 Adjustable shelf support (Knape & Vogt Mfg. Co.).

Figure 4-34 Adjustable shelf standards and support (Knape & Vogt Mfg. Co.).

Figure 4-35 Revolving shelves (Amerock).

may also be used. Revolving shelves such as those shown in Fig. 4–35 may also be purchased.

Drawer Guide Hardware

Roller guide systems are usually either mounted on the drawer sides or under the center of the drawer. A set of side roller guides is shown in Fig. 4–36. See the section on drawers in Chapter 2 for information on installation.

Figure 4-36 Drawer side guides (Accuride).

Specialty Hardware

Hardware manufacturers offer many specialty items that can enhance the quality and utility of woodworking projects. These include castors, lid supports, dropleaf table hinges and leaf supports, locks, index followers for file drawers, folding door hardware, and many kitchen cabinet convenience aids.

5 Wood Finishing

The finishing phase of a woodworking project can be a very rewarding time because you finally get to see the end result of a lot of hard work. The finishing phase is also a very critical part of a project because it is possible to ruin an otherwise good project with the wrong finish or with a finish improperly applied.

The best finish for a project depends on the type of wood used, what the project is to be used for, and what finish application equipment is available. Once the finish is selected, it must be applied according to the manufacturer's directions.

FUNCTIONS OF WOOD FINISH

Wood finishes have several important functions. The most obvious is esthetic. They enhance the beauty of the wood. A good finish will emphasize the natural grain pattern and coloring of the wood. Stains can change the appearance of the wood, can be used to prevent the natural color fading that occurs with some woods, and can be used to color sapwood streaks.

Wood finishes also help keep wood surfaces clean. Raw wood is quite porous and absorbent and would quickly become dirty looking in normal use. Finishes can seal the surface to prevent dirt from becoming lodged in the wood pores, and they make it easy to remove dirt from the surface.

Finishes also slow down the rate at which wood absorbs and gives off moisture. This helps eliminate much of the swelling and shrinkage that otherwise occurs as wood is exposed to different humidity levels. Some finishes are better than others in this respect.

Some wood finishes, such as the penetrating oil finishes, actually increase the hardness of wood near the surface, thus increasing its scratch and wear resistance.

PREPARING WOOD FOR FINISHING

One of the most critical steps of any finishing process is preparing the surface for finish. This preparation usually begins after the project has been assembled, although some preliminary sanding may have been done before assembly.

One of the first steps is to remove any excess glue that may have gotten on the project during assembly. These smears of glue can be hard to see on raw wood, but they must be removed or they will show up when the wood is stained or finished. The glue should be scraped or cut from the surface.

If there are small dents in the wood surface, they may be soaked or steamed to raise the wood fibers back up flush with the surrounding surface. Very small dents can be raised by placing a drop of water in the dent. Larger dents will require steaming. This is done by placing several thicknesses of a wet rag on the dented area and applying a source of heat, such as a soldering iron, wood-burning pencil, or even a clothes iron over the dent. The steam formed will cause the wood fibers in this area to swell. After the wood has dried, it can then be sanded smooth.

Dents in which the wood grain has been crushed or broken and other holes such as nail holes can be filled in one of several ways. Commercial wood fillers are available in a variety of wood colors and can be applied with a putty knife and sanded and finished. Some of these will accept stains and some will not. You should experiment on scrap material when using a filler with which you are not familiar.

High-quality repairs can be made with lacquer sticks although they are more difficult to use. These sticks of solid lacquer are available in many colors and are chosen to match the final finish rather than the raw wood, since they will not accept stain. They are applied by heating the blade of a knife and using the hot knife blade to melt a small quantity of the lacquer stick. It is then quickly pressed into the hole before the lacquer cools (Fig. 5–1). As soon as the lacquer cools, it can be sanded and finished over.

Another category of fillers is designed to be used after the finish is completed. These are wax-based fillers that are rubbed into nail holes after the finish is dry. Any excess filler is wiped off with a rag. These fillers are available in sticks or jars and in a very wide range of colors to match almost any wood finish.

Sanding is another important step in preparing wood for finishing. All final sanding should be done with the wood grain, and all sharp corners should be eased with the final sanding. The final sanding grit will probably be between 150 and 220, depending on the wood and the type of finish being used. To get a very smooth surface, the wood surface can be dampened with a sponge, allowed to dry, and resanded with the final sanding grit. Wetting the wood causes severed grain fibers to stand up. When dry, they can be cut off with the final sanding. This will minimize grain raising when staining, especially when water-based stains are to be used.

Figure 5-1 Using a lacquer stick to repair a small hole.

After the sanding is complete, all dust should be removed by blowing the surface with compressed air, if available, or brushing with a soft brush and then using a tack rag for final cleaning.

FINISHING MATERIALS

Selecting the best finish for a project can be confusing since there are so many different finish products on the market. Some of them are not compatible with each other, and not all work equally well in all situations. Each has its own advantages and limitations. Some finishes use a number of different products, and others may consist of only one product, such as a penetrating oil finish.

For example, a typical finishing schedule for a piece of fine furniture might consist of the following:

- Presealer
- Stain
- Wash coat
- Grain filler
- Sealer

- Several coats of lacquer
- Rub and polish
- Wax

Another finishing schedule might consist merely of several coats of a penetrating oil. The desired result will determine the actual finishing schedule to be used.

There are basically two types of transparent finishes for woodworking, surface finishes and penetrating finishes. Surface finishes protect the wood by forming a hard film on the surface of the wood. They include lacquer, varnish, polyurethanes, shellac, and acrylic finish. Penetrating finishes, on the other hand, penetrate into the wood and harden, but usually do not leave a film on the surface. They include Danish oil, tung oil, and some combination wax and oil products. Stains can be used with either type.

One of the first decisions a woodworker must make is which type of finish to use. Surface finishes will offer somewhat better moisture protection and better protection against penetration from spills. They are easier to clean and do not require the occasional "renewal" coat that some penetrating finishes require. If a high-gloss finish is required, it is much easier to obtain with a surface finish.

Penetrating finishes are generally easier to apply. They require less skill to apply, are less sensitive to dust in the air during application, and do not require any equipment such as a brush or spray gun. They are easy to repair in the event they are scratched by merely sanding out the scratch and applying more finish. They give the wood a very natural appearance since they do not leave a film on the surface. There is no film to crack or peel with age.

They do, however, tend to get dull or dry looking after several years. This requires another coat of the finish to renew the fresh appearance.

The actual choice of type of finish will depend on the appearance desired, the use of the product, and the type of finishing equipment available. Common wood finishing products are described next.

Presealers.   Presealers are sometimes used before staining wood to assist in obtaining a more uniform stain color. They are especially useful on wavy grain woods or woods with uneven grain texture. Such woods otherwise tend to absorb stain unevenly.

They also retard the excess absorption of stain on wood end grain. The end result is a stain of more uniform color. They give the wood additional moisture resistance. They may be used as part of a surface finish schedule or with penetrating finishes. If a presealer is to be used, it would normally be the first finish product applied.

Stains

Stains include a wide range of products designed to change the color of wood. Unless a presealer is used, the stain is the first finishing product applied if the wood color is to be changed.

Stains can be used under surface finishes or penetrating finishes. In fact, many penetrating finishes are available with stain colors incorporated in the finish. Some of the more common stain types are described next.

Oil stains.   Oil stains are the most popular stains for general woodworking because they are relatively easy to use and they do not raise the wood grain. There are two general types of oil stains. One is a wiping or pigmented stain and the other is a penetrating stain or dye stain.

The wiping or pigmented stain has the coloring pigments suspended in the oil. When the stain is applied to the wood, most of the pigment remains at or near the surface of the wood. When the wood has achieved the desired darkness, the excess is wiped off. It is easy to control the final color this way.

Penetrating oil stains have an oil-soluble dye as the coloring agent. The dye penetrates into the wood with the oil, so the finisher does not have as much control over the final color. However, the color penetration into the wood is considered good since a scratch in the finish will not show the original wood color. Oil stains take longer to dry than most of the other types, and their color is not as permanent as water stains when exposed to sunlight.

Water stains.   Water stains are preferred by some woodworkers because of their excellent clarity and for their resistance to fading with age and exposure to sunlight. They do, however, have one serious disadvantage that limits their popularity. Their water base causes the wood grain to swell, leaving a rough surface. This can be partially overcome by pre-sponging the surface as previously described. Water stains will not penetrate previously finished wood, so they are only used for new work.

Water stains are usually purchased in powder form and mixed with hot water. Mixed stains can be kept for later use. They may be applied with a brush or sprayed. End grain should be dampened with water first to prevent it from absorbing an excessive amount of stain. After the stained surface has dried overnight, it is lightly sanded. If a darker finish is desired, another coat of stain may be applied.

Spirit stains.   Alcohol and certain other fast-drying solvents are used as the vehicle for spirit stains. This gives them a very fast drying time. They are used primarily for touch-up work and for staining sapwood. Their very fast drying time makes uniform application difficult on a large project unless the stain can be sprayed.

Nongrain-raising stains (NGR).   These stains were developed for commercial work in an effort to achieve the clarity and color permanence of water-based stain, but without the grain-raising problem. They use soluble dyes in vehicles including alcohol, toluol, glycol, and ketones. Their major use is in production woodworking, but they are available through some hobby and mail-order woodworking outlets.

Chemical stains.   Unlike the other stains, chemical stains do not color the wood with pigments or dyes, but rather through a chemical reaction between the chemical and substances in the wood. For example, the fumes from ammonia will change the color of oak. This process, in fact, is the basis for fumed-oak finishes and is one of the more popular chemical staining processes.

To obtain a fumed-oak stain, the project is placed in a large plastic bag such as a garbage bag or some other container that can be made nearly airtight. An open container of ammonia is set inside the bag with the project and the bag is tied closed. The treatment time depends on the concentration strength of the ammonia and the wood. The actual time may vary from several hours to several days. The color should be checked periodically.

Chemicals such as copper sulfate, iron sulfate, lime, acetic acid, and potassium dichromate may be used to create color changes in certain woods.

Bleaches. It is sometimes desirable to remove color from wood. This might be the case when a very light colored finish is desired or when a project is made using boards that are not uniform in color. The darker boards could be bleached before the project is stained. Wood bleaches will remove much of the natural color from wood.

Most wood bleaches are two-part solutions. Some are mixed before being applied, and others require the application of one solution followed by the application of the other after a specified interval. Wood bleaches should be mixed in a glass or earthenware container and rubber gloves should be used.

Other stains. There are other products on the market designed to change the color of wood. Some of these are combinations of stain with other finishing products, such as grain fillers or varnish. While they may shorten the finish process, they usually do not produce the fine appearance that is possible by using separate stains, fillers, and top coats.

However, two of these combination products work very well. These are tung oil or Danish oil combined with stain and some of the oil and wax finishes combined with stains. These penetrating finishes are available in many popular stain colors.

Wood Grain Fillers

These fillers are designed to fill the pores of open-grain woods, thereby providing a level surface for clear finish coats. Woods with large, open pores, such as mahoganys, oaks, and ash, are often filled. Woods with smaller open pores, such as walnut, cherry, and birch, are sometimes filled with a liquid filler.

Fillers are seldom part of a penetrating oil finish, but they are often used when a clear top coat such as lacquer, varnish, or polyurethane is to be used. Fillers are necessary if a perfectly smooth, clear finish is to be obtained on an open-grain wood. Figure 5-2 shows an open-grain wood without filler and Fig. 5-3 shows the same wood with a filler. Lacquer top coats were used in both cases.

Wood fillers are made from silex, a rock that is ground to a very fine powder. This is combined with solvents, driers, and binders. When it dries, it forms a very dense, hard substance that permanently fills the surface pores of the wood.

Figure 5–2 Open-grained wood without filler.

Figure 5–3 Open-grained wood with a filler.

If the wood surface has been stained, the filler must be either colored to match the stain, or fillers may be purchased to match the stains available from some manufacturers. Standard tinting colors may be used to color the filler, or oil-based stains may be used. For example, if a Danish walnut oil-based stain was used on the wood, the same stain could be mixed with the filler to match it to the stain. Occasionally, fillers that are different from the stain color are intentionally used to create a special effect, such as using a dark filler on a light-colored wood.

Fillers with stains may be applied directly to the raw wood to stain and fill in one operation. However, the staining penetration is not very deep and the results are usually not as satisfactory. Fillers should be thinned with naphtha to the consistency of white glue or slightly thicker for vertical surfaces or for woods with very large pores.

Fillers are worked into the wood pores with a stiff brush or by hand. The important thing is to be sure that the wood pores are packed full of filler with no voids. The filler must then be allowed to dry just to the point where it is firm enough so that it will not be torn from the pores when the excess is wiped from the surface.

This drying usually takes about 15 to 30 minutes. The filler loses its wet look and looks hazy on the surface. At this point, the filler is removed from the surface using a coarse cloth such as burlap and wiping *across* the wood grain. A final light wiping with the grain may be done with a soft cloth to remove any cross-grain streaks. If the filler is left to dry too long, it becomes so hard that it is almost impossible to remove. It is best to fill small sections of a project at a time so that the filler can be wiped from the surface at the right time.

After the excess filler has been removed, the surface should be examined carefully to see if all the pores have been filled. A magnifying glass will help. If any pores are open, the filling process should be repeated. This can be done immediately.

After the filling process is completed, the filler should be allowed to dry at least 24 hours before any other finish products are applied.

Sealers

Sealers are used under some clear finishes. For example, a lacquer sanding sealer is usually used under lacquer finishes. Varnish sanding sealers are sometimes used under varnish. Polyurethanes, on the other hand, are usually used without sealers.

A sealer provides several benefits. It seals in stains to prevent their lifting or bleeding into the top coats. Sealers are also designed to adhere to the surface and are especially useful when oil-based stains have left the surface slightly oily. They help bond the top coat to the surface. Sanding sealers are formulated to sand easily. The material removed by sanding comes off as a powder, rather than clogging the abrasive paper. This makes it easy to get a very smooth surface for the final top coats.

Top Coats

The most common clear top coat finishes used for woodworking are lacquer, varnish, polyurethane, and shellac. Some clear acrylic finishes are used by the furniture industry. Even though these clear finishes may look somewhat similar to each other on the completed project, they are very different chemically and have quite different properties.

Lacquer.   Lacquer is very popular in the furniture and cabinet industry because of its very rapid drying time. It is less popular with amateur woodworkers because it dries so fast that it must be sprayed on the surface. However, for people who have spray equipment available, it offers some very attractive advantages as a clear finish.

Lacquer dries to the touch in as little as 2 to 5 minutes. Thus it is much less likely to collect airborne dust than a finish that remains wet for an hour or more. It is also somewhat less likely to run for the same reason.

Another advantage of lacquer is that the finish has a very "thin" appearance, giving the wood a more natural appearance compared with some of the other clear finishes, which tend to look thick on the surface.

Lacquer is also easy to rub out in order to obtain a perfectly smooth, furniture-quality finish. Lacquer is the easiest of the clear surface finishes to repair.

The disadvantages of lacquer, in addition to the fact that it must be sprayed, include its cost, the health and fire hazards from spraying, and its lack of durability for exterior or high-moisture conditions.

The cost of lacquer is usually not any greater than other clear finishes, but because of the waste inherent in the spraying operation, the cost of finishing a project in lacquer may be greater than for brush-on finishes. The lacquer thinner needed to clean up finishing equipment is also much more expensive than paint thinner. A suitable exhaust system should be used when spraying lacquer, along with a respirator mask designed for organic materials.

Early lacquers were noted for their poor moisture resistance and were not used, for example, on bathroom cabinets. Modern lacquers are better in this regard if at least three coats are applied. However, normal wood lacquers are not suitable for exterior applications.

Lacquer must be sprayed in wet coats. If the gun if too far from the surface or if the gun is moved too fast, the surface will be dry and powdery. When the gun is too far from the surface, the lacquer partially dries before hitting the surface and does not flow out smoothly.

The normal method of applying a lacquer finish is as follows:

1. Spray a thin, but wet coat of lacquer sanding sealer on the surface. (The surface may be raw wood, stained wood, or stained and filled wood.)
2. Let the sealer dry for 30 minutes to 1 hour and lightly sand with a fine abrasive paper (220 grit or finer).
3. Spray two or three wet coats of clear lacquer at 30-minute to 1-hour intervals. These coats do not need to be sanded unless the surface appears to be rough. In that case, additional drying time should be allowed before sanding.
4. The finish can be rubbed out as described later after 24 hours of drying time.

(If the finish is to rubbed out, there should be at least three coats of lacquer in addition to the sealer to provide adequate film thickness.)

Even though lacquer finishes are dry to the touch after just a few minutes, they are not completely hard for several days. They should be handled carefully and should not have heavy objects placed on them during this time.

Although lacquers are generally applied by spraying, there are brushing lacquers made with slower-drying solvents. The popular clear finish, Deft, is similar to a brushing lacquer.

Varnish. Natural varnish was a very popular furniture finish years ago, but has been largely replaced in the furniture industry by other finishes. It does, however, offer some advantages to the amateur woodworker, especially if spray equipment is not available.

Varnish is relatively easy to apply by brushing. It flows out well and leaves a professional looking finish. It may be applied with either a good, natural-bristle brush or one of the inexpensive disposable foam brushes. It is one of the easier clear finishes to apply by brush.

The drawback of varnish is that it is very slow drying. Thus a dust-free environment is necessary to get a good finish. Natural varnish also has a tendency to turn yellow with age, especially when exposed to sunlight.

Varnishes are formulated in different ways depending on their intended use. Long-oil varnishes (high percentage of oil in relation to solid resin content) are used to make spar varnishes for exterior application. These varnishes are tough and remain somewhat flexible. Medium-oil varnishes are somewhat harder, but still very tough. They are sometimes used to finish hardwood floors. Short-oil varnishes are very hard, but somewhat brittle. They are usually used on furniture.

Polyurethane. Polyurethane finishes were originally developed as a synthetic varnish, with synthetic resins replacing the natural resins used in conventional varnish. Polyurethanes form a very hard, durable, clear finish that is resistant to water and many other substances. They do not yellow with age. They are slightly more difficult to apply smoothly than the best conventional varnishes and, compared with lacquer, they tend to look thicker on the surface of the wood.

Shellac. Shellac is another very old, natural, clear finish. It is made from the secretions of the lac bug found mostly in India. These secretions are stripped from tree branches and processed into a solid shellac, which is shipped to paint manufacturers. It is then dissolved in alcohol, packaged, and sold ready to use.

Shellac dries very quickly because of the rapid evaporation of the alcohol. If it is applied by brushing, it must be brushed very quickly with the wood grain. It forms a very tough, clear finish. Normal orange shellac will give a finish that is slightly amber in color, especially on light-colored woods. Bleached white shellac is available if a perfectly clear finish is needed.

Shellac is noted for its ability to bond even to slightly oily surfaces and to seal in stains. It also prevents resins in the wood from bleeding into the finish. Shellac makes an excellent sealer for oily woods or woods that have been stained with oil stains.

The big drawback that keeps shellac from being more widely used as a wood finish is its short shelf life. It deteriorates over a period of time, even when sealed in its original container. The deterioration accelerates after the container has been opened.

Shellac is also very sensitive to moisture until it is cured. A small amount of water from a wet paint brush, for example, will ruin a container of shellac. Old shellacs should be tested on a piece of scrap material before being used on a project. Shellac that is bad will remain sticky on the surface rather than hardening. It should be hard in 30 minutes or less.

Rubbing and Polishing Clear Finishes

Rubbing and polishing is done to remove slight irregularities in the finish such as brush marks or orange-peel texture from spraying and to produce a smooth glossy or satin finish. The procedure usually consists of sanding with 600-grit abrasive paper, rubbing with pumice, rubbing with rottenstone, and finally waxing the surface.

Lacquers can be rubbed out in as little as 24 hours, although it is best to wait several days. Varnish and polyurethane finishes are more difficult to rub out. They must be thoroughly cured. It is best to wait at least 3 weeks before rubbing varnishes or polyurethanes.

Sanding the surface is usually done with 600-grit, waterproof, silicon carbide paper and water. The paper is folded into three thicknesses and is used without a backup block. This sanding will level any brush marks or other irregularities. It will also leave the surface very dull because of the fine sanding scratches. These sanding scratches are removed later with the pumice and rottenstone.

After sanding, the surface is rubbed with pumice. Pumice is a fine abrasive available in powder form. It is mixed with water to make a paste and is used with a felt pad or a pad made of cotton cloth. It is rubbed on the surface using medium pressure and circular strokes. It should be rubbed long enough to rub out all the sanding scratches. Excessive rubbing should be avoided since the pumice continues to cut the finish film thinner as long as it is being rubbed on the surface. It is possible to rub completely through the finish. As soon as the pumice rubbing is completed, the pumice should be removed from the surface with a clean, damp cloth and the surface wiped dry.

The final rubbing step is to rub the surface with rottenstone. It is an even finer abrasive than the pumice and produces a very smooth surface with a high luster. Rottenstone is available in powder form and is mixed with water to make a paste. It is applied in the same way as pumice and must be cleaned from the surface in the same way.

A coat of paste wax may be applied and buffed out for an even higher luster and for additional protection for the surface.

Following the preceding steps will produce a truly beautiful finish that enhances the natural beauty of the wood. It is, however, very important that each product be applied properly and allowed adequate drying time before the next product is applied. It is also important that the finishing area and equipment be clean to avoid getting dust or other foreign material in the finish.

Steel wool and wax rub out.   A finish may be rubbed out with fine steel wool paste wax rather than the sanding and rubbing method just described. The steel wool and wax rub method is much faster and produces satisfactory results in many situations. It leaves a low-luster or satin finish. It works expecially well on sprayed lacquer surfaces when there are no serious surface irregularities to be removed.

Fine steel wool (0000) is dipped in paste wax and is then used to rub the surface, rubbing with the wood grain. The steel wool cuts the surface flat and applies a coat of wax at the same time. The wax is then buffed off the surface with a soft cloth after it has dried to a haze.

Penetrating Finishes

Penetrating finishes are quite different from the surface finishes just described in that they penetrate into the wood and harden, rather than forming a film on the surface of the wood. The most popular penetrating finishes are tung oil and Danish oil, although there are some finishes that contain oil and waxes. Some tung oil finishes contain polyurethane. These have the advantage of being applied like an oil finish (with a rag), but offer additional protection because of the hardness of the polyurethane.

Penetrating finishes can be used alone or in conjunction with some of the other finishing products previously mentioned. The simplest penetrating finish consists of applying several coats of one of the penetrating finishes. Most of the penetrating finishes are available in an assortment of colors, so a penetrating finish could consist of one or more coats of a colored penetrating finish, with the final coats using a clear penetrating finish of the same type.

The presealers previously mentioned can be used under penetrating finishes. Penetrating finishes can also be used over most of the stains previously mentioned, provided they are completely dry. Penetrating finishes can also be used over a surface with wood-grain filler, although this is not often done.

Tung oil and Danish oil finishes.   Even though these two products are different in chemical makeup, they are used in much the same way and the end results are quite similar. Danish oil finishes are usually made with a linseed oil base and a number of other chemicals. Tung oil is made from the nuts of a China wood tree. They are both applied by wiping oil liberally on the wood surface, allowing it to penetrate for a specified time, and then wiping the surface dry with clean rags.

Some manufacturers recommend sanding the first coat into the wood with fine waterproof sandpaper. The first coat may use clear oil or one of the many colors available in the penetrating finishes. Subsequent coats may either be clear or colored depending on whether a darker finish is wanted.

The first coat should be allowed to dry 6 to 8 hours for tung oil or overnight for Danish oil before a second coat is applied. Two coats are adequate for some projects, but a much richer, more lustrous finish can be obtained by applying four to six coats, allowing the required drying time between each coat.

Some porous woods such as red oak will absorb quantities of oil that bleeds back to the surface for several hours after the excess oil has been wiped from the surface. These little pools of oil must be wiped from the surface before they harden.

After the final coat is dry, a coat of wax may be applied or the oil finish may be used as is.

Paints.   Some types of furniture have traditionally been painted rather than being stained or clear finished. Children's furniture is also often painted.

Paints designed for furniture and other interior woodwork include enamel, polyurethane paint, and occasionally lacquer with color added. Enamel is very similar to woodworking varnish with pigment added to give it color and hiding power. It is usually brushed and has many of the same characteristics as varnish. It makes a hard, durable surface that is easy to clean.

Polyurethane paints are similar to the clear polyurethanes used for wood finishing. They make a very hard surface and are noted for their bright pure colors and lack of color fading.

Lacquer paints are not as readily available as enamels and polyurethanes, but they are advantageous when a very fast drying finish is needed and spray equipment is available.

FINISHING EQUIPMENT

Finishing equipment required for a job may range from clean rags to expensive spray guns. One reason for the popularity of penetrating oil finishes is that they require no special finishing equipment. Varnishes, polyurethanes, and shellacs may be successfully applied by brushing. Lacquers usually must be sprayed.

Brushes.   High-quality brushes are necessary to produce a furniture-quality finish with varnish or polyurethane. The best bristles for a high-quality paint brush are tapered and oval in cross section and have flagged (forked) ends to hold a large quantity of finish. Unfortunately, the only animal that produces such a bristle is a rather rare wild Chinese hog. Therefore, pure hog bristle brushes are very expensive. They are often used in conjunction with other natural bristles to make high-quality brushes. Very good quality nylon bristle brushes are available that have most of the same characteristics and will wear longer than natural bristles.

Inexpensive brushes with round, straight bristles make it very difficult to obtain a good quality finish. Their cheaper construction also often allows bristles to come out while the finish is being applied.

Natural bristles are very good for varnish, polyurethane, shellac, and even brushing lacquers. They should not be used for latex paints or water-based stains. Water will soften the bristles and the brush will not hold its shape.

Nylon bristles may be used with varnish, polyurethane, and any water-based finish. They should not be used for shellac or lacquer because the solvents may attack the nylon.

A good quality brush is expensive. With good care, though, it will last almost indefinitely. Cleaning the brush properly is the most important factor in making a brush last. As soon as the finishing job is completed, the brush should be cleaned in the proper thinner for the finish used.

Paint thinner is used for varnish and polyurethane, alcohol for shellac, and lacquer thinner for lacquer. Many finishers keep used thinner in a sealed container to be used for cleaning the finish from the brush first. The brush is then cleaned in clean thinner. The bristles are rubbed between your fingers (wear rubber gloves) in the thinner.

The brush is then wiped dry with a clean cloth and washed several times with mild soap and warm water. This will remove any trace of finish from the brush. The bristles are then partially dried with a rag and shaped by hand. The brush is hung in a dry area to finish drying. When dry, the bristles will be as soft and pliant as when new. If the bristles are stiff and hard when dry, a small amount of finish remained and has hardened on the bristles.

Spray equipment.   Spray finishing equipment represents a major investment unless an air compressor is already available. A spray finishing system consists of an air compressor with air lines or hoses, an air pressure regulator, a moisture extractor, and a spray gun.

Air compressors are rated according to their air volume output in cubic feet per minute. Spray guns (as well as other air-powered tools) are rated by their air consumption in cubic feet per minute. It is very important that the air compressor have adequate capacity for the spray gun and any other tools that might be operated at the same time. For example, a compressor with an output of 5 cubic feet per minute could operate a spray gun rated at 8 cubic feet per minute until the air in the compressor tank was used; the air pressure would then drop and the operator would have to stop and wait for the compressor to "catch up." This is not practical when spraying a large panel.

The pressure regulator is necessary to set the air pressure at the level recommended for each material being sprayed. Wood lacquer is usually sprayed at 35 to 40 pounds per square inch.

Any moisture in a finish will cause problems. Unfortunately, when air is compressed, it is heated, and when it cools down in the tank and air lines, water condenses out of the air. If this moisture is not removed, it will pass through the air lines and the spray gun and ruin the finish.

Moisture extractors are placed in the air line as near as possible to the spray gun to prevent this problem. There are small moisture extractors that can be attached directly to the spray gun at the air inlet. An air line moisture extractor is shown in Fig. 5-4, and a small extractor for mounting on a spray gun is shown in Fig. 5-5. It is best to use both if moisture problems are encountered.

The spray gun is the most important part of the spray finishing system. It must be capable of thoroughly atomizing the finish, must spray the proper-shaped pattern, and must spray consistently with no sputtering or missing.

The small orifices in the gun that the fluid and air must pass through must be very accurately machined. This makes a good-quality spray gun quite expensive. Cheap spray guns usually do not atomize the finish material finely enough to get a high-quality finish.

Spray guns may be classified in one of several ways. They may be external or internal mix; that is, the air and fluid are mixed either outside or inside the spray tip. External mix guns are used for fast-drying finishes such as lacquers. Internal mix guns are often used for slow-drying finishes such as varnishes and enamels.

Spray guns may also be either suction (siphon) feed or pressure feed. In the case of a suction feed gun, the fluid is drawn out of the spray cup by the low pressure created when air passes by the fluid pickup tube. On a pressure feed gun, the fluid cup is pressurized to force the fluid through the gun. Pressure feed guns may also

Figure 5-4 Air line moisture extractor.

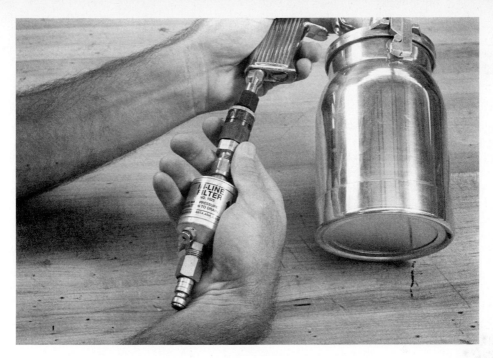

Figure 5-5 Small moisture extractor for mounting at the spray gun.

use remote paint pots for large jobs, eliminating the need of frequently refilling the paint cup on the gun and also eliminating the weight of the paint and cup on the gun.

Most furniture and cabinet finishing, other than production work, is done with a suction feed gun. It sprays the light-bodied wood lacquers very well and is easy to clean since it has no fluid hoses to be flushed out after each use.

A good spray gun has an adjustment for the spray pattern and an adjustment for material flow. The pattern can be adjusted from the normal fan-shaped pattern to a round pattern. The material flow adjustment is an adjustable stop behind the trigger to control the volume of fluid being sprayed.

A typical external mix, suction feed gun used for spraying furniture finishes is shown in Fig. 5-6.

Figure 5-6 Typical suction feed, external mix gun.

Spraying technique.   To spray a piece of furniture, the spray gun is normally adjusted to spray an oval or fan-shaped pattern. The spray gun must be perpendicular to the surface being sprayed and must travel parallel with the surface. A common mistake is to use a sweeping arc motion when spraying. This brings the gun close to the surface in the center of the arc, leaving a very heavy coat in that area. The gun moves away from the surface near the end of the arc, leaving a very thin, dry coat.

Whenever possible, the spray should always be started just off the surface before moving the gun past the surface, and then the spray is stopped after the gun passes the far side. For the next pass, the gun is aimed at the edge of the wet area left by the first pass and the procedure is repeated. It is best to stop the spray at each end of each pass.

When spraying lacquer, each coat must be wet. If the gun is too far from the surface or if it is moved too fast, the surface will be rough and powdery. The pattern for spraying a flat surface on a piece of furniture is shown in Fig. 5–7. The process is repeated for each flat surface. Legs, rails, and other narrow surfaces are usually sprayed with the gun moving along the length of the item, with the fan pattern perpendicular to the item.

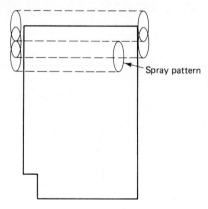

Spray pattern

Figure 5–7   Pattern for spraying a flat surface.

6 Equipping the Home Shop

Perhaps you have taken several woodworking classes and enjoyed them. However, you are finding that getting into the shop once or twice a week is not enough—your list of projects is growing faster than you can complete them. The woodworking bug has truly bitten, and the only relief appears to be having your own woodworking shop. This is a very big step, but it can be a rewarding lifelong hobby (and even a source of some extra spending money).

Several important questions should be answered before you start buying woodworking equipment: Do you have suitable space for a woodworking shop, and what type of woodworking do you plan on doing?

The question of what type of woodworking you plan on doing should be dealt with first because it will determine both the space requirements and the type of equipment to be purchased. If you are planning on working with hand tools only (there are a growing number of woodworkers who do not use power tools or machines) and if you are planning small projects, an unused room in a house or apartment will suffice. A basement would be even better. If you want to use power tools and machines, the noise and dust factors must be taken into consideration. A basement may still be satisfactory, but if it is directly under children's bedrooms or a TV viewing area, the noise may still be a problem. Garages have been used successfully by many woodworkers. Some of them have machines equipped with casters so that they can be rolled aside so that a car may be put in the garage. Others just leave the poor car outside!

Some serious woodworkers have built small shops. This is probably the ideal situation if money and space permit. The actual space requirement will vary greatly, depending on the size of projects contemplated.

Another important consideration is the electrical service to the shop area. Most portable power tools and smaller woodworking machines require 115-volt power, so in this case a number of normal household 110- to 115-volt outlets would be adequate. Some of these motors draw quite a few amperes, so you must be sure not to have too many motors on at one time on the same circuit.

Some larger machines have motors that can be wired for either 110 *or* 220 volts or 220 volts only. In the latter case, one or more 220-volt circuits would be necessary. In the case of motors that can be wired for 110 or 220 volts, they will draw one-half the amperage on 220 volts that they would on 110 volts, so it is better to use 220 volts given a choice.

Another consideration is heating a woodworking shop. Many woodworkers like to use wood-burning stoves so they can burn scrap material to reduce the cost of heating. A wood stove or any source of heat with a flame can ignite an explosion in a wood shop given a high enough concentration of dust in the air, so it is very important that a vacuum be attached to machines to keep the dust down. Many machines come equipped with dust hoods or they can be purchased as options. A portable shop vacuum can then be moved from machine to machine as necessary. Lacking this, shop-built hoods can be fabricated as shown in Fig. 6–1.

The type of woodworking that you plan on doing will also determine the type of equipment that you want to buy. If you are primarily interested in carpentry, such as doing an addition to your house, remodeling, or building a greenhouse, you need

Figure 6–1 Homemade exhaust hood. The hose at the bottom is attached to a shop vaccuum.

equipment that can safely handle large boards, but you probably do not need the ultimate in smooth, accurate cuts. If you are building cabinets and larger furniture, you need equipment that will handle plywood sheets and make accurate cuts. If you are doing small items, such as wooden toys, you will need equipment that can safely and accurately machine small parts.

We will next look at some of the machines, portable power tools, and hand tools usually found in woodworking shops.

EQUIPMENT SELECTION

Table Saw or Radial Arm Saw?

One of the most often asked questions is, Should I get a table saw or a radial arm saw? This is a very important question because the saw, table or radial arm, is the most important piece of equipment in most home shops. Although they are quite different in construction and operation, they are capable of performing many of the same operations, such as ripping, crosscutting, and cutting dados, rabbets, miters, and even moldings. The answer to the question, then, depends on the type of work to be done.

Radial arm saws are best for crosscutting long boards. With proper extension tables, boards of almost any length may easily be crosscut. This makes the radial arm saw a logical choice for building construction projects, since framing lumber can easily be cut to length. The radial arm saw also works well for cutting miters and cross dados.

The table saw (with proper extension tables) is easier to use for cutting sheet material such as plywood and particle board. Ripping boards is also easier and safer on the table saw than on the radial arm saw. For many operations, the table saw is more accurate and capable of smoother, straighter cuts. This is due to the difference in the construction of the two saws. There are more adjustments on the radial arm saw that could be misadjusted or worn. With a radial arm saw, the workpiece is placed on a table and the saw travels along an arm that is suspended over the table. Any sideways movement of the saw caused by improper adjustment or wear in the tracking system will result in uneven cuts. In contrast, the design of the table saw allows the saw to be more rigidly mounted under the table.

To answer the original question of which saw to buy, the radial arm saw is probably best for building construction. For building cabinets, furniture, or other wood items, especially if sheet material is going to be used, the table saw is best.

I would go even further and recommend that if you are serious about woodworking you buy the best table saw that you can afford, even if it means going without or delaying the purchase of some other pieces of equipment. Some lower-priced table saws do not have sufficient rigidity to do accurate work or do not have adequate power to cut through a 2-in.-thick hardwood board. Don't overlook the possibility of buying a used, light industrial model table saw (see the section on buying used equipment later in this chapter).

Selecting a table saw.   Most table saws are built in one of two ways. Cabinet model saws (Fig. 6–2) have an enclosed cabinet and are designed to set on the floor. The works (motor, trunions, arbor, etc.) are mounted in the top part of the cabinet. The table top is then bolted to the top of the cabinet, allowing the table top and its miter gage slots to be easily aligned with the blade.

Bench top saws (Fig. 6–3) are usually somewhat smaller and are designed to be set on a bench or mounted on a separate stand. The works are usually bolted to the underside of the table top. Bench top saws are usually found in home shops and are often used by building contractors because of their portability.

Cabinet model saws are usually found in cabinet shops, school shops, and other areas of the woodworking industry. However, the cabinet-type saw should not be overlooked for home shop use, especially if you are planning on cutting thick (2 in. and up) materials or sheet materials. They usually have heavier trunnion assemblies and more rigidity in the bearing and arbor area, and the table tops are often larger. For cutting plywood, it is important to have a table top or extension and a fence that allows cutting 48 in. to the right of the blade so that you can cut to the center of an 8-ft sheet.

Other things to check when selecting a table saw include the table top. It should be made of cast iron and should be machined to a smooth surface so that wood will

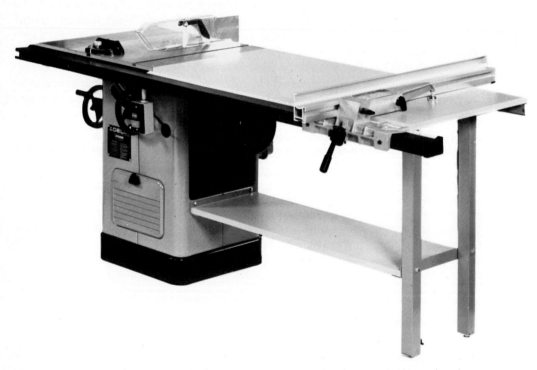

Figure 6–2   Cabinet model table saw (Delta Industrial Machinery Corp.).

Figure 6–3   Bench model table saw (Sears, Roebuck & Co.).

slide smoothly over it. It should be fairly large if you are planning to work with sheet materials.

The rip fence is a real trouble area with many small table saws and even some large ones. It should slide smoothly across the saw table, yet should lock securely in position in perfect alignment with the blade every time it is locked. It should *not* be necessary to have to measure the distance from the fence to the miter gage slot at the front and rear of the saw in order to align the fence each time it is locked.

In fact, this problem with many original-equipment rip fences has provided the impetus for a thriving business for several companies providing high-quality, after-market rip fences. Two of these are shown in Figs. 6–4 and 6–5.

The gears used to raise, lower, and tilt the saw blade should be checked. Larger gears will usually last longer and operate more smoothly over the life of the saw. These gears should be shielded from the stream of sawdust coming from the blade. Raise and lower the blade several times and tilt it to 45°. The crank handles should turn smoothly, but with little excess play. Some saws tilt to the right and some tilt to the left. There are proponents for both types among professional woodworkers.

Equipment Selection

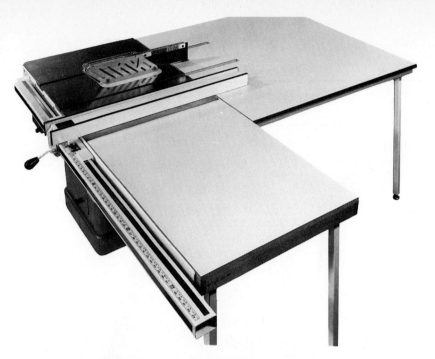

Figure 6-4 Biesemeyer T-square fence (Biesemeyer Manufacturing Corporation).

Figure 6-5 Paralok table saw fence (Quintec Manufacturing, Inc.).

Equipping the Home Shop   Chap. 6

Motor horsepower ratings can be somewhat deceiving, but for most purposes a 10-in. table saw should have at least 2 horsepower and preferably 3.

Table saws are often designated by maximum blade size (i.e., a 10-in. saw or 12-in. saw, etc.). A 10-in saw is adequate for most home shop situations unless cutting of very thick material is planned.

Table saws are much more useful with a table behind the saw to support long stock and a table or rail to the left of the saw to support wide stock. Building these could be one of your first shop projects.

A relatively new, but very useful accessory for table saws is becoming very popular. This is the rolling or sliding table. These were originally found only on large industrial saws but are now available on many medium-size saws. One of these is shown in Fig. 6–6. This attachment makes it easy to crosscut large boards such as glued-up table tops, as well as making many other operations easier and safer.

As an alternative to a rolling table, a sliding crosscut jig, such as the one shown in Chapter 8, could be built for the table saw using the plans provided.

Figure 6–6   Table saw equipped with a rolling table (Powermatic, a division of Stanwich Industries, Inc.).

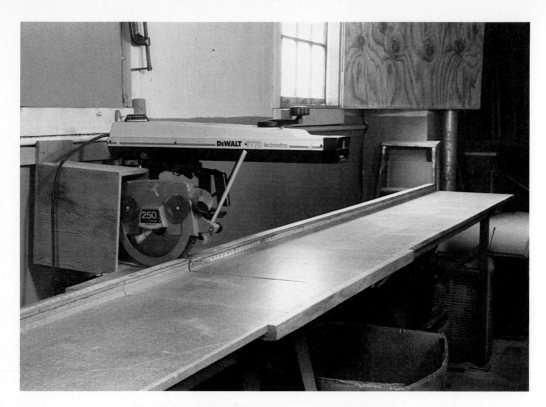

Figure 6–7 Long extension tables make the radial arm saw easier to use.

Selecting a radial arm saw. As previously mentioned, radial arm saws, because of their design, have more potential sources for unwanted movement of the blade than do table saws. Therefore, if the radial arm saw is to be the central piece of equipment in the shop, the saw should be thoroughly checked for sturdy construction. Compare different brands for column and arm size. Also check the bearings in the saw tracking system. Several different designs are used by different manufacturers. The saw should track freely along the arm, but should have no sideways play. Also, check the controls for raising and lowering the blade and for changing angles.

Many radial arm saws are designed so that the arm pivots at the column for cutting miters. Because the saw blade is located to the left of the arm, this limits the width of the miter that can be cut to the left. Some saws are designed so that the tracking arm pivots about its center, which overcomes this problem.

The small table that comes with most radial arm saws is almost useless when it is necessary to cut long material. A table extension, such as the one shown in Fig. 6–7, makes the saw easier to use.

Selecting a jointer. Jointers are rated according to the width of the cutter head or, in other words, the maximum-width board that can be planed. Most home shop models are either 4 or 6 in. wide. Industrial models are available in 8- to 16-in. widths. If you are purchasing planed lumber and using the jointer only to true the edges of boards, a 4-in. jointer would be adequate. However, a 6-in. jointer will usually have a longer table, which is useful for handling longer boards.

Regardless of size, the most important feature of a jointer is that the infeed table and outfeed table must be absolutely parallel with each other and must remain so throughout the adjustment range. It will be impossible to get a straight edge on a board if either table tilts or sags. This can be checked with a straight edge using the following procedure:

1. Move the guide fence back as far as it will go.
2. Remove the blade guard or move it to the outside of the table and block it.
3. Raise the infeed table so that it is level with the outfeed table.
4. Set the straight edge along the infeed table at the back of the jointer as shown in Fig. 6-8. The straight edge should contact both tables over their entire length.
5. Now move the straight edge to the center of the table and check again.
6. Check the front edge of the table in the same way.
7. Finally, check the table diagonally in both directions as shown in Fig. 6-9.

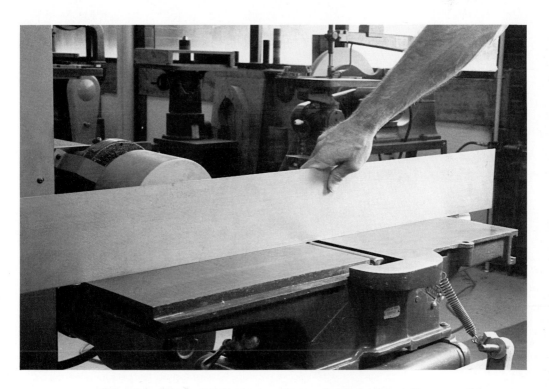

Figure 6-8 Using a straight edge to make sure that both jointer tables are parallel.

Equipment Selection

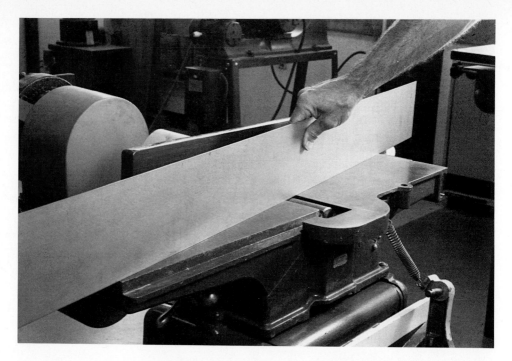

Figure 6–9 Checking the jointer table diagonally.

Figure 6–10 Jointer with a front-mounting fence (Delta Industrial Machinery Corp.).

Equipping the Home Shop   Chap. 6

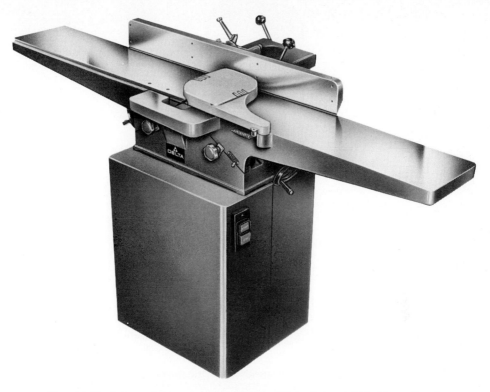

Figure 6–11 Jointer with a center-mounted fence (Delta Industrial Machinery Corp.).

For most work, a ½-horsepower motor is adequate on a 4-in. jointer and a ¾-horsepower motor is adequate on a 6-in. jointer.

Jointers are adjusted for depth of cut by moving the infeed table up or down. Most jointers have an adjustable outfeed table also. It is rarely necessary to adjust the outfeed table except when new knives are installed. The outfeed table is then adjusted tangent to the cutting arc as described in Chapter 7. However, some home shop jointers do not have an adjustable outfeed table. In this case, the knives must be set in the head at exactly the correct height.

The jointer fence may be mounted on the front or center of the machine as shown in Figs. 6–10 and 6–11. However, some fences mount at the rear. The center-mounting system is probably more rigid, but for most applications this probably would not be a significant factor.

Band Saw or Scroll Saw?

Both of these saws are designed for cutting curves and other irregular shapes. The band saw (Fig. 6–12) is much faster and less troublesome. It can also be used for resawing (slicing thick boards into thinner ones). The scroll saw (Fig. 6–13) is better

Figure 6-12 Band saw (Powermatic, a division of Stanwich Industries, Inc.).

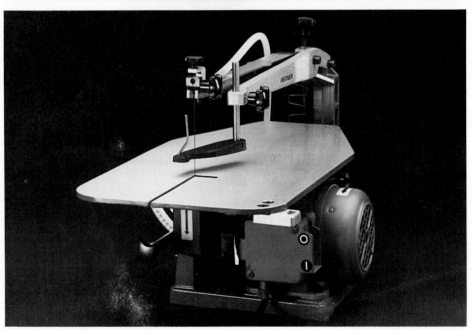

Figure 6-13 Scroll saw (Advanced Machinery Imports, Ltd., New Castle, DE).

Equipping the Home Shop   Chap. 6

for sharp curves and very intricate shapes. The scroll saw may also be used to make internal cutouts by drilling a hole in the area to be cut out, mounting the blade through this hole, and making the cutout. Although the band saw is not necessarily considered a particularly dangerous machine, a scroll saw is much safer if it is to be used by youngsters. Sanding attachments are available for scroll saws as well as for some band saws.

In general, the band saw is more useful for general woodworking, and the scroll saw would be selected for very intricate work.

Selecting a band saw. Band saw size is determined by wheel diameter or distance from the blade to the body in the case of three-wheel machines. In either case, this represents the maximum width of cut that can be made on the left side of the blade. Ten- to fourteen-inch machines are the most popular for home shops with ½- to ¾-horsepower motors.

The top wheel is usually adjustable vertically to tension the blade and is adjustable for tilt to control the tracking of the blade. The wheels are crowned (or slightly convex in cross section) to aid in blade tracking. They are covered with a rubber tire to keep the blade from slipping and to protect the set in the teeth.

There are side blade guides above and below the table to keep the blade from twisting and blade support bearings to prevent the blade from being pushed off the main wheels. Blade side guides may be either hardened steel blocks or ball bearings. In either case, they should be adjustable from side to side for different blade widths. The table can usually be tilted in at least one direction for making angle cuts.

Selecting a scroll saw. Two types of scroll saws are manufactured. One type has a fixed top arm that holds the top blade chuck using a spring-loaded assembly that allows the blade to move up and down. The other type has the blade clamped between reciprocating arms (Fig. 6–13).

The first type has a rather complex mechanism for transforming the rotary motion of the motor drive shaft to reciprocating motion for the blade. This causes some vibration, so parts need to be checked periodically for adjustment. This mechanism usually runs in an oil sump, so the oil level must be maintained. This type of saw works well when properly maintained and adjusted and was the only type readily available for many years.

The second type of scroll saw has been used in Europe for quite some time, but is relatively new to the United States. The blade mounting and tensioning system seems to be more successful, and it is capable of very intricate work.

Planer

The planer is an expensive piece of equipment and consequently is not often found in home workshops. It is usually possible to have planing work done at a local cabinet shop.

However, having a planer does offer some advantages to a woodworker. Rough lumber can be purchased, often saving money compared with buying planed lumber.

A planer (along with a jointer) allows a woodworker to straighten crooked lumber. One big advantage of a planer is having the capability of gluing boards together to form large surfaces and then planing the large board flat.

For example, to make a table top that is $\frac{3}{4}$ in. thick, one can start with 1-in. rough lumber, joint and plane it to about $\frac{7}{8}$ in. thick, glue it together, and then plane it to its final $\frac{3}{4}$-in. thickness. By comparison, if no planer were available, one would start with $\frac{3}{4}$-in.-thick boards and make sure that each board is straight and flat. Then the boards would be glued, being very careful to keep all the glue joints perfectly aligned. Then the surface would have to be scraped and sanded smooth.

The typical home shop planer is a 12-in. model, although smaller models are available and occasionally good buys can be had on large, used industrial models. Twelve-inch planers require a 2- to 3-horsepower motor.

Industrial planers have a number of features and options such as segmented infeed roll, adjustable table rolls, and variable-speed feeds. However, these features are usually not available on smaller models. The main thing to check is to see if the machine has adequate power to take a reasonable cut on a full-width board. Also look at the planed surface of a board to see that it is smooth and does not have "snipes" or dips near the end of the board.

Planers are more complex than most other woodworking equipment, so there are more parts to get out of adjustment. It is a good idea if possible to talk to owners of models that you may be considering. Some planers have been quite troublesome.

Most planers have at least two power-driven feed rolls that may be driven by the main cutter head motor or by a separate motor. These rolls must be free to move up and down to accommodate stock of varying thicknesses. They may be driven by belts, chains, gears, or a combination of these. The rolls are usually adjustable for height. There is a chip breaker just ahead of the cutter head and a pressure bar just behind the cutter head to hold the wood down on the table. A cross section of a typical planer is shown in Chapter 7.

Drill Press

Light-duty drill presses suitable for woodworking are relatively inexpensive and are very useful for a number of jobs. In addition to their basic hole-drilling function, they can be used for sanding with a suitable sanding drum and for making small wood wheels using hole saws or circle cutters. They are sometimes used for router work, although they are not designed for that purpose and the results are usually disappointing.

A drill press for woodworking should have at least four speeds so that it can run small bits at their ideal high speeds or be slowed down for running a circle cutter or a sanding drum. Drill presses in this range usually have a $\frac{1}{2}$- or $\frac{3}{4}$-horsepower motor.

A very handy feature to look for on a drill press is a rack gear on the column that allows the table height to be changed with a crank rather than by lifting the table manually. The chuck should have a $\frac{1}{2}$-in. capacity. This will accommodate most bits used for woodworking. There should also be an adjustable depth stop.

After the drill press is purchased, you will need something to make holes with. It may come as a shock to find that you can easily spend more than the price of the drill press for drill bits. For general woodworking, it is nice to have a set of twist drill bits for smaller holes, such as screw pilot holes, a set of brad point bits for doweling, and a set of either Foerstner bits, multispur bits, or power bore bits for larger holes.

Other nice-to-have items include plug cutters, countersink bits, circle cutters, and hole saws. Mortising conversions are available to convert a drill press to a hollow chisel mortiser. Most of these bits and accessories can be purchased one at a time as needed.

Shaper

A shaper is another of those nice-to-have machines, but one that is not essential for most woodworking. Shapers are used for making moldings, shaping edges, cutting rabbets, making raised panels, cutting tenons, and making matching stile and rail parts for doors and other panels. Many operations that would be done on a small shaper can also be done with a router, especially if a router table is available.

The shaper has a vertical shaft or spindle on which various cutters may be mounted. On most home-shop-size shapers, this shaft is $\frac{1}{2}$ in. in diameter. Many cutters are available in either high-speed steel or carbide for this spindle size. This spindle is adjustable up or down to change the cutter height. Shapers also have an adjustable guide fence. The infeed and outfeed portions of this fence should be adjustable independently from each other. Shapers in this range usually have at least a 1-horsepower motor.

Sanders

The most popular stationary sander for home shops is the combination disc and belt sander, as shown in Fig. 6–14. This takes care of most sanding and grinding opera-

Figure 6–14   Combination disc belt sander (Sears, Roebuck & Co.).

tions. A flap wheel sander that can be mounted on a motor shaft is handy if a lot of free-form work is to be done.

Lathe

The lathe is somewhat outside the mainstream of woodworking machines. The usefulness of a lathe depends on the type of woodworking to be done. Some woodworkers find little use for a lathe; others find it a valuable machine for making various parts for furniture, and the like, while still others center their woodworking hobby around the lathe, making mainly bowls, platters, goblets, lamps, candlestick holders, and other turned objects.

It is important that the wood lathe have several speeds, since the speed must be changed when changing from small- to large-diameter work and from rough cutting to finish cutting to sanding. It should have a drive center or spur center and "tail center" for spindle turning. Better lathes have a ball-bearing tail center that turns with the workpiece. This is a worthwhile feature if much turning is to be done. The lathe should have several different-size face plates for turning bowls, platters, and so on. A set of lathe tools consisting of a gouge, skew, parting tool, and round-nose and diamond-point tool will be necessary.

Combination Machines

The machines we have discussed so far have been special-purpose machines, each designed for a specific purpose. If you had purchased one each of these machines, you would have a very well-equipped shop, but you would need a very large shop to hold the equipment and you would have spent a very large sum of money!

In an effort to minimize space requirements and to reduce costs, a number of manufacturers have developed combination woodworking machines. These combination machines range from jointer–planer combinations to entire woodworking shops, including table saw, jointer, planer, shaper, boring machine, and more combined in one machine. Several of these machines are shown in Figs. 6–15 to 6–18.

Figure 6-15 Combination planer–jointer (Makita USA, Inc.).

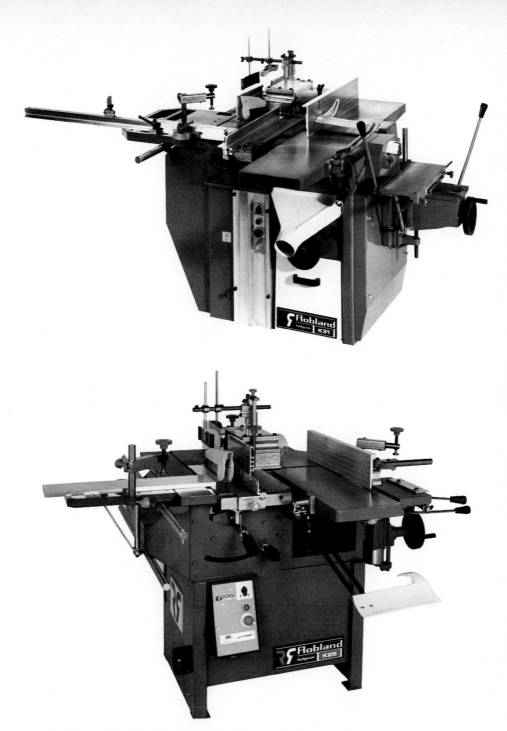

Figure 6-16 Combination woodworking machine featuring a table saw with rolling table, spindle shaper, jointer, planer, boring table, and mortiser (Laguna Tools).

Equipment Selection

273

Figure 6–17 Another combination machine (courtesy of VAMAC, Belgium).

Figure 6–18 Large, industrial-quality combination woodworking machine with a 12-in. circular saw with rolling table, 12-in. jointer and planer, shaper with $1\frac{1}{4}$-in. tilting spindle, and a boring and mortising table (Advanced Machinery Imports, Ltd., New Castle, DE).

Compared with individual machines capable of the same operations, combination machines offer the following advantages:

1. They generally require much less space than individual machines.
2. They almost always cost less than individual machines of comparable quality. This is due in part to the fact that several machine functions are often powered by a common motor and use common tables and stands, and so on.
3. There is less potential for mechanical problems since there are fewer motors and other parts.

Combination machines also have several potential disadvantages compared with individual machines:

1. They often have to be changed when switching from one operation to another. Even though these changeovers may take only a few seconds on some of the better designed machines, it still means changing a setup that you may want to come back to later. Thus it will take a little longer to build some projects with a combination machine than it would with individual machines.
2. Sometimes the function of the combination machine is compromised because of the fact that it combines a number of machines. For example, work table surfaces are often smaller than they would be on individual machines. This makes it more difficult to handle large boards or sheets of plywood. Also, because of the added number of adjustments necessary to convert from one machine to another, the machine may not be as rigid and vibration free. The better machines are very good in this regard, however.

In summary, combination machines offer the biggest advantage when space is at a premium. They also offer the potential of substantial savings in equipping a shop. You should plan on having your projects take slightly more time to complete because of the time loss in converting the machine from one function to another.

Before buying a combination machine, arrange to watch a demonstration of the machine performing a variety of operations and being changed from one function to another. Notice the time it takes for setups. Even more importantly, notice the quality of work the machine does. Also notice if the work appears to be awkward or unsafe in any way.

If you are watching machines being demonstrated at a woodworking show, the operators are probably highly skilled and will demonstrate operations that best suit the machine. If this does not represent the type of woodworking you plan to do, you should arrange to see a demonstration, perhaps in the dealer's show room, of the type of work that you plan to do.

Used Machinery

The stationary machines that we have been discussing represent large investments. These can often be purchased used at a substantial savings. Used machines that are several years old, but in good condition, will usually sell at 50% to 60% of the new price.

Sources of used machines. Private parties are one possible source of woodworking machines. Look in the classified newspaper ads under tools or machinery and in the free want ad papers circulated in most communities. Buying from a private party gives you a chance to talk to the owner and find out about the machine.

Used machines are sometimes taken as trade-ins on new machines at equipment dealers. These machines are likely to be somewhat more expensive than those purchased from a private party, but they are often checked over and may have worn or damaged parts replaced. They may also carry a warranty. You probably will not find smaller used home shop equipment at these dealers, but you may find anything from small cabinet shop equipment on up.

Another possible source of used equipment is an auction. Occasionally, cabinet shops, pattern shops, model shops, or maintenance shops will go out of business and the equipment will be sold at auction. Look under auction notices in the classified section of the paper.

Surplus school shop and government agency equipment is sometimes sold to the highest bidder through sealed bids. These sales are also usually advertised in the newspaper.

Things to check when buying used machinery. When buying used machinery, you should check all the things that you would check when buying new equipment plus the following items.

One of the first things to check on any piece of machinery is the motor. Electric motors are either single phase or three phase. Single-phase motors may be either 110 to 115 volts or 220 volts. Single-phase, 110- to 115-volt motors will plug into any household outlet, so these should work in any shop. Some motors can be wired to run on either 110 or 115 volts or 220 volts, so these should present no problem either. Some single-phase motors can only be used with 220-volt power, so your shop would require a 220-volt circuit to use such a motor. Larger portable air compressors, for example, usually require 220-volt power.

Three-phase motors are another story. Three-phase power is not even available in most residential areas. Your power company can tell you. If you are in an area with three-phase power, but do not already have it, there will be a hookup charge and probably a separate monthly service charge. Check with your power company. The only thing that makes all this worth pursuing is the fact that most cabinet shop machinery has three-phase motors, and it is sometimes possible to get a good, used, cabinet-shop-quality table saw, for example, for the price of a new home shop quality saw. For heavy duty or continuous use, three-phase motors are much better because they do not need separate starting windings and do not have any internal switches to arc and start dust fires. They are generally much more trouble free, have higher stall resistance, and are less expensive in sizes larger than 1 horsepower.

If you find an otherwise good deal on a machine with a three-phase motor, you may be able to do one of the following:

1. Get a three-phase hookup if it is available in your area.
2. Sell the three-phase motor and buy a single-phase motor for the machine. On some machines, standard motor mounts are used and this is relatively easy; on others it is almost impossible. Any machine with a direct drive, such as a radial arm saw, would be very difficult to change. Check this out before buying the machine.
3. Phase converters are available for converting incoming single-phase power to three phase. There are two types of phase converters. The first is a rotary phase converter, which is somewhat like a large electric motor that is run in series with other three-phase motors. It is run whenever other three-phase motors are on. It is quite expensive and will usually cost at least as much as a major piece of equipment. Such a converter would probably not be worthwhile, unless you were planning to equip most of your shop with three-phase machines. The other phase converter is an electronic solid-state model. It is less expensive, but is generally considered to be less efficient from a power-consumption standpoint.

The condition of the machine, of course, should be checked carefully as well. Avoid machines with any of the major casting broken. It can be expensive to replace, if even available. If the machine is still in production, minor parts should still be available. This is something worth checking. In recent years, there have been a number of machine lines imported and sold for a while and then removed from the market. Finding repair parts for these machines could be nearly impossible.

Some parts such as ball bearings, belts, and pulleys are usually readily available through bearing houses. Metric-size ball bearings are readily available.

Most of the better machines have an almost unlimited service life with reasonable care, since the items subject to wear, such as bearings, belts, and pulleys, can be replaced. It is not uncommon for a woodworking machine to last 30 to 40 years even in daily use.

Another thing to check before buying a machine is to see if the cutters or tools are standard and readily available. For example, there are table saws with nonstandard arbor sizes or shapes, jointers that use nonstandard knives, sanders that use nonstandard-size sanding belts, and so on. Getting a good buy on a machine does not mean much if you cannot get cutters for it or if you have to pay a premium to have cutters specially made.

Rust is another thing to look for. Many woodworking machines are made of cast iron. Machined surfaces such as table tops, trunnions, dovetail ways, and other parts can rust easily if not protected. Light surface rust on a table top, for example, can be cleaned up with fine sandpaper or steel wool. Heavy rust will leave deep pitting in the surface and may have made sliding surfaces loose, affecting the accuracy of the machine.

Other items to check include gears used to raise, lower, and tilt cutters. These gears and the sliding surfaces they control, if neglected, get a buildup of dried lubricant and sawdust making them difficult to turn. If they are forced, the gear teeth may break or become badly worn. Sometimes these teeth are machined on a major casting and cannot be replaced without replacing the entire casting. On some machines, the gears can be replaced separately. This should be checked if there is a problem in this area.

In summary, the major things to check when buying used equipment are as follows:

1. The motor is compatible with your power source.
2. The major parts of the machines are not damaged.
3. Parts are still available for the machine.
4. The machine is not badly rusted.
5. The gears are in good shape or are replaceable.
6. You may be able to save some money on a machine that needs bearings, belts, or pulleys if you don't mind the work involved in replacing them. Otherwise, it is best to look for a machine in good condition. A machine with noisy bearings, worn belts, and deeply worn pulley grooves will sound terrible, but can be repaired for relatively little expense if nothing else is wrong.

Specific machines. Some common woodworking machines and some potential problem areas for each that should be checked are discussed next.

Table saw. Check gears for raising and tilting blade. Make sure gear teeth are not broken or badly worn. Turn the motor on and off several times and watch the blade for any run out. This could indicate a bent arbor or just a warped blade.

The rip fence *should* lock down parallel with the miter slots. Unfortunately, even on many otherwise good saws, this is not the case. This can sometimes be corrected. See Chapter 7 on machine maintenance.

Make sure that the saw motor has enough power for the type of work you are planning.

Jointer. The most important feature of any jointer is that the two tables must be absolutely parallel with each other on all planes. A good straight edge is necessary to check this. Put the fence all the way back and set the infeed table at the same height as the outfeed table. Set the straight edge across both tables along the back edge of the table; then check the front edge and check the diagonals. The straight edge should set flat on the table for its entire length.

Tables can get out of true through wear on the dovetail ways or by too much play at that point. Cast-iron tables have been known to warp during curing. A jointer that has been through a fire could have warped tables.

The infeed table should move up and down freely, but without excess play.

Radial arm saw.   Radial arm saws with a lot of running time tend to develop wear in the first part of the tracking arm, since most cuts do not require pulling the saw through its full travel. There is usually a wear adjustment, but if it is set to provide tight, accurate tracking in the wear area, then it will be too tight when it is necessary to make a full-width cut. This can be checked by pulling the saw out about 6 in. and then taking the motor and trying to rock it back and forth. There will be a small amount of play, but it should not be excessive. Then move the saw out near the end of its travel. The play should be the same. If there is more play in the first 6 in. of travel than in the last 6 in., there is probably no way to repair this.

Planer.   Planers are considerably more complex than other woodworking machines. There are quite a few major castings that should be checked for cracks. The corrugations on the infeed roll should be "sharp" so that they will pull the wood through.

The table should move up and down freely, but with no excess play, and should be the same height on both sides. This can be checked by slipping a block of wood under the cutter head near one end and raising the table until the block just touches the head (not the knife). Then slip the block out and move it to the other end of the head without moving the table. It should just slip under the head. If it does not, make sure that there is an adjustment for leveling the table.

It is best if you can listen to a planer run, both at idle and planing lumber. Listen for any unusual noises. It is not uncommon for planers to be quite noisy, but you can usually recognize signs of mechanical distress.

You can tell quite a bit about a planer by looking at a planed board. If the surface is smooth with small mill marks, it is probably in proper adjustment. If the mill marks are very large, it is likely that one knife is set higher than the others. If the board is tapered across its width, the knives (or a knife) could be higher on one side than the other or the table may not be level with the cutter head. If the boards have "snipes" or dips near the ends, the table rollers could be too high or the pressure bar is too high. These things can usually be adjusted, but make sure that these items are adjustable if the planer shows any of these problems. See Chapter 7 for more detail on planer adjustment.

Band saw.   A visual inspection of a band saw should reveal any serious problems such as a broken casting. Most other problems that occur with band saws can be remedied with proper adjustment or replacement of minor parts. The ball-bearing blade support guides (behind the blade both above and below the table) tend to wear out rapidly if not properly adjusted. Fortunately, these are usually readily obtainable standard bearings. The blade side guides may be either ball bearings or hard steel blocks. These also are easy to replace.

If all the guides are adjusted properly (see Chapter 7) and the blade still will not track properly, the most likely cause is bad tires on the band saw wheels. These rubber tires can be replaced. A blade that has been welded with the joint improperly aligned will also track erratically.

Portable Power Tools

Reasonably good quality portable power tools can sometimes be purchased for less money than a good quality hand tool designed to do the same job. This makes them quite attractive for the home shop. Most portable power tool manufacturers make tools in a range from very light duty homeowner models to heavy industrial models. For example, one manufacturer's catalog shows a $\frac{3}{8}$-in., variable-speed reversing drill for less than $30 and another one for $130, with several models priced in between. The $30 drill will have less power and lighter-duty motor windings, so it will be less resistant to heat buildup from stalling or overloading. It will also have a lighter-duty switch, bushings rather than ball or roller bearings, a light plastic cord rather than a heavy rubber one, a lower-quality chuck, and probably an all-plastic housing, whereas the $130 drill will probably have a metal housing in the areas where bearings are housed. Comparable differences can be found in other power tools.

The bottom-line tools are designed for occasional light-duty use and will not stand up well to heavy use or abuse. They would probably not be satisfactory for most serious woodworkers. The intermediate lines, however, are usually quite good and usually represent good value for the money. It is probably not worth buying the very top industrial-line portable tools unless you are doing woodworking full time and using the tools continuously.

Router. The router is an amazingly versatile woodworking tool. With the right cutters, it can be used to make moldings, dados, rabbets, mortise and tenon joints, box joints, dovetail joints, dovetail dados, door stiles and rails, raised panels, flutes, inlays, to trim plastic laminates and veneers, and for many other operations. As with several other woodworking machines, though, the router is only the first part of the investment. The cost of cutters can run many times the cost of the router.

Adequate power is an important consideration in selecting a router. A router with a 1-horsepower motor is usually adequate for cutting narrow dados, small dovetails, and most molding shapes. A $1\frac{1}{2}$-horsepower motor should handle almost anything most woodworkers would want to do.

There are several other things to consider in selecting a router. One of these is the system for locking bits in the collet. Some routers have a built-in shaft lock, so only one wrench is required for tightening or loosening a bit. Others require two wrenches, one to hold the shaft and one to lock the bit. This is less convenient, but is probably one less thing to give trouble as the router gets older. Most smaller routers come with a $\frac{1}{4}$-in. collet, but if the router will also accept a $\frac{1}{2}$-in. collet, it will allow the use of some of the industrial-type bits. Bits with $\frac{1}{2}$-in. shanks are much less prone to vibration and chatter and will provide smoother cuts than bits with $\frac{1}{4}$-in. shanks.

The method of changing depth settings should also be checked. There should be a fine adjustment for depth settings that is smooth and easy to control in fine increments.

There are also routers with a plunge base. This allows you to start the router with the base flat on the work surface, plunge cut to a predetermined depth, complete the cut, and then retract the cutter. This feature is very handy for cutting blind dados and other recessed cuts.

Several accessories are worth considering for a router. One of these is a dovetail jig. Another is a guide fence that mounts on the base of the router. A router table is also very handy for some operations. These can be purchased or built.

Saber saw.   Saber saws are used primarily for curved cuts. If the shop has a band saw or scroll saw, the saber saw will probably not be used so extensively, so an inexpensive one should be adequate. If no band saw is available, a better saber saw would be advisable. Some features found on better models include orbital rather than straight-line stroke, chip blowers, tilting bases, variable speeds, and more power. A few models have scrolling features that allow the saw to cut in any direction without turning the saw itself.

Circular saw.   The portable circular saw is another tool that does not find a great deal of use in the average woodworking shop, although they are sometimes used to cut large pieces to more manageable sizes. They are not designed for precision work, but rather are a contractor's tool, where they are very valuable for building construction.

There are two types of portable circular saws, the top handle or direct drive and the worm drive, both shown in Chapter 3. The blade speed is geared down in the worm drive model so they have a lot of power and resistance to stalling. They are usually preferred for heavy construction.

Miter saw.   A miter saw can perform several of the most common operations done on the radial arm saw, and they cost considerably less. They are very handy for crosscutting smaller stock and for cutting miters of any angle up to 45°. They can even be used for cutting compound miters if a beveled board is used on the table to support the workpiece at the proper angle.

Sanders.   Belt sanders and finishing sanders are the two most popular sanders for woodworking. Belt sanders are used primarily for removing machine marks such as saw marks or planer mill marks and for removing stock (sanding parts to fit).

Belt sanders are designated for size by belt width and length. Most belt sanders are either 3 or 4 in., meaning that they use a 3-in.-wide or a 4-in.-wide belt. Popular belt lengths are 21, 24, and 27 in.

Belt sanders may be either belt driven, in which case the motor sets transversely on the sander, or gear driven, in which case the motor sets longitudinally on the sander. The lower-cost home shop models are usually belt driven. Belt-driven models are usually somewhat lighter and usually require no lubrication. Gear-driven models are usually very heavy duty industrial models and require a special oil in the gearbox.

Belt sanders should have a lever to release belt tension for changing the belt and a control to adjust belt tracking; some newer sanders have automatic belt tracking.

Finishing sanders may be either electric or air driven and may use either rectangular sheets of paper or adhesive-backed discs. Their action may be orbital, straight line, or random orbital (dual action). Orbital sanders are more popular than straight-line sanders. They are generally faster, but they do leave orbital sanding marks on the wood. If their final sanding on a project is done with a fine-grit abrasive, it does not take too much hand sanding to remove these orbital marks. Straight-line sanders do not leave these marks, but are somewhat slower.

Dual-action sanders are very popular in cabinet shops and other woodworking industries. The disc rotates, but also has a very high speed orbital action. These sanders are usually air driven and are very fast. Their air consumption is fairly high, so a good-sized compressor is needed for this type of sander.

Many electric finish sanders use either one-fourth or one-half of a standard abrasive paper sheet. Others require special paper sizes. Some finish sanders use adhesive-backed abrasive discs, which are more expensive, but are handy, especially if the sander is in constant use for long periods.

Power planes. Portable power planes are very useful for work that is done on a job site, such as installing cabinets, hanging doors, and other finish carpentry. However, if most of the work is done in a shop equipped with a jointer, they are not as essential as some other tools. Power planes are similar to a jointer in operation in that the infeed bed (table) is adjusted to regulate the rate of cut. The back bed is tangent with the cutting circle of the cutter.

Portable drills. A good portable drill is an essential part of any woodworking shop. It is usually designated as $\frac{1}{4}$, $\frac{3}{8}$, or $\frac{1}{2}$ in. depending on the maximum capacity of the chuck. A $\frac{3}{8}$-in. drill is popular for general woodworking. Variable-speed and reversing features are popular because the drill can then be used as a power screwdriver.

The price difference between the bottom and the top of the price range in drills is probably more apparent than for other portable power tools. For most woodworking, a medium-duty drill is very satisfactory.

A dowel jig is very useful for many woodworking projects. It will ensure that dowel holes are properly aligned and are perpendicular to the surface in which they are drilled. Some dowel jigs are self-centering. Others locate the dowel hole a specified distance from the face of a board. This is a good feature when it is necessary to join boards of varying thickness that must be flush on one side. However, the self-centering type has one less adjustment to make during setup.

Hand Tools

Most common hand woodworking tools are described in Chapter 3. The assortment of hand tools needed for a home shop will vary with the amount of stationary and portable power equipment and with the type of work a person anticipates doing. A typical shop designed to do a variety of woodworking projects would probably have some or all of the following:

- 13- or 16-ounce curved claw hammer

- Brad hammer
- Wood mallet
- Set of wood chisels (¼, ½, ¾, and 1 in.)
- Block plane
- Bench plane (jack plane or similar)
- Rabbet plane
- Scraper blade
- Assortment of straight slot and Phillips screwdrivers
- Scratch awl
- Framing square
- Try square
- Combination square
- Bevel square (sliding T-bevel)
- Measuring tape
- Dividers or compass
- Auger brace and set of bits
- Pliers and diagonal cutter pliers
- Back saw
- Hand crosscut saw
- Compass saw
- Coping saw
- Utility knife
- Sharpening stones

Other tools that may be handy, depending on the type of work contemplated, include:

- Carving tools
- Router plane
- Other specialty planes
- Spokeshave
- Dovetail saw
- Veneer saw
- Miter box
- Marking gage
- Dividers and calipers (inside and outside)
- Level
- Trammel points
- Hand drill

- Push drill
- Spiral ratchet screwdriver
- Wood rasps

Vise and Clamps

A good woodworking vise (Fig. 6–19) and an assortment of clamps are essential. Bar clamps or pipe clamps are used for assembling cabinets or other larger projects. Hand screw clamps are used for many gluing operations, as well as for holding parts in place for machining or other operations. They are one of the most used clamps in woodworking. Speed clamps are useful for some operations requiring deep clamp jaws. A few C-lamps and spring clamps are always handy. Band or web clamps are good for complex assemblies such as chairs.

Toggle clamps (Fig. 6–20) are probably the least appreciated clamp, but they can be invaluable for use on jigs and fixtures designed to hold small parts for machining. They can hold a small part securely to a jig so that you can perform machining operations on it without getting your fingers near the cutters.

Figure 6–19 Woodworking vise.

Figure 6–20 Toggle clamp. These are very handy for holding parts on jigs and fixtures (De-Sta-Co).

EQUIPPING THE SHOP IN STAGES

As nice as it would be to go out and buy a whole shop full of equipment, it usually is not possible. However, a great deal of woodworking can be accomplished with a few basic machines, especially if supplemented with a few hand tools and a portable router. In fact, if you had all the machines and equipment described in this book, you would probably find that the majority of your work would be done on a few basic machines.

It is therefore good to prioritize the purchase of equipment so that the first pieces purchased are the most useful and versatile. The following discussion assumes that individual pieces of equipment are to be purchased; however, one of the combination machines as described earlier may be a better solution and should not be overlooked. In any case, you should consider the type of work you plan to do. The following suggestions may need to be changed to suit your needs.

Stage I: The Basics

A basic shop that would allow you to do a wide range of projects would include the following:

- Table saw
- Band saw (or scroll saw)
- Jointer
- Portable router with a router table
- Finish sander
- ⅜-in. portable drill and dowel jig
- Several pipe or bar clamps and hand screw clamps
- Some basic hand tools, as described earlier

Equipping the Shop in Stages

A lathe may also be included in this group, depending on the type of work to be done. A portable saber saw may be substituted for the band saw for awhile, although it is less convenient for many operations.

This basic group of tools will allow the woodworker to build many items, such as furniture, cabinets, other household items, and toys.

This equipment should be the best that the budget will allow because it will continue to be the core of the shop, even if other machines and tools are added later. This is especially true of the table saw. It is the important machine in most wood shops and is used on almost every project.

Stage II: The Next Step

There are several machines that will make some woodworking operations easier or faster. These include:

- Drill press
- Power miter saw
- Combination disc–belt sander

Figure 6–21 Heavy-duty dust collector (Delta Industrial Machinery Corp.).

- Dust collector
- Portable belt sander

The drill press can be used with a sanding drum as a spindle sander and can be fitted with a mortising attachment to serve as a hollow chisel mortiser.

It may be hard to spend money on a dust-collection system when there are other neat woodworking machines that you could spend the money on, but a dust collector will make woodworking much more enjoyable and healthy. It may be nothing more than a heavy-duty shop vacuum that can be wheeled from one machine to another as needed. The shop vacuum should have a 2½-in.-diameter hose, rather than the smaller 1¼-in. size. Many machines are available with dust hoods to fit this size of hose or hoods can be built from plywood or sheet metal.

There are also larger dust systems that mount on standard metal 55-gallon drums. Some of these have several hoses so they can handle several machines at once. These are machines for the seriously addicted woodworker! A heavy-duty dust collector is shown in Fig. 6–21.

Stage III: The "Nice-to-Have" Machines

Just about any machine could be included in this category, but some of the most useful ones include:

- Planer
- Shaper
- Overarm router
- Radial arm saw
- Band resaw
- Bench grinder

The planer allows you to plane boards to exact thicknesses. If you need ½-in.-thick drawer sides, for example, with a planer you can easily make them. It also allows you to buy rough lumber rather than finished lumber, with some savings. (You would have to buy a *lot* of rough lumber to save the cost of a planer, but it may help ease your conscience for spending money on a planer!)

One big advantage of a planer is that, after edge gluing boards, you can run them through the planer to make them perfectly flat. With a jointer and planer, you can also straighten warped or crooked boards by face jointing one face flat on the jointer and then planing the other surface parallel with the planer.

The shaper is excellent for making moldings found on some types of traditional furniture. It also makes it relatively easy to make frame and panel doors.

The overarm router is usually considered to be an industrial machine, but in recent years several manufacturers have come out with smaller models or models that use a normal, heavy-duty portable router (Fig. 6–22). They make it easy to do blind dados, internal routing, and routing with patterns.

Figure 6-22 Overarm router that uses a portable router (Sears, Roebuck & Co.).

Band resaws are somewhat specialized for the average home shop, although some are designed to accept a narrow blade and can be used as a normal bandsaw. For the serious woodworker who has access to wood such as small logs or large branches, the machine could pay for itself in lumber cost savings.

The bench grinder can be used (along with an oil or water stone) to sharpen hand tools. A wire wheel can also be mounted to remove rust from metal objects.

The machines described in this chapter represent a very large investment if all are purchased at the same time. However, it is not necessary to have all of them in order to enjoy woodworking. Many of these machines can be purchased used and, if they are given reasonable care, can be sold later at no loss if you decide to buy a better model.

7 Equipment Adjustment and Maintenance

Equipment that is properly adjusted and maintained is a joy to use and contributes to good-quality work. On the other hand, using equipment that is out of adjustment is unpleasant and even dangerous. Even new woodworking equipment is not always properly aligned and adjusted, so it is good for the woodworker to be familiar with the basic machine adjustments. The adjustment and alignment settings are the same in most cases, regardless of the brand name of the machine. Only the method of making the adjustment will change.

In this chapter, we will discuss lubrication for woodworking machines, general maintenance checks, troubleshooting procedures, and then maintenance and adjustments for some of the common woodworking machines. The final section will describe the procedure for sharpening hand tools and machine cutters. Always be sure to unplug the machine or turn off its circuit breaker before performing maintenance on any machine.

LUBRICATION

Lubrication of woodworking machines is a big problem because of the difficulty of keeping sawdust from the lubricant. Most conventional petroleum-based lubricants catch and hold fine sawdust. This dust mixes with oil or grease and makes a thick paste that eventually becomes dry and hard, making it almost impossible for moving parts to slide. This can be a real problem in gears used to raise or tilt a table saw blade, for example. Other problem areas are sliding ways on jointers and planers and trunnions on table saws. Fortunately, the bearings on most of these machines are sealed ball bearings, so dust is not a problem there.

There are three lubricants that work well in the problem areas. One of these is paste wax (Johnson's paste wax works very well). Paste wax can be used for many sliding surfaces such as table saw trunnions and bed ways on jointers and planers. The same paste wax should be used on all machine surfaces on which wood must slide. The table tops on table saws, jointers, planers, band saws, and shapers should be waxed and buffed periodically. The same is true for guide fences. Many of these table surfaces are machined cast iron. The wax will fill the pores in the metal and prevent rust from humidity in the air, from moisture from fingerprints, and the like. It also makes it easy to push the wood through the machine.

The second lubricant is a silicone spray or a very light spray lubricant such as WD-40. This can be used for sliding surfaces that are inaccessible for applying paste wax.

The third lubricant is a white lithium grease such as Lubriplate. This is used where you *have* to have grease, such as the worm and rack gears for a table saw. This grease does not have as much tendency to build up with sawdust as other greases.

If a machine has grease fittings for bearings or other purposes, use the grease recommended by the manufacturer. If no instructions are available, a multipurpose automotive chassis grease is usually used.

Some machines such as scroll saws may have an oil reservoir. Again, the manufacturers' recommendations should be followed.

Some portable power tools have worm drive power transmission systems. Some portable saws and belt sanders are so equipped. The lubrication requirements on these machines are very critical, and only the special lubricants supplied or recommended by the manufacturer should be used. The sliding loads on the gear surface are very high, and using an improper lubricant for even a short period of time can result in gear failure.

OTHER COMMON MAINTENANCE CHECKS

For most woodworking machines, the power is transmitted from an electric motor to the machine through pulleys and one or more V-belts. This system is normally quite reliable and efficient, but it can be the source of many mysterious noises and vibrations.

V-belts can look good, but be worn out. With age and wear, the sides (which transmit the power) can become glazed and slick, causing them to slip under load. They also may not be worn evenly, causing vibration or thumping noises.

Many machines use common V-belts that can be purchased at a hardware store or automotive parts store. If the machine has two or more belts running together, they should be replaced as matched sets so that they will transmit power equally.

Setting the tension on a new V-belt requires judgment. It is sometimes recommended that the tension be adjusted so that the belt can be moved back and forth $\frac{1}{2}$ in. when moved at the center of a span between two pulleys. However, this would probably result in the belt being too loose if the span were very short or too tight if the span were very long. If the belt is too tight, it will place unnecessary loads on the bearings in both the machine and the motor and will cause rapid wear of the belt and pulleys. It is best to set the belt only as tight as necessary to prevent slipping under maximum load.

Pulleys should be checked when changing belts. Most pulleys on woodworking machines are made of a fairly soft metal. If the grooves are worn wide enough that the belt touches the bottom of the groove, the belt will slip and be very noisy. V-belts are designed to transmit power *only* on the *sides* of the belt. If the pulley grooves are badly worn, the pulley should be replaced.

Another common problem with pulleys is set screws that work loose. Most pulleys are keyed to the shaft with a small key and then locked in place with a set screw. If this set screw works loose, the pulley will rock back and forth on the shaft and the hole in the pulley will become elliptical. This will cause very bad vibration in the machine. In some cases, the key will work its way out of the groove and then the pulley will merely spin on the shaft.

The cure for self-loosening set screws is to use one of the commercial thread-locking compounds, such as Locktite. It is a good idea to use this even when assembling a new machine. Locktite comes in different grades, and some of them are so strong that you would have to destroy the threads to disassemble the parts. Others can be reused. Be sure to get the right one. If using the Locktite brand, the blue-colored thread locker is the one to use for this application. Make sure that the thread surfaces are clean and free of any oil. Put a few drops on the threads and assemble as usual. The lock screw will not back out from vibration, but can still be disassembled if necessary. Locktite is available at automotive parts stores.

Adjusting the preload on sliding assemblies is another common operation with woodworking equipment. The places where this is done are on the dovetail ways on jointer tables, the sliding ways on planer tables, and the column clamp on radial arm saws. These must be adjusted loosely enough so that the surfaces will slide freely for adjustment, but tightly enough to limit excess play. For example, if you grab the end of a jointer table and lift, you should not feel any free movement, but it still must be loose enough to slide freely when the table is adjusted up or down.

This adjustment is usually made by tightening or loosening a row of set screws that act on gibs in the sliding mechanism. The procedure is to loosen all the screws so that the table can be adjusted freely up or down. Then tighten one set screw until the table cannot be adjusted. Then back off the set screw until the table can just be moved freely. Repeat this in turn with each of the other set screws. These set screws usually have locknuts that should be tightened to keep the adjustment from changing.

TROUBLESHOOTING MACHINE NOISES OR VIBRATIONS

When a machine is running, it can sometimes be difficult to determine the source of an unusual noise. It is best if you can isolate possible sources of noise by removing belts and only running part of the machine.

For example, to troubleshoot a band saw, the drive belt could be removed and the motor run alone to check for vibration. Check the pulley and set screw as well as the drive belt. If everything is satisfactory, replace the drive belt, but remove the blade. In this way you can run the bottom wheel only, to check for vibration. If none is found, then check the blade for being bent or misaligned at the weld and place it on the wheels. The rubber tires on the wheels should be checked at this time to see if they show any cracks or lumps. Then mount the blade and run the entire machine. This procedure of isolating and testing various parts of a machine will usually pinpoint the source of noise or vibration. A mechanics stethoscope is also handy for locating the source of unusual noises.

TABLE SAW ADJUSTMENT

One of the most critical adjustments on a table saw is to align the miter gage slots in the table with the blade. They must be exactly parallel with the blade to obtain accurate crosscuts and miters. They are also utilized to align the rip fence. These miter slots may be aligned in one of two ways, depending on the construction of the table saw. Most large, floor-model table saws have the saw works mounted in the cabinet, and the table is bolted to the cabinet. In this case, it is merely necessary to loosen the three or four bolts that mount the table and then move the table in relation to the blade.

On many smaller bench-top saws, the saw works are hung from the underside of the table. In this case, you must find the bolts under the table and loosen them so that the saw blade can be moved relative to the table.

Figure 7–1 Using a miter gage and pencil to align the miter slot with the saw blade.

In either case, the alignment procedure is the same once the table top or saw assembly is loose. To align the saw, you need a sliding miter gage and a pencil or wood dowel with a nearly sharp point on one end. Place the miter gage in the miter slot and use the dowel or pencil against the face of the miter gage to locate the edge of a saw tooth as shown in Fig. 7-1. (The blade should be at its maximum height for this operation.) Mark the tooth used and rotate the saw blade backward until the marked tooth is at the table level at the back of the blade. Slide the miter gage back to the rear of the blade, being careful not to move the pencil or dowel. Check the same tooth as in Fig. 7-2. The pencil or dowel should just rub on the edge of the tooth if the miter slot is parallel with the blade. Move the miter gage and marked tooth back to the front and try it again. If necessary, the table can be rotated slightly until the miter slot is parallel with the blade. (On bench model saws, the motor and blade assembly will have to be moved under the table.) When the slot is aligned, tighten the bolts and check it once more.

The rip fence can then be aligned with the miter slot. Most rip fences have an adjustment for front-to-back alignment. Different systems of adjustment are used by different manufacturers. One system is shown in Fig. 7-3.

In any case, the rip fence should be either exactly parallel with the miter slot or should angle to the right at the rear by $\frac{1}{64}$ to $\frac{1}{32}$ in. In this case, the fence will be slightly farther from the blade at the rear than at the front. The latter is better than having the fence exactly parallel with the miter slot, because wood will have less tendency to bind or "pinch" between the blade and rip fence. If the rear of the

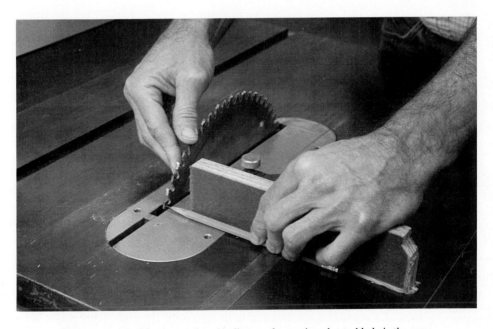

Figure 7-2 Checking to see that the distance from miter slot to blade is the same at the rear of the blade as it was at the front.

Table Saw Adjustment

Figure 7-3 Adjusting the rip fence parallel with the miter slot.

fence is angled much farther away from the saw, however, boards will tend to pull away from the rip fence.

After the fence has been aligned, it should be moved and then locked down next to the miter slot to see that it always assumes the same setting each time it is locked. Some saw fences lock on a rail in front and in back of the machine. In this case, they have a linkage between the front and rear of the fence that must be adjusted so that the fence locks to the front rail first. As the lock handle is pushed downward, the fence should lock to the front rail and align itself. As the lock handle is fully engaged, the rear of the fence should lock to the back rail. If this linkage is out of adjustment, the rear lock may lock first, thus not allowing the fence to "self-align," or the rear may not lock at all.

Most table saws have adjustable stops on the blade tilt mechanism. These stops should be adjusted to stop the blade at 0° (perpendicular to the table) and at 45° for miter cuts. The stops are usually found inside the saw cabinet. A combination square can be used to check the adjustment.

Some miter gages have adjustable stops for making 90° and 45° cuts to the left and right. These can both be set using a framing square as shown in Figs. 7-4 and 7-5.

To set the miter gage at 90°, put the short leg of the framing square along the face of the miter gage and the long leg along the right-hand miter slot.

To set the miter gage at 45°, put the long leg of the square against the face of the miter gage and rotate the miter gage to approximately 45°. The exact setting

Figure 7-4 Using a framing square to set the miter gage at 90°.

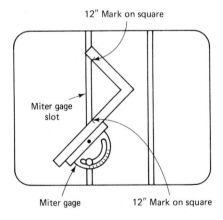

12″ Mark on square

Miter gage
slot

Miter gage   12″ Mark on square

Figure 7-5 Using a framing square
to set the miter gage at 45°.

is made by aligning the 12-in. marks on the inside scales of both legs of the square with one edge of the miter slot.

After the adjustments are made, the trunnions and other sliding surfaces can be lubricated with paste wax and the gears lubricated with a light coat of Lubriplate. Apply a coat of paste wax to the table surface, the rip fence, and the rails that the rip fence slides on. Buff the wax when it is nearly dry.

Table Saw Adjustment

Saw blades that have pitch or resin burned on them can be cleaned by spraying oven cleaner on them, letting them set for a few minutes, and rinsing with water. Read and follow the precautions on the oven cleaner can.

JOINTER ADJUSTMENTS

The most critical adjustment on a jointer is the height of the outfeed table in relation to the cutting arc of cutters. The outfeed table must be at exactly the same height as the knife when it is at the top of the cutting circle (Fig. 7–6.)

If the outfeed table is low, the result will be a "snipe" on the trailing edge of each board as the back end of the board leaves the infeed table and drops into the cutter. This is shown in Fig. 7–7.

Knife arc

Figure 7–6 Jointer outfeed table must be at same height as knife at top of cutting arc.

Figure 7–7 A jointer outfeed table that is set too low will produce a "snipe" on the trailing end of the cut.

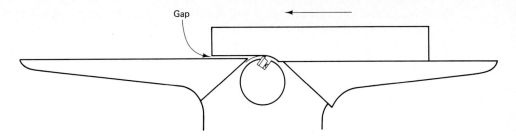

Gap

Figure 7-8 Gap under planed surface when outfeed table is set low.

If the outfeed table is high, the board will climb off the infeed table as it travels by the cutters. The cut will become shallower as the board moves along until it quits cutting altogether. The result will be a tapered cut. The beginning of the cut will be the full depth, but will taper off to nothing. If another cut is attempted, the result will be the same. Eventually, the board will become much narrower on the front than the back.

The easiest way to set the outfeed table is to set it low to start with. Use a board such as a 1 in. by 6 in. about 24 to 30 in. long. Set the infeed table to take a $\frac{1}{16}$-in. cut. Start the machine and run the board over the cutters about 6 in. If the outfeed table is low, there will be a gap between the board and the outfeed table (Fig. 7–8). Raise the outfeed table until it just touches the board. Complete the cut, making sure that the machine does not snipe the end of the board. A double-check can be made by running the board about 1 in. into the machine and backing it out. Pencil an $\times$ on the just cut surface. Reverse the board and run it all the way through. If the outfeed table is correct, the jointer knives will just touch, but not remove the $\times$. It may take several tries to get it right.

Some jointers do not have adjustable outfeed tables. In this case, the knife height in the cutter head must be adjusted. This is much more difficult, but must be done if the machine is to cut properly. This procedure is described later under *installing knives*.

Some jointers have adjustable stops to set the fence at 90° to the table or at 45°. These can be adjusted with a combination square.

Installing jointer knives.   Sooner or later the knives get dull or nicked and must be changed. If they get a nick, but are otherwise sharp, it is possible to move one knife slightly to the left and the other to the right so that the nicks in the knives are not in line. This will eliminate the ridge that nicked knives would otherwise leave on the board. This procedure should not be used, however, if the jointer is to be used for cutting rabbets.

Installing jointer knives is a very critical operation, especially if the outfeed table is not adjustable. It is desirable to have two sets of knives for a jointer so that they can be changed one knife at a time, rather than removing the entire set and then installing them after sharpening. If all the knives are removed, it "unloads" the cutter head. Then, when the first knife is installed and tightened, the head is slightly distorted.

When the second knife is installed, it will distort the head some more and will actually change the knife height and the torque on the locking screws on the first knife. Thus, after these knives have been installed, it will be necessary to go around the head at least one more time, resetting and retightening each knife. If an extra set of knives is available and one knife only is removed and replaced at a time, this will not be necessary.

In any case, the knife height should be set to the outfeed table. There are several ways to do this. The Magna-set knife-setting jig shown in Fig. 7–9 works very well for this purpose.

Another method that can be used requires placing a piece of straight hardwood on the outfeed table so that it extends about 2 in. over the cutter head. Put a pencil mark on the wood block right at the front edge of the outfeed table as shown in Fig. 7–10. Then rotate the cutter head in its normal direction until the knife moves the wood block forward slightly, and put another mark on the board where it now rests over the front edge of the outfeed table (Fig. 7–11). Adjust the knife height so that it pulls the board about ¼ in. forward as a knife is rotated through its cutting arc. Now check the knife height at the right, left, and center of each knife.

If the knife is level, it will drag the board the same distance each rotation. With the two marks on the board, you merely set the board on the outfeed table, with the first mark on the front edge of the outfeed table, and then rotate the cutter. The board should be moved forward until the second mark lines up. If the board is not moved far enough, raise the knife and try again. If it is moved too far, lower the knife. The center of each knife must also be checked because it is possible to bow the knife when tightening the locking screws.

Each knife in turn should be set the same way. This will get all the knives level and at the same height. The outfeed table can then be set as described earlier. This procedure can be used for jointers with nonadjustable outfeed tables, but the marks on the board should only be about ⅛ in. apart.

Figure 7–9 Magna-Set magnetic jointer knife setting jig (Quest Industries).

Equipment Adjustment and Maintenance   Chap. 7

Figure 7-10 Marking the edge of the outfeed table on a hardwood board.

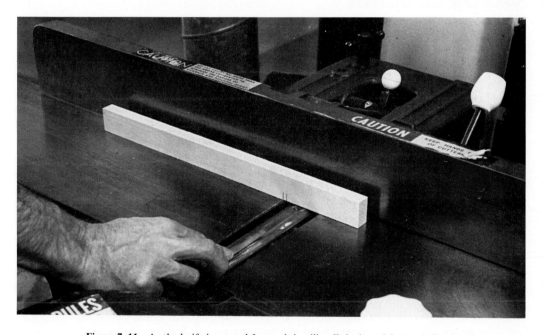

Figure 7-11 As the knife is rotated forward, it will pull the board forward slightly. The new position is then marked. Each knife is then set so that it moves the board the same distance.

Jointer Adjustments

Sharpening jointer knives. Much has been written on how to sharpen your own jointer knives, but it is almost impossible to get really good results in a typical home shop. It is best to send them out to someone who is equipped to do it right. The sharpening shop should have a grinder that provides coolant to keep the knives from overheating and expanding while being ground. Knives have come back from a sharpener with the cutting edge over $\frac{1}{32}$ in. lower in the center than at the outsides. This indicates that the knife got hot and expanded, causing the center to rise while being ground. When it cooled, the center was low. These knives are useless until being reground straight.

Even though good-quality knife sharpening seems expensive, it does not have to be done very often if only clean lumber is used. Avoid running wood with paint or other finish on it. Wood that has had nails in it or that has been set on the floor where bits of rock and sand can be embedded in it should also be avoided.

Knives that are slightly dull but otherwise good can be honed with a fine oil stone without removing them from the machine. This can prolong the time between grindings.

After the knives have been installed, the depth scale pointer can be adjusted by raising the infeed table so that, when running a board over the knives, they just touch but do not cut. The depth-of-cut pointer should then be adjusted to read zero.

The table and fence surfaces should then be waxed and buffed.

BAND SAW ADJUSTMENTS

The main adjustments on a band saw are the blade tension, the blade tracking, the adjustment of the side guides, and the adjustment of the blade support guides. If the band saw is very old, the condition of the rubber tires on the blade wheels should be checked. If they are badly cracked or have grooves worn in them, the blade will not track properly and they must be replaced. Tires should be available from the machine manufacturer. Some are stretched on and others are glued with an adhesive such as plybond cement. They must be stretched evenly to avoid stretching the rubber thin in some areas, which will cause uneven running.

If the tires are in good shape, the first adjustment in installing a new blade is to set the tension. Most band saws have a scale for setting tension according to the width of the blade. The top wheel is generally adjusted upward to increase the tension.

To set the tracking, the side and rear blade guides should be moved well away from the blade so that they will not interfere with the blade tracking. The tracking adjustment is made by tilting the top wheel while turning the blade by hand. The wheel is adjusted until the blade tracks on the center of the wheel. At this point, you should also see that the blade tracks at the center of the lower wheel. If not, the set screw holding the top wheel to the shaft can be loosened and the wheel moved in or out on the shaft as necessary.

After the tracking has been properly adjusted, the blade side guides can be adjusted. These guides may be either ball bearings or hard steel blocks. There will be a set of guides above the table and a set below. They should be adjusted very close to the blade, but not quite touching. One way to do this is to wrap a piece of paper around the blade and adjust the guides so that they just touch the paper. Lock them in place and remove the paper. The blade should not touch these guides when the saw is running. The side guides are to prevent the blade from twisting when making curved cuts.

The rear blade support guides are adjusted close to the back of the blade, but again not touching. They should not rotate when the saw is idling. They will start to spin as soon as a board is pushed into the saw. They prevent the blade from being pushed off the rear of the wheels while cutting.

The band saw may have a tilting table. This can be set perpendicular to the blade using a try square or a combination square.

RADIAL ARM SAW ADJUSTMENTS

The radial arm saw has a number of adjustments to be checked. They must be checked in sequence, starting at the column base and working toward the saw itself. If adjustments are made to the saw blade, for example, and then an adjustment is made to the arm, this could change the first adjustment.

The first adjustment is usually to remove any excess play between the column and the column base. This is done by loosening all the gib screws on the column so that it can be cranked up and down freely. Then one screw is tightened until the column cannot be adjusted. Then the screw is loosened until the column can just be moved freely. This is repeated with the rest of the screws.

Another adjustment is to check for excess play in the carriage that allows the saw to travel along the arm. There is usually an adjustment to compensate for wear on the track. On some saws, the carriage rides on four ball bearings. The two on the right are mounted on eccentric shafts and can be rotated to take up excess clearance caused by wear in the track.

Other saws have four replaceable round rods mounted inside the arm. These rods form the bearing surface. They can be rotated when they become worn on one side.

The bearings should be tight enough so that the saws have almost no side play, but they must be loose enough so that the saw return spring will pull the saw back freely after a cut.

The arm on the radial arm saw is adjusted perpendicular to the fence by laying a framing square along the fence as shown in Fig 7–12. Adjust if necessary. Most saws have a 0° (or 90°) positive stop that allows the arm to be reset perpendicular to the fence after it has been moved for angle cutting. This stop should be adjusted while the arm is perpendicular to the fence.

The next adjustment is to make sure that the blade is perpendicular to the table. This is done with a try square, as shown in Fig. 7–13. This adjustment must be made with the 90° indexing pin in place so that when the angle is changed it will return to 90° when the pin is engaged.

The next adjustment is to check for heeling. This is a condition in which the

Figure 7-12 Adjusting the arm perpendicular to the guide fence.

Figure 7-13 Adjusting the blade perpendicular to the table.

Equipment Adjustment and Maintenance   Chap. 7

blade is not parallel with the arm as it travels along the arm (Fig. 7–14). This will show up in the form of chipping on the top side of a board being cut. The chipping occurs at the rear of the blade as it comes up through the top surface of a board. It could be on either the right or left side of the cut depending on which way the blade is heeling.

Checking for heeling is more difficult than the other alignment checks. A rough check can be made by using a framing square with the long leg against the fence and the short leg tipped up slightly across the face of the saw blade. The best test, however, is to crosscut a piece of hardwood plywood. The very thin outside veneers found on most hardwood plywoods are very prone to chipping.

If chipping consistently occurs on one side of the cut, the saw should be adjusted. This adjustment involves rotating the motor on a vertical axis in the yoke that holds the motor. On many saws, this is accomplished by loosening set screws on the rear arm of the yoke. To rotate the saw clockwise (from the top), for example, one would loosen the set screw on the right and tighten the one on the left.

A final check is to make sure that the table surface is level with the arm. This is done by shimming under the table surface as necessary. This step is not necessary for normal crosscutting. However, if the saw is to be used for cutting dados and rabbets, the table must be level with the arm or the dado will be deeper on one side than the other. This can be checked by raising the blade so that a small piece of ¼-in. plywood will just slip between the blade and the table. Then move the saw in and out to several positions and check the table height by slipping the plywood block under the blade. Shim the table as necessary. Swing the arm 45° left and 45° right and check the table at those settings also.

The sliding lower blade guards that attach to the hood guard on most saws should be checked to be sure that they slide up and down freely. It may be necessary to file off burrs and wax the sliding surfaces.

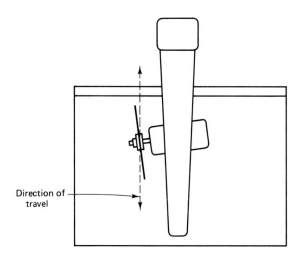

Direction of travel

Figure 7–14 Heeling is a condition in which the blade is not parallel with the direction of travel.

PLANER ADJUSTMENTS

Fortunately, planers do not usually require frequent adjustment, but there are many adjustments on some machines, and they must be accurately set if the planer is to feed properly and produce smooth surfaces. A cross section of a typical planer is shown in Fig. 7–15.

The cutter head is usually mounted in bearing housings machined in the main machine casting. Almost everything else is adjustable. The table can be adjusted on either side to level it with the cutter head, and the idle rolls in the table can be adjusted for height on many machines. The infeed and outfeed rolls can be adjusted up or down on each end, as can the chip breaker and pressure bar.

The first check is to make sure that the table is level with the cutter head (not the knives). If the table is not level, it should be set according to the manufacturer's directions. (The low side should always be raised, rather than trying to drop the high side.) A planer bed gage with a dial indicator is good for checking this setting. However, this setting can be checked by inserting a block of hardwood about 4 in. long under the head on one side and then raising the table until it just touches the head. Move the block to the other end of the head and try it again. If it just slips under both ends, the table is properly adjusted.

The idle rollers on the table can be set for height as per the manufacturer's specifications. If only kiln-dried hardwoods are to be used, the smoothest cut will be obtained by having the idle rollers set flush with the table surface. It will then be necessary to keep the table surface well waxed, since the boards will be sliding on the table rather than rolling. Otherwise, the rollers should be set about 0.005 in.

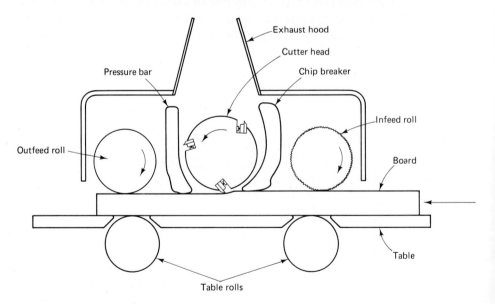

Figure 7-15 Cross section of a typical planer.

above the table surface. If they are set much higher than this, the boards tend to get dips planed into the surface as they roll on and off the rollers.

Installing planer knives is similar to installing jointer knives, except that the knives' height is set relative to the head rather than an outfeed table. A jig such as the one made by Magna Set (Fig. 7–16) makes the job easier. Most planer manufacturers supply a template or jig of some type for setting knife height. If the knife height is not specified, the knives should be set so that there is about $\frac{1}{32}$ in. between the back of the knife bevel and the cutter head, as shown in Fig. 7–17. It is very important that the knives be level with the head from end to end and that each knife be exactly the same height.

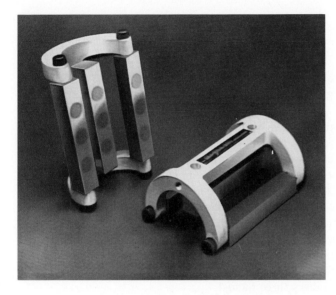

Figure 7–16 Magna-Set planer knife setting jig (Quest Industries).

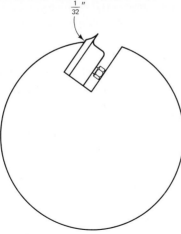

$\frac{1}{32}$ ″

Figure 7–17 Back of planer or jointer knives should extend approximately $\frac{1}{32}$ in. beyond head.

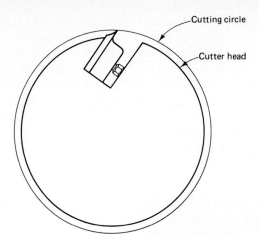

Cutting circle

Cutter head

Figure 7-18 The cutting circle or arc is used as the reference for all planer settings except for leveling the table.

The circle described by the knife edges as they rotate is called the cutting circle or cutting arc. All remaining settings are made relative to the low point on the cutting circle (Fig. 7-18).

If a bed gage is available, it may be put under the knife edge when it is at the lowest point in its arc to establish the cutting circle height. Then, without moving the table, the infeed roller, chip breaker, pressure bar, and outfeed roller heights can be set. The infeed and outfeed rollers are set 0.032 in. below the cutting circle. The chip breaker is set at 0 and the pressure bar is set at 0.005 in. above the cutting arc.

If a bed gage is not available, the settings can be made as follows. Use a block of hardwood about 4 in. long. Put a 0.032-in. feeler gage on the block and slide the block and gage under the cutter head. (A thin, flexible, 6-in. steel pocket ruler is usually about the right thickness and may be used in place of a feeler gage.) Raise the table until the feeler gage on the block just touches the knife at the bottom of its rotation. This usually requires three hands!

After the table height is set, remove the feeler gage, and, using the block alone as a gage, set the infeed and outfeed rolls. The pressure bar height may be set with the block and a 0.036 in. feeler gage. The chip breaker height is set with the block and the feeler gage.

After the planer is adjusted, the table surface should be waxed and buffed. The bottom surfaces of the chip breaker and pressure bar should also be waxed.

Plane a board and accurately measure its thickness and adjust the pointer on the thickness scale accordingly.

COMMON WOODWORKING MACHINE PROBLEMS

Table 7-1 lists some of the most commonly encountered machine problems and their most likely causes.

TABLE 7-1

Problem	Probable cause
Table saw	
Boards pull away from fence when ripping	Fence angled away from blade at rear, or uneven set on saw teeth
Boards bind between blade and fence	Fence angled toward blade at rear
Cannot cut accurate 90° cuts or miters	Miter slots not aligned with blade
Jointer	
Boards are sniped on trailing end of cut	Outfeed table too low
Board "climbs"; the cut gets shallower as the board is run until it quits cutting altogether	Outfeed table too high
Unusually large ripple knife marks	One knife higher than the others, or feed speed too fast
Band saw	
Blade will not track properly	Rubber tires on the wheels are grooved, or the top wheel angle is not adjusted, or the side or rear support guides are set so that they interfere with the blade tracking.
Blade wanders when cutting	Blade dull, or side guides too far from blade
Radial arm saw	
Chipping on top surface of board	Heeling
Blade wobbles during cut	Dull blade or wrong type of blade, or excess play in carriage bearings
Planer	
Boards are hard to feed	Table needs to be waxed, or height adjustment wrong for infeed rollers, or pressure bar too low
Boards are tapered (thicker on one side than the other)	Table not parallel with head, or one of more knives set higher on one side
Boards get a snipe on trailing end of cut	Pressure bar to high
Boards have snipe or ripples near both ends	Table rollers too high
Boards twist when being fed	Infeed or outfeed rollers high on one side

TOOL SHARPENING

Many tools can be easily sharpened by the woodworker with just a little practice. Chisels, plane blades, lathe tools, hand scrapers, auger bits, twist drill bits, and some router and shaper cutters can be sharpened in the typical home shop. Jointer and planer knives and any carbide cutters should be professionally sharpened. Steel circular saw blades and hand saws are sometimes sharpened by woodworkers, but they are quite difficult to do successfully. The cost of having these tools sharpened professionally is surprisingly low when you consider the amount of time it takes an amateur to do the same job by hand.

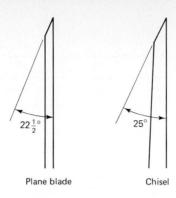

Figure 7-19 Angles for sharpening plane blades and chisels.

Plane blade   Chisel

Chisels and plane blades. The sharpening of chisels and plane blades is quite similar. They are ground with a single bevel as shown in Fig. 7–19. The angle is usually about $22\frac{1}{2}°$ for a plane blade and $25°$ for a chisel. The initial grinding is done on a grinder if possible. If there are any nicks in the cutting edge, these may be ground out by holding the chisel horizontal and grinding the edge blunt until the nick is gone. The bevel is then ground by holding the tool on the tool rest at the proper angle (Fig. 7–20). The tool should be dipped in water frequently while grinding to keep it cool. As the cutting edge gets thinner and thinner during sharpening, it becomes easier to overheat the steel. It will quickly turn blue or black when it is overheated. This spoils the temper in the steel and must be avoided by grinding lightly and cooling the tool often.

After the bevel cutting edge has been ground with the grinder, the edge is honed on an oil stone. (Some people prefer Japanese water stones.) A relatively soft, coarse stone is used first and then a fine, harder stone is used to finish the job.

To hone a chisel or plane blade, put some light oil (for oil stones) on the stone and set the chisel on the bevel. Lift the handle slightly so that just the cutting edge is on the stone (Fig. 7–21). Push the chisel so that you are honing against the cutting edge. When you finish a stroke, lift the chisel off the stone, bring it back, and repeat. After a dozen or so strokes, carefully lay the flat face of the chisel flat on the stone and slide it against the cutting edge to remove the wire edge formed by grinding and honing the bevel edge. This sequence may have to be repeated several times, first

Figure 7-20 Grinding the bevel on a chisel.

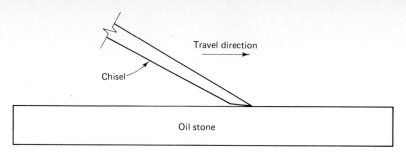

Figure 7-21 Honing a chisel on an oil stone.

on the coarse stone and then on the fine one. Some woodworkers prefer a very hard, fine stone for a final honing.

Chisels and plane blades can usually be rehoned several times without being reground. In fact, they can be sharpened indefinitely by honing only, but it is more work to maintain the proper bevel.

Lathe tools. Lathe tools are sharpened in somewhat the same manner as chisels, but they are a little more difficult because some of them have curved edges. The proper angle for grinding lathe tools is shown in Fig. 7–22. Notice that the skew

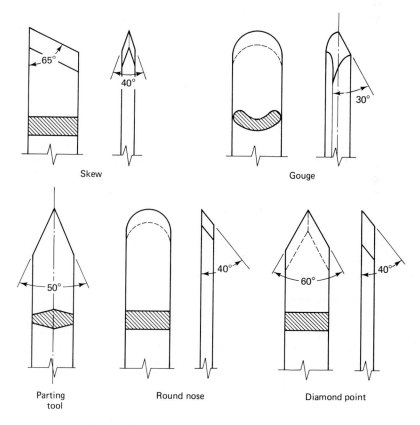

Figure 7-22 Proper angles for sharpening lathe tools.

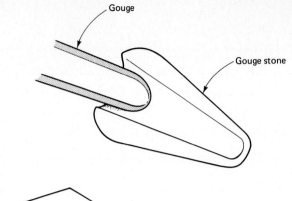

Figure 7-23 The gouge is honed with a gouge slip stone.

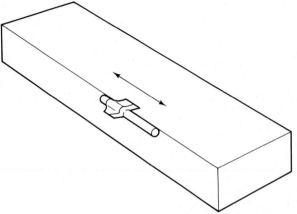

Figure 7-24 Honing the flat side of a router bit on an oil stone.

and the parting tool have bevels on both sides. Other than that, they are ground and honed in much the same way as a chisel.

The gouge is the most difficult to sharpen. Its bevel is ground on the grinder and then it is honed, first on the outside and then the inside, with a cone-shaped gouge slip stone (Fig. 7–23). Care must be taken to keep the slip stone flat on the inside of the gouge so the cutting edge is not rounded.

Some steel router bits and shaper cutters can be touched up on an oil stone. Lay the flat side of one of the cutter wings on the edge of an oil stone and rub it back and forth (Fig. 7–24). It is usually best not to try to work on the bevel of the cutter, because it would be very easy to change the shape of the pattern.

Hand scraper.   The hand scraper is one of the most effective hand tools in woodworking, but it must be *sharp* to be of any use. It takes a little practice to master the technique of sharpening it, but it is worth it. A fine, single-cut file and a burnisher are needed to sharpen the hand scraper.

The first step in sharpening the hand scraper is to remove the old burr from the edge. This is done by laying the blade flat on an oil stone and honing the burr off. Do not use a file for this purpose. A file may scratch the face of the scraper.

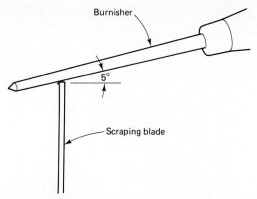

Burnisher

5°

Scraping blade

Figure 7-25 Forming a cutting edge on a scraper with a burnisher.

This will result in a small nick in the cutting burr everytime the scraper is sharpened. After the old burr is removed, the blade is put in a vise and the edge is filed flat and perpendicular to the face.

The final step is to produce the new cutting edge. The burnisher is set on the edge of the scraper at about a 5° angle from horizontal and is then slid along the edge with considerable downward pressure to form a new cutting burr (Fig. 7-25).

Start near the tip of the burnisher and slide it outward as you slide it along the edge of the scraper. This will draw the steel out and form a very small cutting burr on the edge of the tool. It will take several good, firm passes with the burnisher to form a satisfactory cutting burr. This procedure can be repeated on the other corner of the same edge to produce a cutting burr on both sides of the blade.

Auger bits. Auger bits, multispur bits, Foerstner bits, and speed bore bits may be sharpened with an auger bit file. This file has flat tapered ends on both ends of the file. One end has teeth on the face, but none on the edges, and the other end has teeth on the edge, but none on the face (Fig. 7-26). Auger bits are filed on the inside edge of the scoring spurs (Fig. 7-27) and on the top side of the ramp that lifts the chip out of the hole (Fig. 7-28).. Be sure not to file on the outside edge of the scoring spur as this would reduce the cutting diameter of the bit.

Multispur bits are done in much the same way, with each of the spur teeth being sharpened on the front edge.

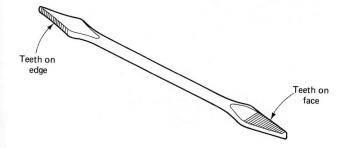

Teeth on edge

Teeth on face

Figure 7-26 Auger bit file.

Tool Sharpening

Figure 7-27 Filing the inside surface of the auger bit spur.

Figure 7-28 Filing the top side of the ramp.

Equipment Adjustment and Maintenance   Chap. 7

Twist drill bits.   Twist drill bits can be ground freehand on a grinder. This also takes considerable practice, but, once mastered, they can be sharpened very quickly. The point and cutting edges should be shaped as shown in Fig. 7-29.

The following procedure can be used for sharpening a twist drill bit. Hold one of the two cutting edges horizontal against the face of the grinding wheel. The shank of the bit will be angled downward approximately 5° from horizontal (Fig. 7-30). The bit should be held between the thumb and forefinger of the right hand about 1 to $1\frac{1}{2}$ in. from the tip and held at the shank end with the left hand. Start grinding against the cutting edge and, while grinding, slowly lower the shank end with the left hand. This will grind the relief angle behind the cutting edge. As the shank end of the bit is lowered, it is also rotated very slightly to the left. The bit is then rotated exactly 180°, and the process is repeated on the other cutting edge. Equal mounts must be ground from both sides to keep the chisel point exactly in the center.

As an aid to learning the proper grinding angle, take a fairly large twist bit with a properly ground edge and darken the ground surface with a dark felt marker

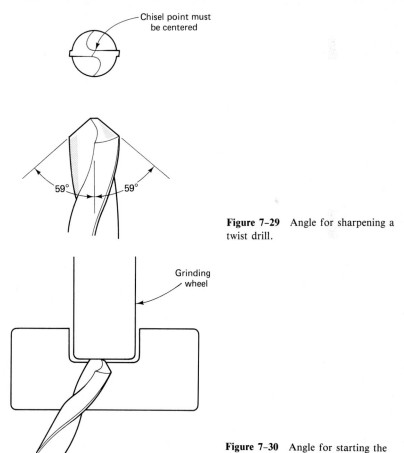

Chisel point must be centered

59°   59°

Figure 7-29   Angle for sharpening a twist drill.

Grinding wheel

Figure 7-30   Angle for starting the grinding on a twist drill bit (top view).

or blue layout dye. Then grind one of the cutting lips. If your grinding angle is not the same as the original, it will be obvious. Practice until you can remove all the dark marking with one light grinding pass.

The reward of working with properly maintained and adjusted machines and sharp hand tools is well worth the effort and practice necessary to learn to do the maintenance.

8 Projects

The following projects range from things that can be done in several evenings up to quite challenging projects. The first projects shown are designed to make your wood shop more efficient. Most of these can be built rather quickly.

SLIDING CROSSCUT JIG FOR A TABLE SAW

A sliding crosscut jig (Fig. 8-1) is an essential accessory for a table saw. It is much easier to use and more accurate than a miter gage for trimming the uneven ends of glued-up panels. It can also be used to cross-cut large plywood parts.

The base is made of ½- or ¾-in. plywood. The front and back boards are straight 2 in. by 4 in. boards or other similar material, and the guide slats are a hardwood such as oak or maple. They are spaced to fit the miter gage grooves in your table saw. If fine sandpaper is glued to the face of the fence, it will help keep boards in place while they are being cut.

It is very important that the guide slats be exactly perpendicular to the guide fence. Use a framing square to align the first slat and glue it in place. Then set the jig on the saw with the first slat located in the miter gage groove. The second slat can now be accurately located by sliding it in the other miter gage groove and gluing it in place.

Figure 8-2 gives the cutting list for this project.

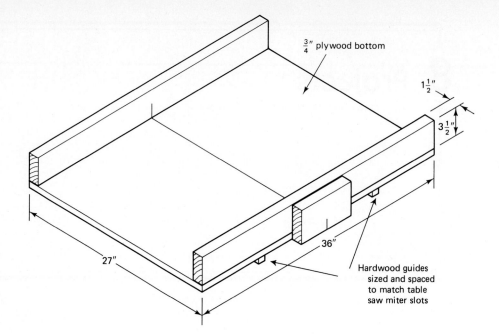

Figure 8-1 Sliding crosscut jig for table saw.

1 pc	¾ × 27 × 36 ″ Bottom (Plywood)
2 pc	1½ × 3½ × 36 ″ sides (solid lumber)
1 pc	1½ × 4¼ × 8 ″ guard (solid lumber)
2 pc	Guide strips sized to match miter grooves in table saw top

Figure 8-2 Sliding crosscut jig cutting list.

OFF-BEARING TABLE FOR A TABLE SAW

An off-bearing table (Figure 8–3) will contribute to the safety and convenience of using a table saw. When the table saw is not in use, the table can be used as a work bench. If storage space in the shop is scarce, an enclosed cabinet may be preferable. The cabinet top can serve as the off-bearing table, and the cabinet can provide storage for extra blades, push sticks, tools, and shop supplies.

The table or cabinet may be finished with a clear varnish, polyurethane, or lacquer or it may be painted.

Figure 8-4 gives the cutting list for this project.

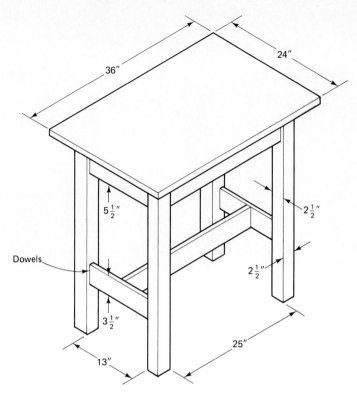

Figure 8-3 Off-bearing table for table saw.

1 pc	$\frac{3}{4} \times 24 \times 36''$	top (industrial particle board)
1 pc	$\frac{1}{8} \times 24 \times 36''$	top (tempered hardboard or plastic laminate)
4 pc	$2\frac{1}{2} \times 2\frac{1}{2} \times 33\frac{1}{4}''$	legs
2 pc	$\frac{3}{4} \times 5\frac{1}{2} \times 25''$	rails
2 pc	$\frac{3}{4} \times 5\frac{1}{2} \times 13''$	rails
2 pc	$\frac{3}{4} \times 3\frac{1}{2} \times 13''$	rails
1 pc	$\frac{3}{4} \times 3\frac{1}{2} \times 27\frac{1}{2}''$	rails
24 pc	$\frac{3}{8} \times 2''$	dowels

Figure 8-4 Off-bearing table cutting list.

WORKBENCHES

Some thought should be given to the type of woodworking you plan to do before building a work bench or benches. If cabinets and larger furniture items are to be built, a low (24 to 26 in. high) bench with a large flat top is best. This bench should

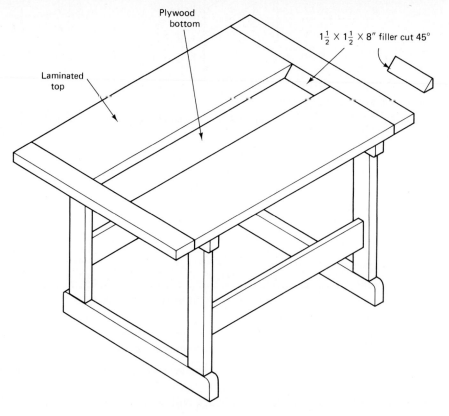

Figure 8-5 Workbench.

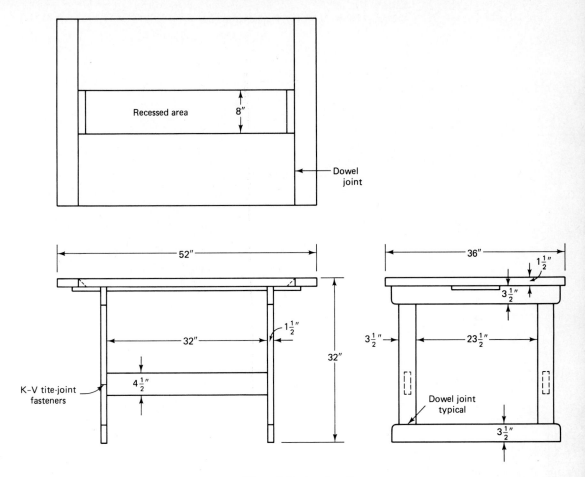

Figure 8-5 (continued)

be positioned away from any walls so that you can work all the way around the bench. Along with this bench, another higher bench (36 in.) would be placed against a wall. This higher bench is used for holding tools, hardware, and project parts that are being used. This bench (or cabinet) would also be equipped with a vise. Hand tools are often hung on the wall behind this bench. A bench such as this, along with a low assembly bench about 30 to 36 in. in front of it, makes a very efficient work area for assembling cabinets, furniture, and other larger projects.

If mostly smaller projects are contemplated, a single higher bench equipped with a vise would probably be best. These benches often have a recessed area near the center of the work surface for setting tools and small parts. Figure 8-5 shows a bench made of hard maple, but other woods may be used. A very serviceable top may be made by laminating two thicknesses of ¾-in. industrial particle board and covering the top with ⅛-in. tempered hardboard.

Workbenches **319**

Eastern hard maple

2 pc $1\frac{1}{2} \times 14 \times 43''$ laminated for top
2 pc $1\frac{1}{2} \times 4\frac{1}{2} \times 36''$ ends for top
4 pc $1\frac{1}{2} \times 3\frac{1}{2} \times 23\frac{1}{2}''$ legs
4 pc $1\frac{1}{2} \times 3\frac{1}{2} \times 32''$ rail and leg base
2 pc $1\frac{1}{2} \times 4\frac{1}{2} \times 32''$ rail
2 pc $1\frac{1}{2} \times 1\frac{1}{2} \times 8''$ filler

Miscellaneous

pc $\frac{3}{4} \times 10 \times 45''$ bottom for table recess (birch plywood)
20 $\frac{1}{2} \times 4''$ dowels
8 Tite Joint fasteners, Knape and Vogt #516

Figure 8-6 Workbench cutting list.

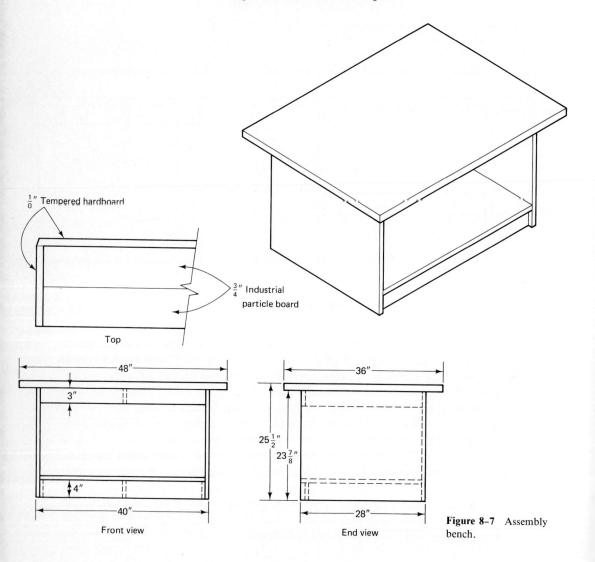

$\frac{1}{0}''$ Tempered hardboard

$\frac{3}{4}''$ Industrial
particle board

Top

48"

3"

4"

40"

Front view

36"

$25\frac{1}{2}''$

$23\frac{7}{8}''$

28"

End view

Figure 8-7 Assembly bench.

2 pc	$\frac{3}{4} \times 36 \times 48''$ top (industrial particle board)
1 pc	$\frac{1}{8} \times 36 \times 48''$ top (tempered hardboard)
2 pc	$\frac{1}{8} \times 1\frac{1}{2} \times 48''$ top edge (tempered hardboard)
2 pc	$\frac{1}{8} \times 1\frac{1}{2} \times 36\frac{1}{4}''$ top edge (tempered hardboard)

Plywood
2 pc	$\frac{3}{4} \times 23\frac{7}{8} \times 28''$ ends
1 pc	$\frac{3}{4} \times 23\frac{7}{8} \times 39\frac{1}{2}''$ back
1 pc	$\frac{3}{4} \times 27\frac{1}{4} \times 38\frac{1}{2}''$ bottom
1 pc	$\frac{3}{4} \times 4 \times 38\frac{1}{2}''$ toe kick
1 pc	$\frac{3}{4} \times 3 \times 38\frac{1}{2}''$ top rail
1 pc	$\frac{3}{4} \times 3 \times 26\frac{1}{2}''$ top brace
4 pc	$\frac{3}{4} \times 4 \times 25\frac{3}{4}''$ bottom supports

Figure 8-8   Assembly bench cutting list.

The dimensions shown on the benches are suggestions only and may need to be altered to fit the space you have available. Bench tops should be finished with clear polyurethane or penetrating oil. Other surfaces may be finished to match or painted.

Figure 8-6 gives the cutting list for the bench shown in Fig. 8-5.

Figure 8-7 shows an assembly bench and Fig. 8-8 provides the cutting list for it.

MITER CUTTING JIG FOR A TABLE SAW

This miter cutting jig (Fig. 8-9) makes it easy to cut accurate miters on the table saw without having to adjust a miter gage each time. The guide slots are attached in the same way as described for the sliding crosscut jig. Toggle clamps can be mounted to hold the parts in position for cutting. If toggle clamps are not available, the miter jig can still be used without them.

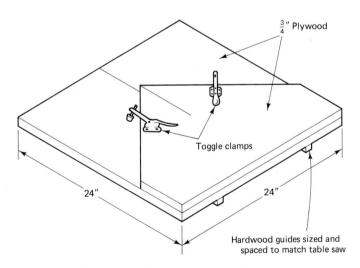

Figure 8-9   Miter cutting jig for table saw.

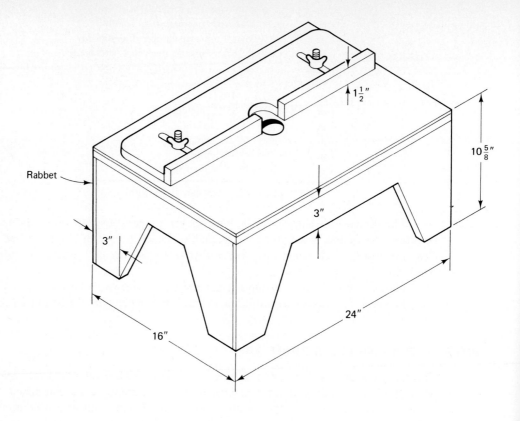

Rabbet

$1\frac{1}{2}''$

$10\frac{5}{8}''$

3"

3"

24"

16"

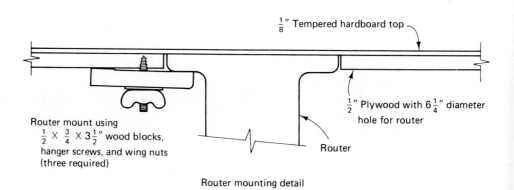

$\frac{1}{8}''$ Tempered hardboard top

Router mount using
$\frac{1}{2} \times \frac{3}{4} \times 3\frac{1}{2}''$ wood blocks,
hanger screws, and wing nuts
(three required)

$\frac{1}{2}''$ Plywood with $6\frac{1}{4}''$ diameter
hole for router

Router

Router mounting detail

Figure 8–10 Router table.

ROUTER TABLE

There are many situations where it is better to have the router mounted in a router table (Fig. 8–10) and move the workpiece by the cutters. Many of the operations that would normally be done with shaper may be done with a router in this manner. In fact, many woodworkers have an extra router that is always mounted in a router table.

Figure 8–11 gives the cutting list for this project.

1 pc	½ × 16 × 24″ top (plywood)
1 pc	⅛ × 16 × 24″ top (tempered hardboard)
2 pc	¾ × 10 × 24″ sides (plywood)
2 pc	¾ × 10 × 15½″ ends (plywood)
1 pc	½ × 6 × 23″ fence base (plywood)
2 pc	¾ × 1½ × 10″ fence (hardwood)
3 pc	½ × ¾ × 3½″ mounting blocks
Hardware:	3 hanger screws (1½″)
	3 wing nuts

Figure 8–11   Router table cutting list.

WOODWORKING TOOL BOX

The tool box shown in Fig. 8–12 is designed to be mounted on a wall behind a work bench and serve as a tool panel. It can, however, easily be taken down from the wall, closed, and taken to a job. The dimensions may have to be changed to suit your tool collection.

This cabinet is made of 12-mm Baltic birch plywood, which is sold in metric dimensions for thickness. It has nine plys, all of uniform thickness. The core plys are all birch, so the exposed edges are quite attractive and do not need to be covered. Finland birch is another similar product. These plywoods may not be available at lumberyards, but they are often available from cabinet shops where they are used to make drawer sides.

The corners of the box unit are box joints, as described in Chapter 3 in the section on the table saw. The tool holders are hard maple and must be designed to fit each tool. Use your imagination! The finish is clear satin lacquer.

Figure 8–13 gives the cutting list for this project.

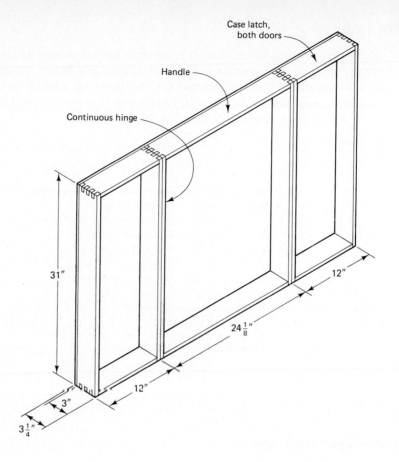

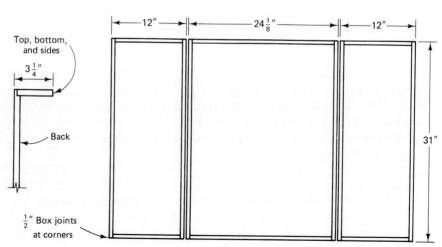

Figure 8-12 Woodworking tool box.

Figure 8-12 (continued)

½" (12 mm) Baltic birch

1 pc   24⅛ × 31" back
2 pc   12 × 31" backs
2 pc   3 × 24⅛" top and bottom
4 pc   3 × 12" top and bottom
6 pc   3 × 31" sides

Miscellaneous

Maple for tool holders

2 pc   continuous hinge, 30"
2   case latches
1   handle
Bugle-head screws for tool holders

Figure 8-13   Woodworking tool box cutting list.

KNIFE HOLDER

The kitchen knife holder shown in Fig. 8–14 can be set on a counter top and protects the blades while providing easy access to the knives. This rack is made of ¾-in.-thick red oak, but almost any wood could be used.

Figure 8-14   Knife holder.

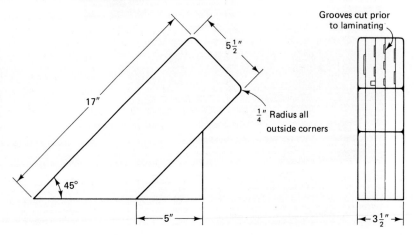

The slots for the knives are cut in the individual boards before they are glued together. They can be cut with a dado head on a table saw. When gluing the boards together, be careful not to use so much glue that it runs into the knife slots. After the boards are glued, the base end is cut off at a 45° angle and the cut-off piece is used to form the support.

The corners are all rounded with a router, the project is stained if desired, and then finished with a tung oil or Danish oil finish.

WOOD CLOCK

This contemporary wood clock (Fig. 8–15) will blend well with many contemporary furniture styles. The one shown is red oak, but walnut, cherry, maple, or other woods may be used. The clock works are inexpensive, battery-powered movements available

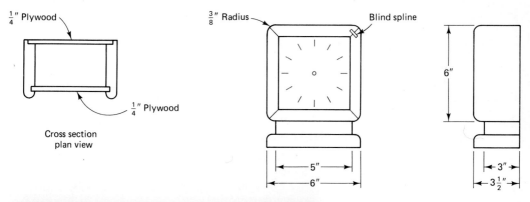

Figure 8–15 Clock.

¾″ Red oak or other hardwood	
4 pc	3½ × 6″ sides
1 pc	3½ × 6″ base
1 pc	3 × 5″ base top
Miscellaneous	
1 pc	¼ × 5 × 5″ front (oak plywood)
1 pc	¼ × 5½ × 5½″ back (oak plywood)
1	kit (clock motor, hands, and numbers)

Figure 8–16 Clock cutting list.

at many department stores in the crafts section. The finish is stain and tung oil, but a lacquer may also be used.

Figure 8–16 gives the cutting list for this project.

JEWELRY CABINET

This jewelry cabinet (Fig. 8–17) presents a challenging project that does not require large quantities of material. The drawers can be divided if desired to provide organized storage for earrings. The one shown is made of black walnut and the drawer sides are made of hard maple. The drawer bottoms and the cabinet back in the drawer section are made of tempered hardboard. The drawer bottoms are covered with felt.

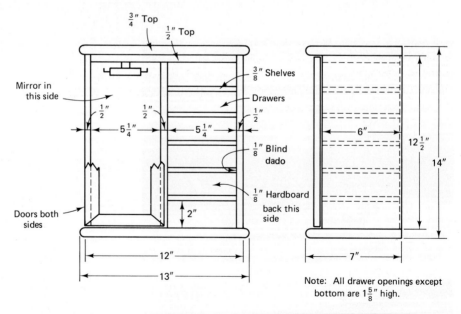

Figure 8–17 Jewelry box.

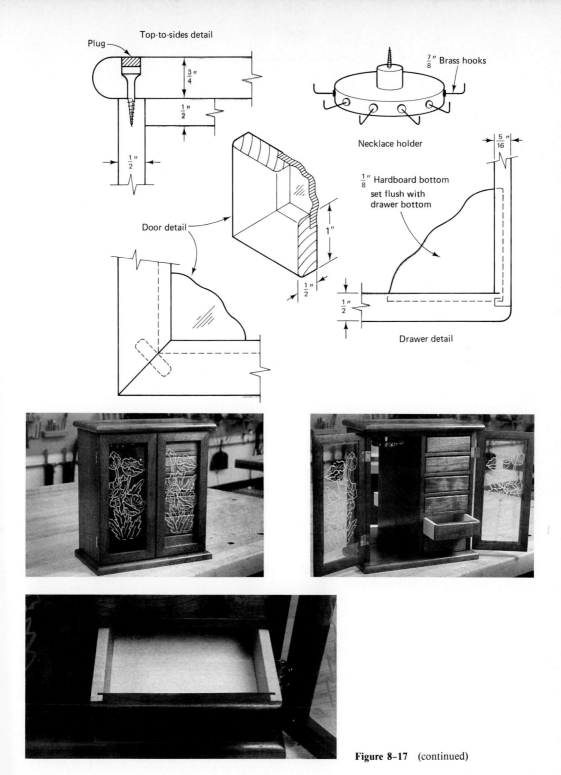

Top-to-sides detail

Plug

$\frac{3}{4}''$

$\frac{1}{2}''$

$\frac{1}{2}''$

$\frac{7}{8}''$ Brass hooks

Necklace holder

Door detail

$\frac{1}{8}''$ Hardboard bottom set flush with drawer bottom

$\frac{5}{16}''$

1"

$\frac{1}{2}''$

$\frac{1}{2}''$

Drawer detail

Figure 8–17 (continued)

Jewelry Cabinet

329

Black walnut
- 2 pc   ¾ × 7 × 13″ top and bottom
- 1 pc   ½ × 5⅞ × 11″ false top
- 1 pc   ½ × 5⅞ × 12″ partition
- 2 pc   ½ × 6 × 12½″ sides
- 4 pc   ½ × 1 × 12½″ door stiles
- 4 pc   ½ × 1 × 6″ door rails
- 5 pc   ½ × 1⁹⁄₁₆ × 5³⁄₁₆″ drawer fronts
- 1 pc   ½ × 1¹⁵⁄₁₆ × 5³⁄₁₆″ drawer front
- 1 pc   ½ × 2½ × 2½″ necklace holder

Walnut or other hardwood
- 10 pc   ⁵⁄₁₆ × 1⁹⁄₁₆ × 5¼″ drawer sides
- 2 pc   ⁵⁄₁₆ × 1¹⁵⁄₁₆ × 5¼″ drawer sides
- 5 pc   ⁵⁄₁₆ × 1⁷⁄₁₆ × 4¹⁵⁄₁₆″ drawer backs
- 1 pc   ⁵⁄₁₆ × 1¹³⁄₁₆ × 14¹⁵⁄₁₆″ drawer backs

⅛″ Tempered hardboard
- 6 pc   4⅞ × 5⅛″ drawer bottom
- 1 pc   5¾ × 13″ back in drawer section

Miscellaneous
- 1   mirror, ⅛ × 5¾ × 13″
- 6   springs for drawers (approx. ⁵⁄₁₆″dia.)
- Fabric to line drawers
- 12   brass hooks (⅞″)
- 2 pr   1 × 1″ brass butt hinges
- 2 pc   glass (³⁄₃₂ × 4½ × 11″)

Figure 8-18   Jewelry box cutting list.

One interesting feature of this jewelry cabinet is the spring system used to open the drawers. To avoid using drawer pulls on the drawers, a small coil spring is mounted in the back of each drawer. When the front of the drawer is pushed inward and released, it springs out enough to grasp it and pull it out.

The coil spring is epoxied into a shallow hole drilled into the drawer back. The drawer is then inserted and pushed in until the spring hits the cabinet back. The coil spring is then cut to length so that it stops the drawer when the front is flush with the front of the cabinet.

The dado-rabbet joints between the drawer fronts and drawer sides were cut on a table saw using a thin rim blade. The glass was glued into the wood door frames with clear silicone sealer. The mirror behind the necklace compartment was attached in the same way. The finish is five coats of clear tung oil and one coat of liquid satin wax.

Figure 8-18 gives the cutting list for this project.

DRAFTING TABLE

A drafting table will make it easier to draw plans for future woodworking projects! This table (Fig. 8-19) can be adjusted for height and the table top can be tilted.

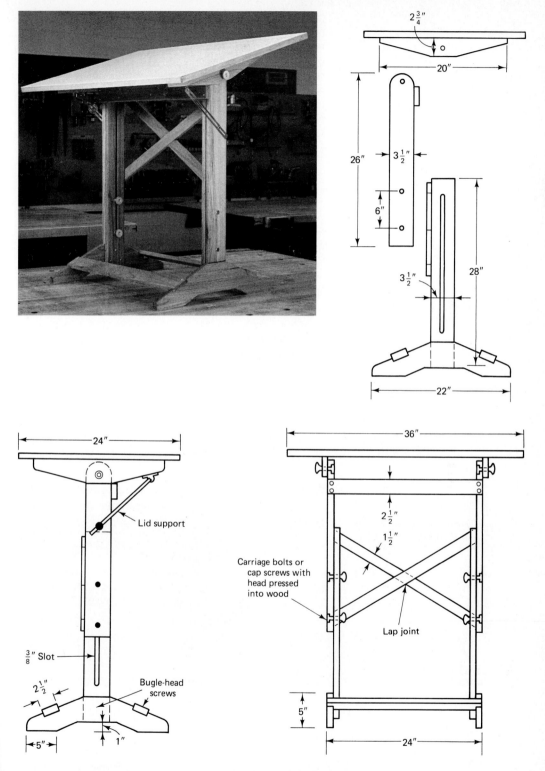

Figure 8-19 Drafting table.

¼" Red oak

2 pc	3½ × 28"	ends
2 pc	3½ × 26"	ends
2 pc	5 × 22"	feet
2 pc	2¾ × 20"	top support
3 pc	2½ × 24"	cross braces
2 pc	1½ × 27"	diagonal braces
1 pc	¾ × 24 × 36"	top (particle board)
1 pc	24 × 36"	plastic drafting surface

Edge banding for top (oak)

Hardware

6	cap screws (⅜ × 2")
2	lid supports
6	plastic knobs
20	bugle-head screws (2")
8	bugle-head screws (1¼")

Figure 8–20 Drafting table cutting list.

A special cover material for drawing board surfaces is available from many office supply stores. Large wing nuts may be used for the height adjustment or plastic knobs can be purchased from Frey Industrial Supply, P.O. Box 777, Burbank, CA 91510.

This table is made of red oak with a tung oil finish.

Figure 8–20 gives the cutting list for this project.

DESK TOP ORGANIZER

This desk top organizer (Fig. 8–21) can be used on a table top, counter top or desk top to provide very compact and neat storage for bills, envelopes, stamps, pencils, and all those other things that you can never find when you need them!

Figure 8–21 Desk top organizer (Designed & built by Scott McCulloch).

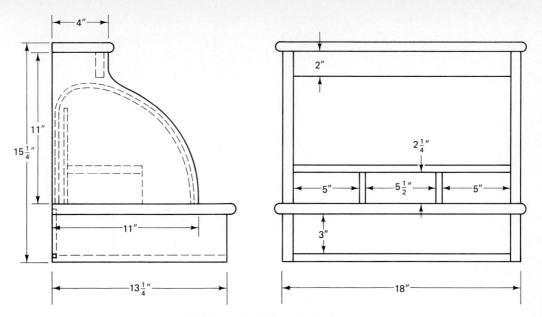

All joints are butt joints with dowels.

Figure 8–21 (continued)

Red oak
    1 pc $\frac{3}{4} \times 13\frac{1}{4} \times 16\frac{1}{2}$" bottom
    1 pc $\frac{3}{4} \times 14 \times 19$" shelf
    1 pc $\frac{3}{4} \times 4\frac{1}{2} \times 19$" top
    2 pc $\frac{3}{4} \times 11 \times 11$" ends
    2 pc $\frac{3}{4} \times 3\frac{3}{4} \times 13\frac{1}{4}$" ends
    1 pc $\frac{1}{2} \times 6 \times 16\frac{1}{2}$" shelf
    2 pc $\frac{1}{2} \times 6 \times 2\frac{1}{4}$" partitions
    1 pc $\frac{1}{4} \times 3\frac{3}{4} \times 16\frac{3}{4}$" back
    1 pc $\frac{1}{4} \times 7 \times 16\frac{1}{2}$" back
Roll top
Drawers

Figure 8–22 Desk top organizer cutting list.

The project is made of red oak with a tung oil finish. Figure 8–22 gives the cutting list for this project.

FILE CABINET

A good file cabinet is always useful. The cabinet in Fig. 8–23 is quite simple to build since most of the joints are simple butt joints attached with the now popular bugle-head screws (sometimes sold as dry-wall screws).

File Cabinet

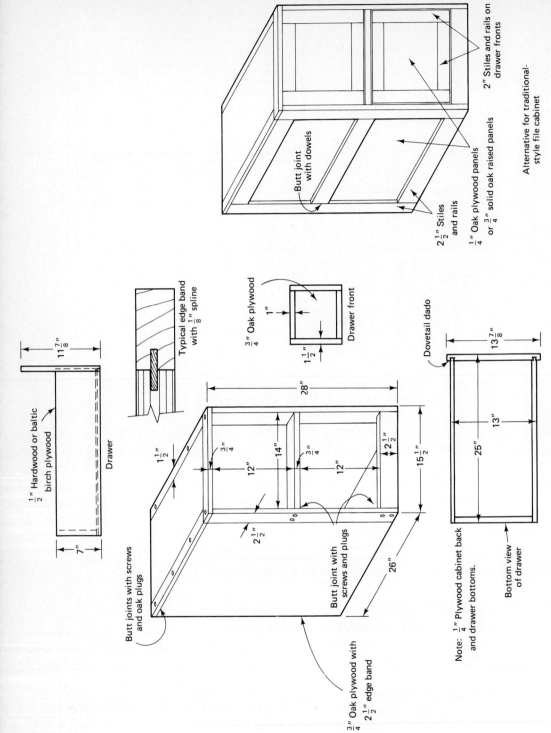

2" Stiles and rails on drawer fronts

Alternative for traditional-style file cabinet

Butt joint with dowels

$2\frac{1}{2}$" Stiles and rails

$\frac{1}{4}$" Oak plywood panels or $\frac{3}{4}$" solid oak raised panels

$11\frac{7}{8}$"

Typical edge band with $\frac{1}{8}$" spline

$\frac{1}{2}$" Hardwood or baltic birch plywood

Drawer

7"

$\frac{3}{4}$" Oak plywood

Drawer front

1"

$1\frac{1}{2}$"

Dovetail dado

$13\frac{7}{8}$"

13"

25"

Bottom view of drawer

Butt joints with screws and oak plugs

28"

$1\frac{1}{2}$"

$\frac{3}{4}$"

14"

$\frac{3}{4}$"

12"

12"

$2\frac{1}{2}$"

$15\frac{1}{2}$"

$2\frac{1}{2}$"

26"

Butt joint with screws and plugs

Note: $\frac{1}{4}$" Plywood cabinet back and drawer bottoms.

$\frac{3}{4}$" Oak plywood with $2\frac{1}{2}$" edge band

Figure 8–23 File cabinet.

334

Figure 8-23 (continued)

The sides, top, and drawer fronts are ¾-in. red oak plywood with solid oak edges attached with splines and glue. The cabinet back and drawer bottoms are ¼-in. plywood. The drawer sides are 12-mm (½-in.) Baltic birch. The drawer sides are attached to the drawer fronts with a dovetail dado cut with a router and table saw, as described in Chapter 3.

Adjustable file followers are used in both drawers. These are available from several woodworking supply sources. Full-extension roller guides, available from the same sources, are used.

The file cabinet pictured here is very contemporary in style. A traditionally styled file cabinet could easily be made by substituting frame and panel assemblies for the plywood cabinet sides and drawer fronts.

Figure 8–24 gives the cutting list for this project.

¾″ Oak plywood
    2 pc   23½ × 27¼″ sides
    1 pc   23½ × 12½″ top
    2 pc   9⅞ × 10⅞″ drawer fronts
    2 pc   6⅜ × 12″ drawer backs
½″ Hardwood or plywood
    4 pc   7 × 24⅝″ drawer sides
¼″ Plywood
    1 pc   15 × 27¾″ cabinet back
    2 pc   12⁷⁄₁₆ × 24½″ drawer bottoms
Solid oak lumber
    2 pc   ¾ × 2½ × 27¼″ edge band for sides
    1 pc   ¾ × 2½ × 15½″ edge band for top
    2 pc   ¾ × 1½ × 23½″ edge band for top
    4 pc   ¾ × 1½ × 11⅞″ edge band for drawer fronts
    4 pc   ¾ × 1 × 10⅞″ edge band for drawer fronts
    2 pc   ¾ × 2½ × 14″ cross stretchers
Miscellaneous
    2   sets 24″ full-extension drawer guides
    2   drawer pulls
    2   letter-size file followers
    16   bugle-head wood screws (2″)
    16   oak wood plugs (⅜″ dia.)

Figure 8–24 File cabinet cutting list.

TYPING OR COMPUTER DESK WITH TWO FILE DRAWER UNITS

This typing table (Fig. 8–25) is made by putting a top over two two-drawer file cabinets. These file cabinets are designed a little differently than the previous file cabinet project to make them as low as possible. This allows the top to be at a comfortable typing height.

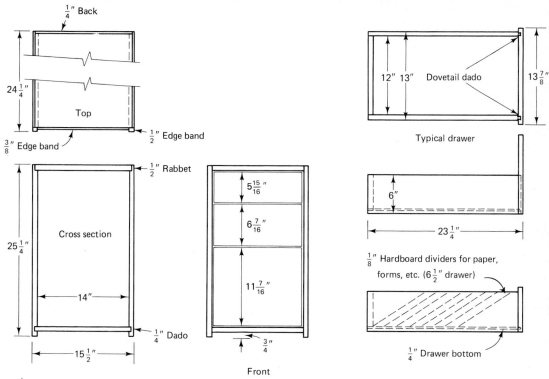

Figure 8–25 Typing desk with file cabinets.

Typing or Computer Desk with Two File Drawer Units

There are three standard file drawers, a shallow drawer for supplies, and another drawer with angled dividers for storage of several types of paper, letterhead, and other forms.

The cabinet is made of birch plywood. The sides are painted and the drawer fronts are stained and finished with satin lacquer. The top is industrial particle board covered with plastic laminate.

Figure 8-26 gives the cutting list for this project.

$\frac{3}{4}$ " Hardwood plywood

    4 pc $23\frac{3}{4} \times 25\frac{1}{4}$ " sides

    2 pc $23\frac{3}{4} \times 15$ " tops*

    2 pc $23\frac{1}{2} \times 14\frac{1}{2}$ " bottoms*

    3 pc $13\frac{7}{8} \times 11\frac{7}{16}$ " drawer fronts

    1 pc $13\frac{7}{8} \times 6\frac{7}{16}$ " drawer fronts

    1 pc $13\frac{7}{8} \times 5\frac{15}{16}$ " drawer fronts

    *Any plywood or particle board; top and bottom will not show.

Miscellaneous

    2 pc $\frac{1}{4} \times 15 \times 24\frac{1}{4}$ " plywood backs

    8 pc $\frac{1}{2} \times 6 \times 22\frac{7}{8}$ " drawer sides (plywood or solid lumber)

    2 pc $\frac{1}{2} \times 5 \times 22\frac{7}{8}$ " drawer sides (plywood or solid lumber)

    4 pc $\frac{3}{4} \times 5\frac{3}{8} \times 12$ " drawer backs (plywood or solid lumber)

    1 pc $\frac{3}{4} \times 4\frac{3}{8} \times 12$ " drawer backs (plywood or solid lumber)

    5 pc $\frac{1}{4} \times 12\frac{1}{2} \times 22\frac{3}{4}$ " drawer bottoms (plywood or hardboard)

    1 pc $\frac{3}{4} \times 24\frac{1}{2} \times 56$ "* plus edge banding and plastic laminate

    *Top may be made any desired length

    6 pc $\frac{1}{8} \times 9\frac{1}{2} \times 14$ " tempered hardboard dividers

Hardware

    5   drawer pulls

    5   sets full-extension drawer guides

    3   file followers (letter size)

Figure 8-26   Typing desk cutting list.

COMPUTER TABLE

This computer table (Fig. 8-27) places the keyboard and viewing monitor at comfortable heights. It provides work space to set documents and space for a printer. There is also generous space to store software documentation and other items.

This table is made in the European style using light-colored surfaces with wood accents. In this case, almond-colored polyester laminated particle board with matching edge banding is used. The table top is a matching plastic laminate. The wood trim is red oak stained and sprayed with satin lacquer.

The wood parts are made, sanded, and finished before the project is assembled. The polyester laminated particle board may not be available at lumberyards, but should be available at local cabinet shops. They also should have matching edge band-

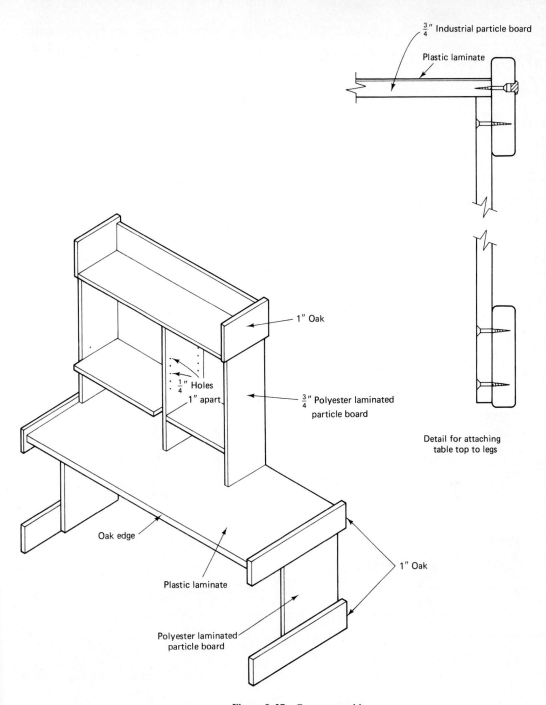

$\frac{3}{4}$" Industrial particle board

Plastic laminate

Detail for attaching
table top to legs

1" Oak

$\frac{1}{4}$" Holes
1" apart

$\frac{3}{4}$" Polyester laminated
particle board

Oak edge

Plastic laminate

Polyester laminated
particle board

1" Oak

Figure 8–27 Computer table.

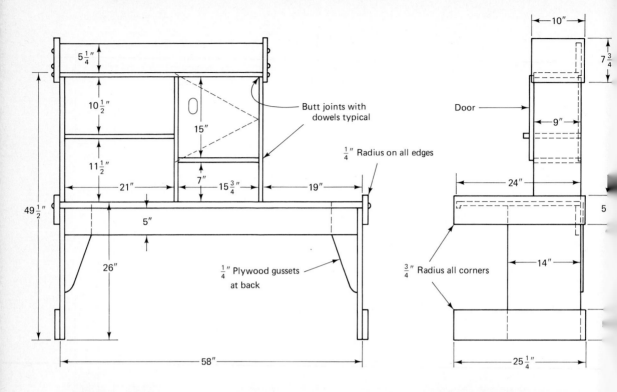

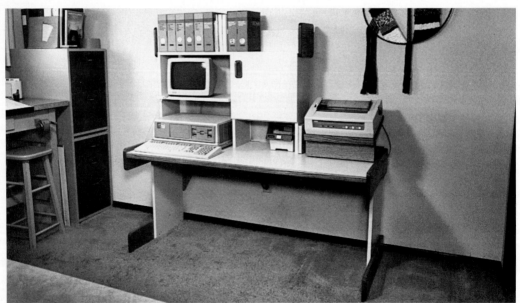

Figure 8–27 (continued)

ing material and would probably edge band the parts for you if you want. The parts are joined with dowels and the wood trim pieces are attached with screws.

The table top height and monitor shelf height are good for people of average height. You may want to change these dimensions to suit your requirements.

Figure 8-28 gives the cutting list for this project.

Oak
- 4 pc $1 \times 5\frac{1}{2} \times 25\frac{1}{4}''$ ends
- 2 pc $1 \times 7\frac{3}{4} \times 10''$ ends
- 1 pc $\frac{3}{4} \times 1\frac{1}{4} \times 58''$ edge for table top

Polyester laminated particle board
- 2 pc $\frac{3}{4} \times 14 \times 25''$ desk ends
- 3 pc $\frac{3}{4} \times 9 \times 22\frac{3}{4}''$ top section ends and partition
- 1 pc $\frac{3}{4} \times 11 \times 21''$ shelf
- 1 pc $\frac{3}{4} \times 9 \times 15\frac{3}{4}''$ shelf
- 1 pc $\frac{3}{4} \times 8\frac{1}{4} \times 15\frac{5}{8}''$ adjustable shelf
- 1 pc $\frac{3}{4} \times 17\frac{1}{4} \times 15\frac{3}{4}''$ door
- 1 pc $\frac{3}{4} \times 5\frac{1}{4} \times 37\frac{1}{2}''$ back for top shelf
- 1 pc $\frac{3}{4} \times 5 \times 56\frac{1}{2}''$ back support for desk top
- 1 pc $\frac{3}{4} \times 9 \times 37\frac{1}{2}''$ top shelf

$\frac{1}{4}''$ plywood
- 1 pc $16\frac{1}{2} \times 15\frac{3}{4}''$ back for door compartment
- 2 pc $5 \times 15''$ gussets for desk ends

Miscellaneous
- 1 pc $\frac{3}{4} \times 23\frac{1}{4} \times 58''$ industrial particle board top
- 1 pc $24+ \times 58 + ''$ plastic laminate for top

Polyester edge band for all polyester laminated parts
- 24 Bugle-head screws ($1\frac{1}{4}''$)
- 8 Bugle-head screws ($2''$)
- 14 Wood plugs ($\frac{3}{8}''$)
- 1 Oak drawer pull
- 4 Adjustable shelf support clip
- 2 European-style hinges for overlay door
- 2 European-style hinge mounting plates

Figure 8-28   Computer table cutting list.

SMALL COMPUTER TABLE

This computer table (Fig. 8-29) is smaller and simpler in construction than the previously described project. It can be made of hardwood plywood with solid hardwood feet. It can easily be cut from one sheet of plywood. A plastic laminate top could be used for added durability and scratch resistance.

Figure 8-30 gives the cutting list for this project.

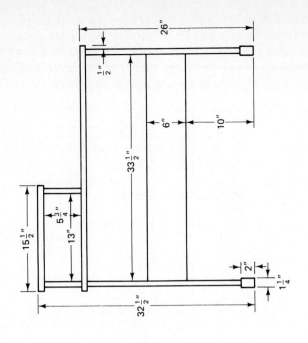

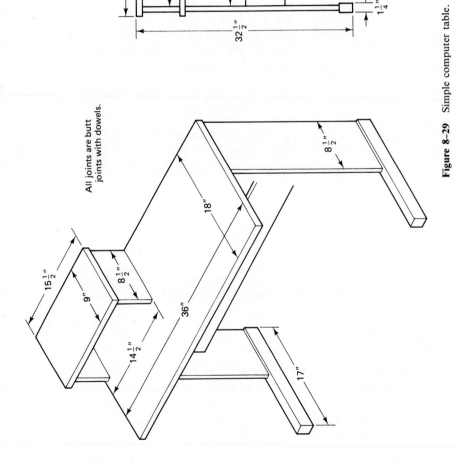

All joints are butt
joints with dowels.

Figure 8–29 Simple computer table.

¾" Oak plywood
- 1 pc   18 × 36" top
- 2 pc   8½ × 23¼" ends
- 1 pc   9 × 15½" shelf
- 2 pc   8½ × 5¾" shelf ends
- 1 pc   6 × 33½" stretcher

Other
- 2 pc   1¼ × 2 × 17" oak feet
- 30   ⁵⁄₁₆ × 1½" dowels
- 22   Linear feet of wood tape edge banding

Figure 8-30 Simple computer table cutting list.

REVOLVING PRINTER STAND

This revolving printer stand (Fig. 8–31) can be used with either of the computer tables shown previously. It has space for storing paper underneath and can be turned to load the printers that load from the back.

Figure 8–32 gives the cutting list for this project.

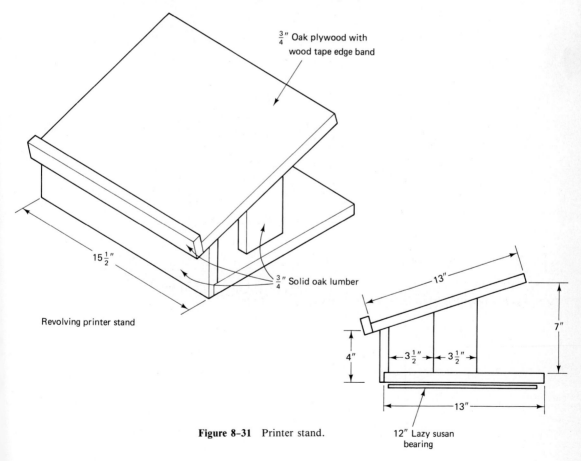

Figure 8-31 Printer stand.

¾" Oak plywood
  2 pc   15½ × 13" top and bottom
Solid oak lumber
  1 pc   ¾ × 4¾ × 15½" front
  2 pc   ¾ × 3½ × 5⅝" side supports
  1 pc   ¾ × 1¼ × 15½" cleat for top

Figure 8-32   Printer stand cutting list.

CHILD'S DESK

This child's desk (Fig. 8–33) provides a lot of storage space in a small area. The flat surfaces are made of industrial particle board, and exposed edges are filled and sanded. Trim pieces are made of alder, and the project is sprayed with satin white lacquer. The desk top is a matching satin-white plastic laminate.

Figure 8–34 gives the cutting list for this project.

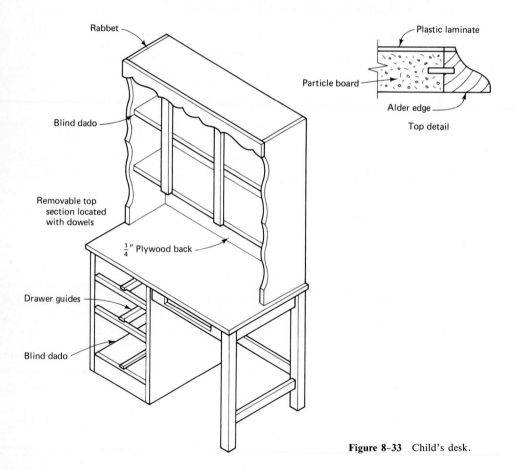

Figure 8-33   Child's desk.

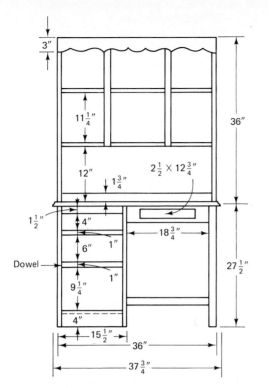

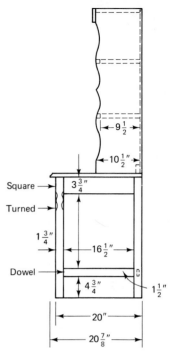

Figure 8–33 (continued)

¾″ Industrial particle board or medium-density fiberboard

2 pc	10½ × 36″	ends (top section)
2 pc	9½ × 35″	shelves (top section)
1 pc	10½ × 35½″	top (top section)
2 pc	20 × 26¾″	ends (desk section)
1 pc	20 × 36″	top
1 pc	14½ × 19″	bottom

Other material

1 pc	¼ × 35½ × 35¾″	back (plywood)

Alder or other hardwood

2 pc	¾ × 1½ × 23¼″	front stiles
1 pc	¾ × 3¾ × 18¾″	front rail
1 pc	¾ × 3¾ × 16½″	side rail
1 pc	¾ × 1½ × 16½″	bottom rail
1 pc	¾ × 1½ × 18¾″	bottom rail
2 pc	1¾ × 1¾ × 26¾″	legs
2 pc	¾ × 1 × 14″	rails
1 pc	¾ × 1½ × 14″	rails
1 pc	¾ × 4 × 14″	rails
1 pc	¼ × ¾ × 19¼″	drawer guide
2 pc	¾ × 1⅜ × 19¼″	drawer guide
1 pc	¾ × 1⅛ × 18¾″	drawer guide
1 pc	¼ × 15 × 22¾″	back (plywood)
2 pc	¾ × ⅞ × 20⅞″	edge band for top (alder)
1 pc	¾ × ⅞ × 37¾″	edge band for top (alder)

Drawers

1 pc	¾ × 4½ × 14½″	front (alder or similar)
1 pc	¾ × 6½ × 14½″	front (alder or similar)
1 pc	¾ × 9¾ × 14½″	front (alder or similar)
1 pc	¾ × 3 × 13″	front (alder or similar)
2 pc	½ × 3¾ × 19″*	sides (alder or plywood)
2 pc	½ × 5¾ × 19″	sides (alder or plywood)
2 pc	½ × 9 × 19″	sides (alder or plywood)
2 pc	½ × 2¼ × 18½″	sides (alder or plywood)
1 pc	¾ × 3⅛ × 12¾″	back (alder or plywood)
1 pc	¾ × 5⅛ × 12¾″	back (alder or plywood)
1 pc	¾ × 9⅜ × 12¾″	back (alder or plywood)
1 pc	¾ × 1⅝ × 11¼″	back (alder or plywood)
3 pc	¼ × 13¼ × 18¾″	bottoms (plywood)
1 pc	¼ × 11¾ × 18¼″	bottoms (plywood)
1 pc	½ × 3¾ × 12¾″	false fronts†
1 pc	½ × 5¾ × 12¾″	false fronts†
1 pc	½ × 9 × 12¾″	false fronts†
1 pc	½ × 2¼ × 11¼″	false fronts†

*Drawers are sized to use plastic guide tabs.

†Drawers are built as a box; then second front is attached.

Miscellaneous

4	drawer pulls
4	sets plastic drawer guides
1 pc	plastic laminate (21 × 37¾″)

Figure 8-34 Child's desk cutting list.

ENTERTAINMENT CENTER

This entertainment center (Fig. 8–35) will accommodate a television set, VCR, receiver, record player, tape player, compact disc player, records, and audio and video tapes. The project is made of red oak with a clear tung oil finish.

The cabinet ends are made from 2-in.-thick oak (planed to $1\frac{1}{2}$ in.) and the panels are from $\frac{1}{4}$-in. oak plywood. The shelves are $\frac{3}{4}$-in. oak plywood with edges banded on the front. The lower section of each unit has a $\frac{1}{4}$-in. plywood back. This back extends from the fixed shelf down to the bottom.

Figure 8–35 Entertainment center.

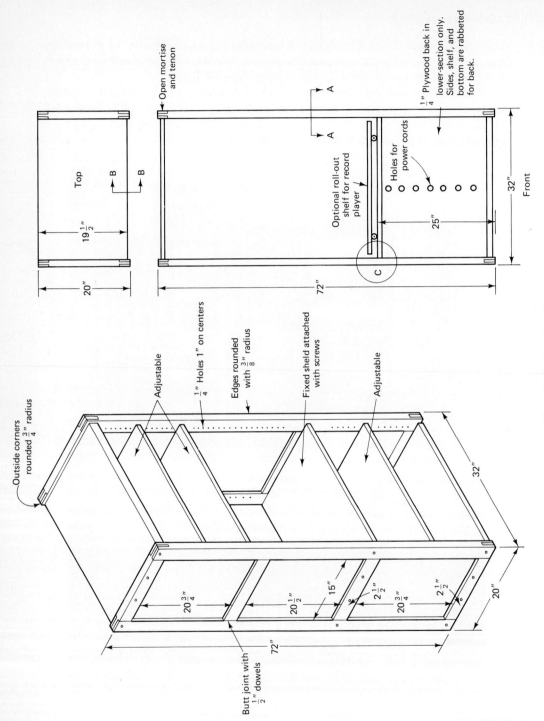

Open mortise and tenon

Top

B

B

$19\frac{1}{2}''$

20"

Optional roll-out shelf for record player

Holes for power cords

A   A

Front

$\frac{1}{4}''$ Plywood back in lower-section only. Sides, shelf, and bottom are rabbeted for back.

32"

25"

C

72"

Adjustable

$\frac{1}{4}''$ Holes 1" on centers

Edges rounded with $\frac{3}{8}''$ radius

Fixed shelf attached with screws

Adjustable

Outside corners rounded $\frac{3}{4}''$ radius

32"

20"

$20\frac{3}{4}''$

$20\frac{1}{2}''$

15"

$2\frac{1}{2}''$

$20\frac{3}{4}''$

$2\frac{1}{2}''$

72"

Butt joint with $\frac{1}{2}''$ dowels

Figure 8-35 (continued)

348

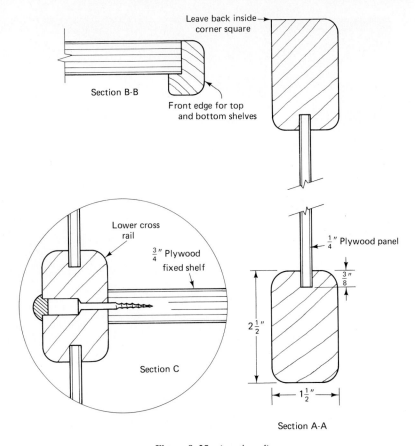

Leave back inside corner square

Section B-B

Front edge for top and bottom shelves

Lower cross rail

$\frac{3}{4}''$ Plywood fixed shelf

Section C

$\frac{1}{4}''$ Plywood panel

$\frac{3}{8}''$

$2\frac{1}{2}''$

$1\frac{1}{2}''$

Section A-A

Figure 8–35 (continued)

Figure 8–36 Jig used for cutting open mortise and tenon joints.

Figure 8–37 Strip of pegboard used to index shelf holes.

Figure 8–38 Open mortise and tenon joint.

The cabinet top and bottom are attached to the ends with 2-in. bugle-head screws, and all other shelves are adjustable. The frame for the cabinet ends is made using open mortise and tenon joints at the corners and dowel joints for the center rails.

If the cabinet is not going to be used to house a TV, the depth could be reduced to 16 in. This will accommodate almost any stereo components and will result in much better plywood utilization for the shelves.

Grant model 308 drawer guides are used for the optional roll-out shelf for the record player.

Figure 8–39 gives the cutting list for this project.

Solid oak lumber
    8 pc $1\frac{1}{2} \times 2\frac{1}{2} \times 72''$ stiles
    8 pc $1\frac{1}{2} \times 2\frac{1}{2} \times 20''$ top and bottom rails
    8 pc $1\frac{1}{2} \times 2\frac{1}{2} \times 15''$ center rails
    4 pc $\frac{3}{4} \times 1\frac{1}{4} \times 29''$ edge band for top and bottom
    2 pc $\frac{3}{8} \times \frac{3}{4} \times 29''$ edge band for fixed shelf
            $\frac{3}{8} \times \frac{3}{4} \times 28\frac{7}{8}''$ edge band for adjustable shelves as needed
$\frac{3}{4}''$ Oak plywood (size does not include edge band)
    4 pc $19 \times 29''$ top and bottom
    2 pc $19\frac{1}{8} \times 29''$ fixed shelves
    *$19\frac{1}{8} \times 28\frac{7}{8}''$ adjustable shelves (make as many as needed)
$\frac{1}{4}''$ Oak plywood
    8 pc $15\frac{5}{8} \times 21\frac{3}{8}''$ top and bottom side panels
    4 pc $15\frac{5}{8} \times 21\frac{1}{8}''$ center side panels
    2 pc $29\frac{3}{4} \times 23\frac{5}{8}''$ backs for lower section
Miscellaneous
    4   adjustable shelf clips for each shelf
    48   Bugle-head wood screws (2$''$)
    48   Wood screw plugs ($\frac{3}{8}''$ dia.)
    1   Set roll-out shelf guides (Grant 308 or similar)

*Adjustable shelves used in bottom section must be cut $\frac{1}{4}''$ narrower ($18\frac{7}{8}''$) to allow for $\frac{1}{4}''$ back in that section.

Figure 8–39 Entertainment center cutting list.

The open mortise and tenon joint used to assemble the cabinet ends is cut on a table saw as shown in Fig. 8–36 and the finished joint is shown in Fig. 8–38. A strip of peg board is used as a guide for drilling the shelf support holes (Fig. 8–37).

PRECISION TOOL CHEST

This precision tool box (Fig. 8–40) is a traditional favorite for storing carving, measuring, and layout tools and other tools that must be protected from damage. It is usually made of oak with an oil or varnish finish. The entire box is assembled and the lid is then cut off with a table saw.

Figure 8–41 gives the cutting list for this project.

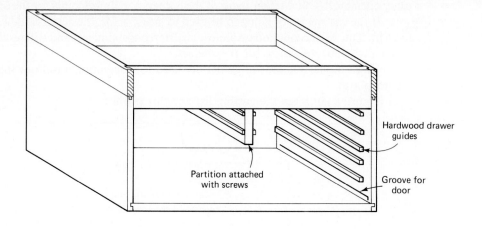

Hardwood drawer
guides

Partition attached
with screws

Groove for
door

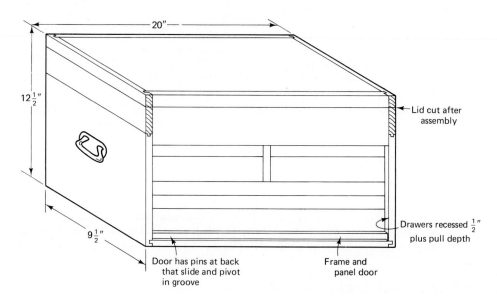

20"

12½"

9½"

Lid cut after
assembly

Drawers recessed ½"
plus pull depth

Door has pins at back
that slide and pivot
in groove

Frame and
panel door

Figure 8–40 Precision tool chest.

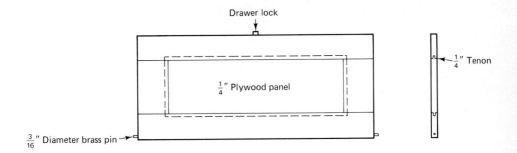

Drawer lock

$\frac{1}{4}$" Plywood panel

$\frac{1}{4}$" Tenon

$\frac{3}{16}$" Diameter brass pin

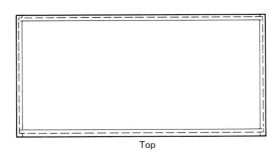

Top

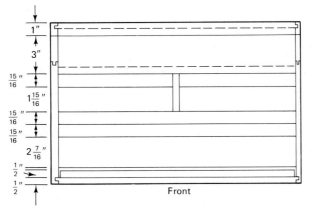

1"

3"

$\frac{15}{16}$"

$1\frac{15}{16}$"

$\frac{15}{16}$"

$\frac{15}{16}$"

$2\frac{7}{16}$"

$\frac{1}{2}$"

$\frac{1}{2}$"

Front

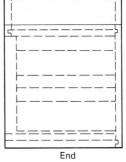

End

Figure 8-40 (continued)

Precision Tool Chest

Red oak
   2 pc $\frac{1}{2}$ × $9\frac{1}{2}$ × $9\frac{1}{2}$" sides
   2 pc $\frac{1}{2}$ × $3\frac{3}{8}$ × $9\frac{1}{2}$" side caps
   1 pc $\frac{1}{2}$ × $12\frac{1}{2}$ × $19\frac{1}{2}$" back
   1 pc $\frac{1}{2}$ × $9\frac{1}{4}$ × $19\frac{1}{2}$" bottom
   1 pc $\frac{1}{2}$ × 4 × $19\frac{1}{2}$" front
   1 pc $\frac{1}{2}$ × 9 × $19\frac{1}{2}$" top
   2 pc $\frac{1}{2}$ × 2 × 19" door stiles
   2 pc $\frac{1}{2}$ × $2\frac{1}{2}$ × $4\frac{1}{2}$" door rails
   1 pc $\frac{1}{2}$ × $1\frac{15}{16}$ × $18\frac{7}{8}$" drawer front
   2 pc $\frac{1}{2}$ × $\frac{15}{16}$ × $18\frac{7}{8}$" drawer front
   2 pc $\frac{1}{2}$ × $1\frac{15}{16}$ × $9\frac{1}{8}$" drawer front
   2 pc $\frac{1}{2}$ × $\frac{15}{16}$ × $9\frac{1}{8}$" drawer front
   1 pc $\frac{1}{2}$ × 3 × 8" partition
   8 pc $\frac{3}{8}$ × $\frac{15}{16}$ × $7\frac{7}{8}$" drawer sides
   6 pc $\frac{3}{8}$ × $1\frac{15}{16}$ × $7\frac{7}{8}$" drawer sides
   2 pc $\frac{3}{8}$ × $1\frac{13}{16}$ × $8\frac{3}{4}$" drawer backs
   2 pc $\frac{3}{8}$ × $\frac{13}{16}$ × $8\frac{3}{4}$" drawer backs
   2 pc $\frac{3}{8}$ × $\frac{13}{16}$ × $18\frac{1}{2}$" drawer backs
   1 pc $\frac{3}{8}$ × $1\frac{13}{16}$ × $18\frac{1}{2}$" drawer backs
Oak plywood
   1 pc $\frac{1}{4}$ × 5 × $14\frac{1}{2}$" door panel
Plywood
   1 pc $\frac{1}{2}$ × 9 × $19\frac{1}{2}$" tray shelf
Tempered hardboard
   4 pc $\frac{1}{8}$ × $7\frac{3}{4}$ × $8\frac{3}{4}$" drawer bottom
   4 pc $\frac{1}{8}$ × $7\frac{3}{4}$ × $18\frac{1}{2}$" drawer bottom
Miscellaneous
   2   handles for cabinet sides
   1   drawer lock for $\frac{1}{2}$" material (for door)
   10   pulls for drawers
   Felt for lining drawers

Figure 8–41 Precision tool chest cutting list.

LIVING ROOM FURNITURE SET

This contemporary living room furniture set consists of a coffee table, an occasional table, two end tables cabinets, and a stereo cabinet. Tambour doors are featured on the end table cabinets and the stereo cabinet.

The set is made of red oak, stained with a pecan stain, and finished with tung oil. Bronze glass is used in the table tops.

The strips for the tambour doors were cut from the edge of $\frac{3}{4}$-in.-thick oak boards and numbered as they were cut. They were then glued to the canvas backing in the same sequence. The edge strip with the finger pull on the tambour doors is thicker than the other strips, but it is cut thin at the ends so that it will fit in the sliding groove.

After the parts are cut and machined, the general assembly procedure is as follows:

1. Assemble the tops as a unit. Shape the outside edge of the top and cut the rabbet for the glass after the top is assembled.
2. Assemble a rail to the legs. You will have four of these inverted U-shaped legs and rail assemblies for each table.
3. Cut the rabbet in the table legs.
4. Glue and clamp the four table leg and rail assemblies together to make the table base.
5. Attach the top.

Coffee table (Fig. 8–42) and occasional table.　These are the simplest pieces in the set. The top is assembled, the outside edges shaped with a router or shaper, and the rabbet for the glass is cut with a router. Figure 8–43 gives the cutting list for the coffee table.

Figure 8–42　Coffee table.

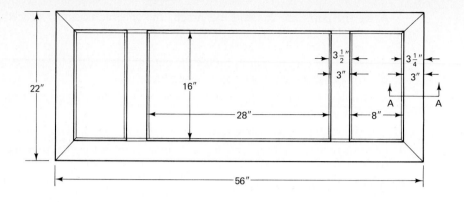

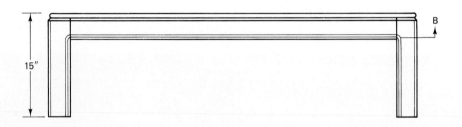

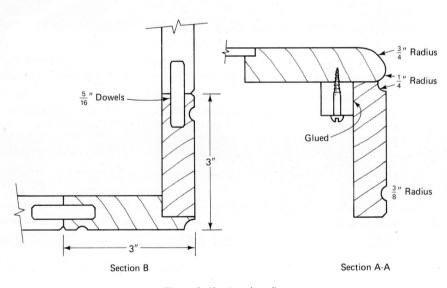

Section B

Section A-A

Figure 8–42 (continued)

¾″ Red oak
    2 pc   3¼ × 56″ table top
    2 pc   3¼ × 22″ table top
    2 pc   3½ × 15½″ table top
    2 pc   3 × 50″ rails
    2 pc   3 × 16″ rails
    4 pc   3 × 14¼″ legs
    4 pc   2¾ × 14¼″ legs
Miscellaneous
    32   dowels, ⁵⁄₁₆ × 1½″
    1 pc   bronze glass, ³⁄₁₆ × 16 × 28″
    2 pc   bronze glass, ³⁄₁₆ × 8 × 16″

Figure 8-43 Coffee table cutting list.

Figure 8–44 shows the occasional table, and Fig. 8–45 gives the cutting list for it.

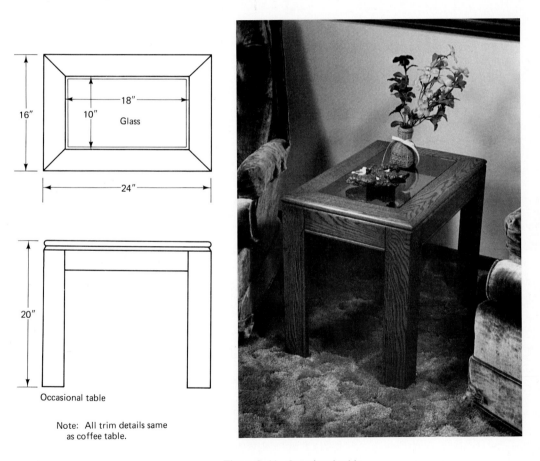

16″

18″

10″

Glass

24″

20″

Occasional table

Note: All trim details same
    as coffee table.

Figure 8-44 Occasional table.

Living Room Furniture Set

¾" Red oak
    2 pc $3\frac{1}{4} \times 24$" top
    2 pc $3\frac{1}{4} \times 16$" top
    4 pc $3 \times 19\frac{1}{4}$" legs
    4 pc $2\frac{3}{4} \times 19\frac{1}{4}$" legs
    2 pc 3×18" rails
    2 pc 3×10" rails

Miscellaneous
    24   dowels, $\frac{5}{16} \times 1\frac{1}{2}$"
    1 pc bronze glass, $\frac{3}{16} \times 10 \times 18$"

Figure 8–45 Occasional table cutting list.

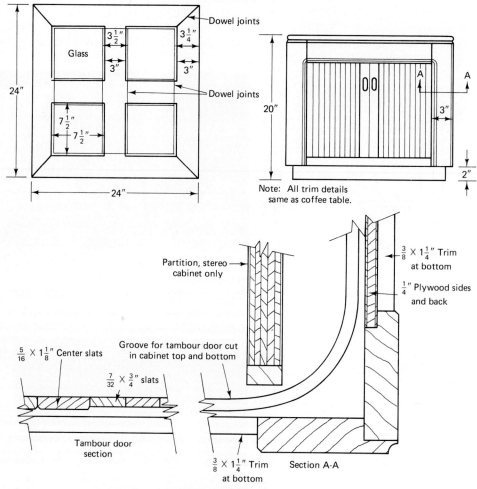

Note: All trim details same as coffee table.

Figure 8–46 End table cabinet.

Figure 8-46 (continued)

End table cabinets. This end table (Fig. 8-46) is enclosed to provide storage for magazines and other items. It is built much like the coffee table except that the sides are enclosed and sliding tambour doors are used. The tambour doors are "trapped" in place when the top is installed. Figure 8-47 gives the cutting list for the end table.

$\frac{3}{4}$" Red oak		
4 pc	$3\frac{1}{4} \times 24$"	table top
1 pc	$3\frac{1}{2} \times 17\frac{1}{2}$"	table top
2 pc	$3\frac{1}{2} \times 7$"	table top
4 pc	3×18"	rails
4 pc	$3 \times 17\frac{1}{4}$"	legs
4 pc	$2\frac{3}{4} \times 17\frac{1}{4}$"	legs
4 pc	2×22"	base
Miscellaneous red oak		
4 pc	$\frac{3}{8} \times 1\frac{1}{4} \times 18$"	bottom trim
26 pc	$\frac{7}{32} \times \frac{3}{4} \times 17$"	tambour slats
2 pc	$\frac{5}{16} \times 1\frac{1}{8} \times 17$"	tambour slats
Miscellaneous		
1 pc	$\frac{3}{4} \times 22\frac{1}{2} \times 22\frac{1}{2}$"	oak plywood bottom
3 pc	$\frac{1}{4} \times 18\frac{3}{4} \times 14\frac{5}{8}$"	oak plywood sides
36	dowels, $\frac{5}{16} \times 1\frac{1}{2}$"	
4 pc	bronze glass, $\frac{3}{16} \times 7\frac{1}{2} \times 7\frac{1}{2}$"	
Canvas for tambour doors		

Figure 8-47 End table cabinet cutting list.

Stereo cabinet.   This stereo cabinet (Fig. 8–48) provides space for a receiver, tape player, record player, and record and tape storage. To leave room along the inside ends of the cabinet for the tambour doors to slide, it is necessary to build partitions just inside the ends of the cabinet. These partitions support the shelves since they cannot extend to the cabinet ends. The back of the cabinet is attached with screws so it can be removed to insert the tambour doors after the cabinet is assembled.

Figure 8–49 gives the cutting list for the stereo cabinet.

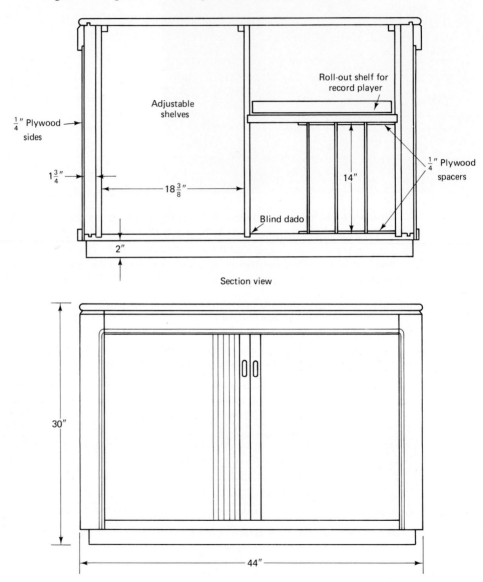

Section view

Figure 8–48   Stereo cabinet.

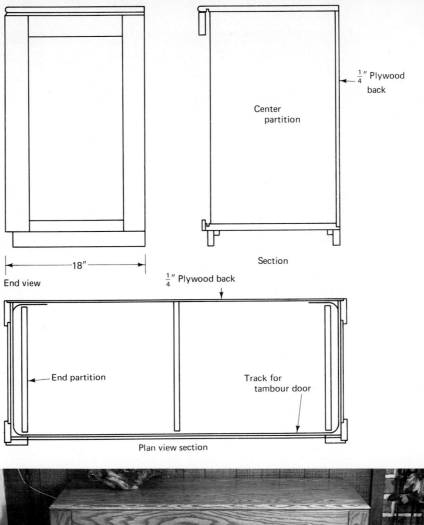

End view

18″

$\frac{1}{4}$″ Plywood back

Center partition

$\frac{1}{4}$″ Plywood back

Section

End partition

Track for tambour door

Plan view section

Figure 8-48 (continued)

Living Room Furniture Set

Figure 8-48 (continued)

¾″ Red oak
  1 pc   18 × 44″ laminated top
  1 pc   3 × 38″ rail
  2 pc   3 × 12″ rail
  4 pc   3 × 27¼″ legs
  2 pc   2¾ × 27¼″ legs
  2 pc   2 × 42″ base
  2 pc   2 × 17″ base
Miscellaneous red oak
  1 pc   ⅜ × 1¼ × 38″ bottom trim
  2 pc   ⅜ × 1¼ × 12″ bottom trim
  50 pc   ⁷⁄₃₂ × ¾ × 27″ tambour slats
  2 pc   ⁵⁄₁₆ × 1⅛ × 27″ tambour slats
Miscellaneous
  1 pc   ¾ × 17¼ × 42½″ oak plywood bottom
  1 pc   ¾ × 16½ × 26¾″ oak plywood partition
  2 pc   ¾ × 15⅞ × 26¾″ oak plywood partition
  1 pc   ¾ × 15⅞ × 18⅞″ oak plywood shelf
  3 pc   ¾ × 15⅞ × 18¼ oak plywood adjustable shelves
  2 pc   ¼ × 12¾ × 34⅝″ oak plywood ends
  4 pc   ¼ × 15⅞ × 14″ oak plywood dividers
  1 pc   ¼ × 43½ × 27½″ fir plywood back
  1 set roll-out tray guides (16″) (Grant 308 or similar), canvas for
  tambour

Figure 8-49 Stereo cabinet cutting list.

PORTABLE CAMPING CABINET

This cabinet (Fig. 8-50) is designed to be set in the back of a van for traveling and then be set outside at a camp site for cooking. It has large wings that fold out to provide large counter top areas on each side of the cabinet. It has space for a pro-

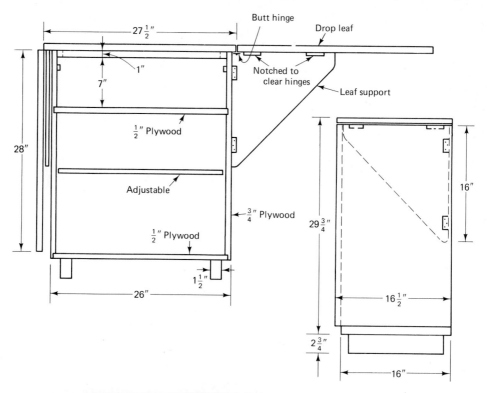

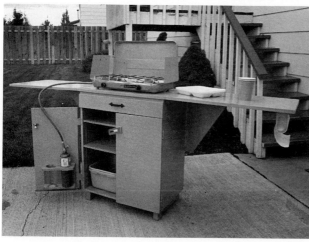

Figure 8-50 Portable camping cabinet.

pane stove and tanks. It is made of ¼, ½, and ¾-in. exterior plywood and painted with an exterior enamel.

Figure 8–51 gives the cutting list for this project.

Exterior A-B plywood
2 pc   ¾ × 16 × 29″ sides
1 pc   ¾ × 16½ × 27½″ top
2 pc   ¾ × 16½ × 28″ drop leaves
1 pc   ½ × 15¾ × 25½″ bottom
1 pc   ½ × 15¾ × 25″ shelf
1 pc   ½ × 15¾ × 24⅜″ adjustable shelf
2 pc   ½ × 15 × 16″ leaf supports
1 pc   ¼ × 25½ × 29″ back
1 pc   ½ × 3¾ × 26″ drawer front
1 pc   ½ × 3 × 23⅜″ front for drawer box
2 pc   ½ × 3 × 15½″ drawer sides
1 pc   ½ × 3 × 23⅞″ drawer back
1 pc   ¼ × 23⅞ × 15″ drawer bottom
2 pc   ½ × 13⅛ × 24½″ doors
Miscellaneous
2 pc   1½ × 2¾ × 15 feet
2 pc   ¼ × ⅝ × 15¼ drawer guides
2 pc   ¾ × 1 × 24½ top rails
2 pc   ¾ × 1 × 14½ side rails
4 pc   adjustable shelf standard, 18″
4   adjustable shelf clips
6 pr   2 × 2″ butt hinges
1   hasp
1   drawer pull

Figure 8–51   Portable cooking cabinet cutting list.

ROLLING TOOL CABINET

This small tool cabinet (Fig. 8–52) can be rolled to a car that is being worked on. The wheels are large enough so that it can be moved outside if the terrain is not too rough. Drawers are divided up to organize wrenches and other tools.

The cabinet is made of ¼, ½, and ¾-in. exterior plywood with a tempered hardboard work surface on the top. The finish is an exterior enamel. The top is finished with polyurethane.

Figure 8–53 gives the cutting list for this project.

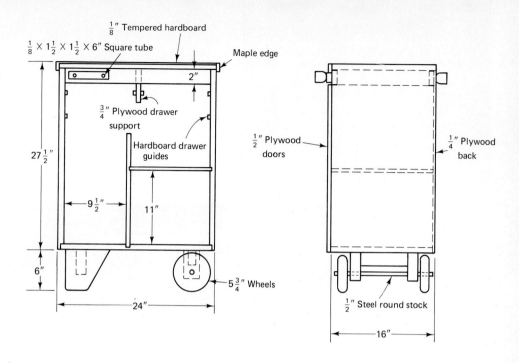

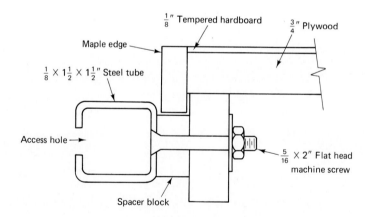

Detail for attaching handle bracket
to front of cart. Back is similar
but does not have spacer.

Figure 8-52   Rolling tool cabinet.

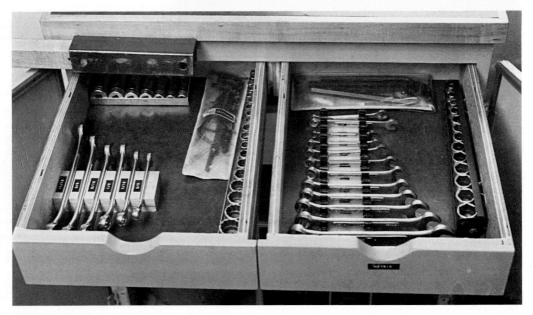

Figure 8-52 (continued)

Exterior A-B plywood

- 2 pc $\frac{3}{4} \times 16 \times 26\frac{3}{4}$" ends
- 1 pc $\frac{3}{4} \times 16 \times 24$" top
- 1 pc $\frac{3}{4} \times 15\frac{3}{4} \times 23\frac{1}{2}$" bottom
- 1 pc $\frac{1}{4} \times 23\frac{1}{2} \times 26\frac{3}{4}$" back
- 1 pc $\frac{3}{4} \times 4\frac{3}{4} \times 15$" drawer support
- 1 pc $\frac{1}{2} \times 15\frac{3}{4} \times 13$" shelf
- 1 pc $\frac{1}{2} \times 15\frac{3}{4} \times 17$" partition
- 2 pc $\frac{1}{2} \times 12\frac{1}{4} \times 25$" doors
- 2 pc $\frac{3}{4} \times 3 \times 11\frac{1}{8}$" drawer fronts
- 1 pc $\frac{3}{4} \times 4 \times 22\frac{3}{8}$" drawer fronts
- 4 pc $\frac{1}{2} \times 3 \times 15\frac{1}{4}$" drawer sides
- 2 pc $\frac{1}{2} \times 4 \times 15\frac{1}{4}$" drawer sides
- 2 pc $\frac{1}{2} \times 3 \times 10\frac{1}{4}$" drawer backs
- 1 pc $\frac{1}{2} \times 4 \times 21\frac{7}{8}$" drawer backs
- 1 pc $\frac{1}{4} \times 21\frac{7}{8} \times 15$" drawer bottom

Other material

- 2 pc $\frac{1}{8} \times 10\frac{1}{4} \times 15$" drawer bottoms (tempered hardboard)
- 1 pc $\frac{1}{8} \times 16 \times 24$" top cover (tempered hardboard)
- 2 pc $\frac{1}{2} \times 1\frac{1}{4} \times 16\frac{1}{2}$" edge for top (maple)
- 1 pc $\frac{1}{2} \times 1\frac{1}{4} \times 25$" edge for top (maple)
- 2 pc $1\frac{1}{8} \times 1\frac{1}{8} \times 18$" handles (maple)
- 2 pc $1\frac{1}{2} \times 6 \times 7$" feet
- 1 pc $1\frac{1}{2} \times 3\frac{1}{2} \times 11$" brace for feet
- 2 pc $1\frac{1}{2} \times 3 \times 4$" axle mounting blocks
- 1 pc $1\frac{1}{2} \times 2 \times 7\frac{1}{2}$" brace

Hardware

- 2 Wheels ($5\frac{3}{4}$" dia.)
- 1 pc $\frac{1}{2}$" round steel for axle (15" long)
- 2 pr $1\frac{1}{2} \times 2$" butt hinges
- 1 elbow catch
- 1 hasp
- 2 pc $\frac{1}{8} \times 1\frac{1}{2} \times 1\frac{1}{2} \times 6$" square tube
- 2 F.H. machine screws and nuts ($\frac{5}{16} \times 2$")
- 2 F.H. machine screws and nuts ($\frac{5}{16} \times 1\frac{1}{2}$")

Figure 8–53 Rolling tool cabinet cutting list.

Index

Index